The Hayduke Trail

The Hayduke Trail

A Guide to the Backcountry Hiking Trail
on the Colorado Plateau

Joe Mitchell and Mike Coronella

THE UNIVERSITY
OF UTAH PRESS
Salt Lake City

The Defiance House Man colophon is a registered trademark of
The University of Utah Press. It is based upon a four-foot-tall,
Ancient Puebloan pictograph (late PIII) near Glen Canyon, Utah.

LIBRARY OF CONGRESS CATALOGING-IN-PUBLICATION DATA
Mitchell, Joe, 1969–
    The Hayduke trail guide : a backcountry hiking trail on the Colorado Plateau of the
American Southwest from Arches to Zion National parks through the Grand Canyon /
Joe Mitchell and Mike Coronella.
      p. cm.
    ISBN 978-0-87480-813-1 (pbk. : alk. paper)
    1. Hiking—Colorado Plateau—Guidebooks. 2. Trials—Colorado Plateau—Guide-
books. 3. Colorado Plateau—Guidebooks. I. Coronella, Mike, 1963- II. Title.
    GV199.42.C63M58 2005
    796.51'09792—dc22   2004017802

Contents

Warning!

. . . .

Because of the extraordinarily challenging nature of this route, you must be an experienced backpacker in excellent physical condition before beginning the Hayduke Trail!

The Hayduke Trail traverses a vast and rugged area subject to dynamic weather changes and conditions. Expect changes and hazards. Your safety is a matter of personal responsibility. Base your choices on experience, personal knowledge, a realistic assessment of your abilities, and the prevailing conditions. The information herein is not a substitute for your own best judgment. **If you have any doubt regarding your ability to hike any of the segments described in this book, do not attempt them.**

Neither the University of Utah Press nor the authors are responsible for personal injury, damage to property, or violation of the law in connection with this guidebook. Any error, omission, or incorrect information is solely the responsibility of the authors. Corrections for future editions are welcome.

Please send all comments and corrections to the authors c/o The University of Utah Press, 1795 E. South Campus Drive, Suite 101, Salt Lake City UT 84112-9402.

MITCH TAKING A BREAK ALONG THE RIVER, GRAND CANYON NATIONAL PARK

Using the Hayduke Trail Guide

This guidebook is intended to provide the necessary information to lead a sensible, well-conditioned, experienced desert trekker through a remarkable portion of the Colorado Plateau. We recommend that anyone who plans to head out on any or all of the sections of this route not only use this guide but also have all of the USGS 7.5 minute topographic maps that are listed for each section. (We found that also having a larger-scale map helped one be able to identify faraway landmarks). The maps in this guide are for reference only. Under no circumstances should they be used alone as a navigational tool.

The book begins with preliminary information about the route, safety, water concerns, and general information about the region before moving into descriptions of each section of the route. We can't stress enough the importance of knowing as much as possible about what you are getting into out there—this can be a hostile and treacherous land. Each of the fourteen Hayduke Trail sections begins with an overview map, ratings for different parts of the section, distance and recommended time, excerpts from Mike Coronella's journals, a general route description with information on trailhead and resupply points, a detailed description, and finally an overlapping series of finer-scaled maps.

This book is meant only as a guide to the route that we have established through the Colorado Plateau region. It is *not* a survival guide, a first-aid guide, or a guide on how to backpack or camp. Neither is it a reference work on desert flora and fauna, geology, meteorology, archaeology, or anthropology. There are many excellent books on these subjects. We strongly recommend that you familiarize yourself with these subjects before you venture into this untamed land. Your backcountry experience will vastly benefit from some knowledge about what you are getting yourself into! (See also the Suggested Reading section at the end of this book.)

George Washington Hayduke, a fictitious defender of the Colorado Plateau, was created by Edward Abbey in his much-acclaimed 1975 novel *The Monkey Wrench Gang*, among other things a book often credited as a catalyst for the formation of the Earth First! movement. While we absolutely do not condone vandalizing private or public properties, we do wish to acknowledge the passion that some people have for this amazing part of our planet. We also seek to pay homage to Edward Abbey for his eloquent defense of these fragile lands. Although we have named our trail as part of this homage to Edward Abbey and the lands he loved, please be aware that this trail (or any of its parts) does not seek to trace any route traveled by any of the characters in Abbey's writings. It is something entirely unrelated to Abbey's works.

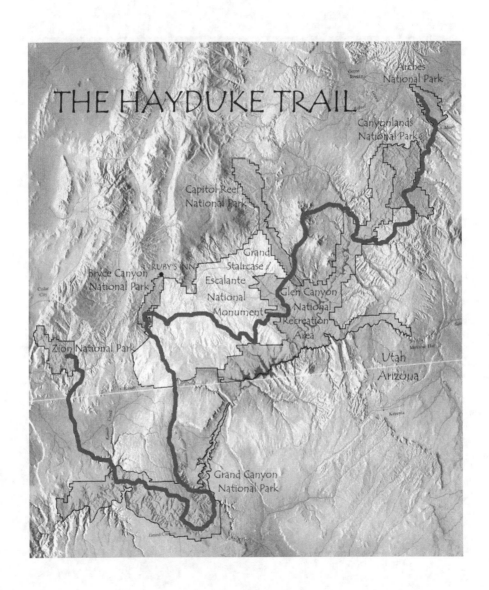

THE HAYDUKE TRAIL

Arches National Park

Canyonlands National Park

Capitol Reef National Park

Grand Staircase / Escalante National Monument

RUBY'S INN

Bryce Canyon National Park

Glen Canyon National Recreation Area

Zion National Park

Utah

Arizona

Grand Canyon National Park

HEADING INTO LOCKHART CANYON

Introduction to
the Hayduke Trail

The Hayduke Trail travels across the arid lands of southern Utah and northern Arizona, with Arches and Zion National Parks at either end. If you intend on traveling the entire Hayduke Trail all at once, you'll need three months or more, not just to complete the route but to actually have time (and energy) to enjoy yourself and the scenery; at times you'll be carrying a pack weighing at least sixty pounds over terrain that often includes climbs of thousands of vertical feet in a single day.

The Hayduke Trail is a challenging 812-mile-long backcountry route that passes through some of the most rugged, desolate and beautiful land in the world. This route, entirely on public land, traverses six national parks (Arches, Canyonlands, Capitol Reef, Bryce Canyon, Grand Canyon, and Zion), a national recreation area, a national monument, and various wilderness, primitive, and wilderness study areas. **This route is not intended to be the most direct way through this region, nor is it always the easiest or even the most logical route through the area.** What you will find is the variety of terrain and experiences that are available in the Colorado Plateau short of highly technical travel. A backcountry route intended for non-motorized use, it truly showcases the diversity of the region, going from 2,000 feet above sea level deep in the Grand Canyon to 11,419 feet above sea level on Mount Ellen's south summit in the Henry Mountains—nearly a two-mile vertical difference in elevation. The thermometer fluctuates greatly as well: a temperature range of more than 100°F may be experienced while trekking through the Colorado Plateau's mountains and canyons.

You'll find natural arches and bridges, spires and hoodoos, cracks and deep, narrow canyons, sand dunes and rock falls, ponderosa and aspen forests, as well as sage and cactus, delicate desert flowers and grizzled old juniper trees, even high alpine peaks—all to be explored in this untamed region. The route passes through the homes of ancient peoples as well as those of horned toad lizards, collared lizards,

HIKING IN A GRABEN VALLEY, NEEDLES DISTRICT, CANYONLANDS NATIONAL PARK

whiptail lizards, and of bullsnakes, rattlesnakes, and racers. There are trophy-sized trout, river chub, salamanders, tadpoles, and all kinds of toads in the desert riparian zones. There are turkey vultures, magpies, canyon wrens, mockingbirds, towhees, flickers, hawks, eagles, falcons, and condors, even great blue heron. While on our exploratory journeys, we saw bobcats, deer, elk, coyotes, weasels, mice, muskrat, beaver, cottontail and jackrabbits, desert bighorn sheep, pronghorn, badger, evidence of many cougar (without ever actually seeing one), and even found the skull of a bear. This is truly a land of superlatives and unimaginable variety.

The Hayduke Trail was first conceived by the authors while on a 94-day-long backpacking trek from Arches National Park to Zion National Park during the spring of 1998. A second trek, in the spring of 2000, lasted 101 days, and helped solidify our plans for the route of the Hayduke Trail. Each trip was the product of a full year's worth of research and Joe Mitchell's uncanny knack for choosing viable routes from topo maps. Much of our trekking fell into the "exploratory" category, and our average daily mileage while hiking through this terrain was a meager-sounding six miles per day. The route was carefully

HIKING IN INDIAN CREEK

planned around available water sources and to take advantage of existing routes whenever possible, though there were places that not only lacked existing routes but where we could find no one who could tell us whether or not we could actually pass through from one end to the other. There are times these existing routes mean that the Hayduke Trail follows dirt roads. While we have tried to avoid this wherever possible, sometimes these were the "paths of least resistance"; the alternative would have been to create a new trail on the land, which is not within our goal of introducing a low-impact recreation opportunity.

This guide thus is designed for the experienced desert trekker who is looking for some new through-hiking experiences on a tested route. Hopefully, we've removed some of the questions about water availability and terrain accessibility.

Mike Coronella grew up in suburban New Jersey and moved to Utah in 1990 for "just a winter, to ski." Joe "Mitch" Mitchell came to Utah to climb and snowboard in 1989, after growing up in the nomadic world of an Army brat. After separately discovering the charms of the Colorado Plateau, and its beautiful, deep desolation, we decided that we needed to try to show people what is here, to showcase these beautiful, unique and threatened public lands, and to try to dispel the notion that they are merely wastelands, good only for their limited resources. We want to help promote the protection and conservation of this incredible region, and we believe that as more people become aware of this region, the more likely they will be to work towards its protection.

"Civilization" seems to be encroaching on any and every piece of possibly (and sometimes questionably) habitable land, and the Colorado Plateau is not ignored by

MITCH (LEFT) AND MIKE (RIGHT) OUT ON THE TRAIL

the spreading masses. At the rate land is being overspread, soon there could be few places that those who need a sabbatical in the deepest recesses of the natural world can go for an escape, or recharge, or whatever it is that they seek. While certainly not everyone has a need for such a reprieve from society, some of us do, and if these lands become lost through development we would feel a serious loss. We need lands where we can explore, where we can go for days on end without seeing another being, where the only footprints to be found are those of wild animals, the only evidence of the modern world the sadly discordant noise of overhead airplanes.

The area discussed here is threatened in many ways, and virtually always with an economic motive. Yet these lands have enormous worth far beyond that of any monetary value that is far too often overlooked and underrepresented; but then, how does one measure the value of a reinvigorated soul?

> *"The wilderness once offered men a plausible way of life, now it functions as a psychiatric refuge. Soon there will be no wilderness. Soon there will be no place to go. Then the madness becomes universal. And the universe goes mad."*
>
> —DOC SARVIS IN *The Monkey Wrench Gang*

Here's what *you* can do to help ensure that this area will be intact for future generations: Contact your state's representatives and insist that they support America's Redrock Wilderness Act. Also contact:

Southern Utah Wilderness Alliance
1471 South 1100 East, Salt Lake City, Utah 84105
(801) 486-3161
www.suwa.org

Red Rock Forests
90 West Center St., Moab, Utah 84532
(435) 259-5640
www.redrockforests.org

Grand Canyon Trust
2601 N. Fort Valley Road, Flagstaff, Arizona 86001
(928) 774-7488
www.grandcanyontrust.org

Glen Canyon Institute
450 S. 900 E., Ste 160, Salt Lake City, Utah 84102
(801) 363-4450
www.glencanyon.org

One thing is certain: If no one speaks up now, the integrity of this area will be lost forever. **Please, get involved!**

ABOUT THE TRAIL

The Hayduke Trail has been broken down into fourteen sections. Each section can be an amazing trek unto itself, or sections can be linked together for extended journeys. All multiple-section hikes will need to be well planned, with careful thought given to methods and places of resupply: food/water caches, meetings, etc. Most sections have adequate water available along the route, but some sections require the bringing of outside water supplies.

Weather needs to be considered when planning a through hike because of the length of time you'll be out there. We recommend a springtime journey. While you never quite know what kind of weather you'll get, you will avoid the hottest season and the flash floods associated with monsoon storms. Water also will be more readily available in the spring.

There are also many other options: day hikes and spur routes that can be accessed from the Hayduke Trail to allow for a unique experience and greater exposure to the many incredible features of this region. A few of these will be mentioned in their appropriate sections.

BEWARE!

The Hayduke Trail is made up of existing trails, known routes, unpaved roads, cattle and game trails, ridges, and drainages. The trail is not always apparent or obvious (in fact, there may be no trail at all!); strong navigational skills are necessary if one is to safely and happily complete a trek in this beautiful, rugged region. This is a backcountry route; it is not a beaten trail like the Appalachian Trail. There are no towns ahead; there are few shelters. There are numerous "dry camps"; so you'll be carrying up to twelve liters of water weight, which means you may have an extra twenty-six pounds of load on your back. The "trail" involves hiking and wading through rivers, often dealing with quicksand and tight brush. It involves scrambling over or around rockfalls, and climbing up, down, and across steep talus slopes. Most likely, there will be no one around, perhaps for days at a time. We once went ten days in one section without seeing another person). This is a desolate region, and care must be taken to enjoy (and survive) trekking through it. This is not "beginner" terrain: getting in over your head in this region can easily end your life.

Always tell someone your itinerary before heading out, so they can sound the alarm if you don't return within a reasonable time. If you do become lost, remember that it's easier for a searcher to find a stationary subject than a wandering subject.

This guide cannot address every possible situation that could potentially be encountered on the Hayduke Trail. Weather can change, drainages could have too much water to enter or to cross, springs dry out, there could be rock/landslides, one could go slower than expected, or any of an unimaginable array of other obstacles may present themselves while you are out there. Plan accordingly! Don't push timetables too closely; always leave yourself enough food and water to deal with unexpected happenings, think about weather conditions before they become an issue, etc. Remember: **the difference between an adventure and an ordeal is how well prepared you are!**

Traveling in the Colorado Plateau region can be a different experience than many are accustomed to. This region is largely uninhabited, undeveloped, and infrequently visited (though that is changing as people search for new places to escape to). There are a couple of reasons for this. One is certainly the terrain; it is not easily navigated or traversed, with its multitude of steep, deep, rock-walled canyons. The biggest reason, however, for this land being left so desolate in this day and age is the lack of viable water sources. Human settlement is dependent on adequate water for agriculture, cooking, and drinking, and water in the Colorado Plateau region generally is not available in such quantities. This is a desert climate. **The deep canyons and desert climate present some hazards that must be carefully considered and require constant vigilance to avoid serious situations such as becoming lost, trapped, or even dying.**

WATER CONCERNS

Water in the Colorado Plateau region is generally found in two quantities: not enough, or much too much. Either situation can be lethal. A general rule for traveling through this area is to plan on the consumption of **at least one gallon of water per day per person.** People traveling in the heat of the summer, where temperatures can easily exceed 100°F, or over more strenuous terrain, will need more than a gallon per day. Dehydration, caused by inadequate water consumption, can become a very serious situation very rapidly.

Hyponatremia, also known as "water drunk," is defined as "abnormally low concentrations of sodium ions in the circulating blood." It is an *extremely* serious condition that usually presents itself only in the heat of the desert (and is of particular concern in the gorge of the Grand Canyon). Profuse sweating and subsequent rehydration without adequate salt/electrolyte intake causes hyponatremia. This condition is very debilitating; vomiting, inability to proceed, seizures, and even death are possible. Be absolutely sure to address this concern while traveling; always have some type of electrolyte and sodium

YOUNG'S CANYON DRAINAGE

replenishment strategy. Sports drinks work, and eating properly will also help prevent this condition; salt tablets are not recommended, as they can be harmful to the stomach. Anyone who is suspected of suffering from this needs *immediate* sodium replenishment, as symptoms will rapidly get worse. One of the authors ran into someone who had become hyponatremic in the Grand Canyon after not eating breakfast on a hot day with a tough climb out of the gorge. He had plenty of water but was soon vomiting and became unable to even stand up. He claimed that he literally thought he was going to die. Eating an energy bar was enough to get him quickly back on his feet, a bit more food and nourishment brought him to capable form again. Moral: **A proper diet and hydration are paramount in assuring your body's ability to function properly.**

There are two main sources of water in the region: surface water and groundwater. Surface water comes in either perennial streams or rivers, or in the form of run-off from snowmelt or storms. Surface water in this region is generally heavily silt laden; we found that letting water settle overnight helped extend the life of our water filters. A coffee filter used as a pre-filter also helps, as does adding a small quantity of alum or prickly pear juice. Groundwater is found at seeps and springs, where underground water spills out between certain layers of rock. Springs are the major source of water along the Hayduke Trail, and most are shown on the USGS 7.5 minute quad maps, although not all springs shown on these maps can be found. Some of these springs have been "developed" for livestock by ranchers. They often run a pipe or hose into the ground to ensure a more reliable flow, occasionally filling stock tanks. Some of the springs are mere trickles, the water dripping from a wall. These trickles, or seeps, can provide water, but sometimes ingenuity is needed to actually extract a useful portion. You could try to soak up water with a bandana or camptowel, then wring the liquid into a container; or you could try leaving a container to catch the drips over a period of time. There are other less-obvious water sources deep in sandy washes or near cottonwood tree groves; we suggest consulting desert survival handbooks to learn more about these potentially lifesaving sources. One last source that we took advantage of while trekking about this parched land was that of the infrequent motorist; such folks are almost always ready to help out backpackers, and they often have extra water.

There are a few considerations about water safety to keep in mind. First, not all water found in these parts is immediately suitable for drinking. Safe consumption involves making certain that the water does not contain any bacteria that will cause a person to become ill. This can be accomplished through one of three methods: boiling the water, treating it with iodine (the *later* addition of a small quantity of vitamin C will reduce the iodine flavor), or filtering the water with a commercially

available water filter (such as SweetWater filters). It is also a good idea to do some research about your water sources; many in the Colorado Plateau contain such toxins as arsenic or uranium and other radioactive materials. **All of the water sources referred to in this guide have been sampled by the authors, but all water should be treated/ filtered, even that from seemingly clean springs.** We can only attest to the existence of these sources as of this writing; but droughts are known to dry up springs.

PUMPING WATER, DIRTY DEVIL RIVER

There is one more very important water consideration to keep in mind: rainfall. While rain is not very common here, one must be aware of the weather, not only where one is but also in the farthest reaches of whatever drainage one might happen to be in. Rainfall can certainly be quite beneficial, making it easy to find fresh water, either in streambeds or "potholes" (water-filled depressions in the rock); but rainfall can also spell disaster. In this land of sand and rock, the rain does not readily soak into the ground, it mostly forms run-off, which has been instrumental in forming the deep gorges that carry water to the Colorado River (by definition, all drainages of the Colorado Plateau eventually empty into the Colorado River). This can create a very dangerous hazard: flash flooding. Even a small storm can cause flooding, or "gully washers," due to the ground's inability to soak up rainfall. Never allow yourself to be in a deep canyon (which will frequently have no "escape zones") without being able to get above the high-water mark when it is storming or threatening to storm. **You must always be aware of flash flood hazards. They are the biggest killer of Colorado Plateau backcountry travelers.** Never camp in a drainage unless you are certain that the weather is clear, and, even then, make absolutely certain that the camp is above the high-water mark. **Remember: clear skies overhead do not ensure your safety.** A distant storm can easily produce enough water to send a raging torrent down the drainage, leaving unsuspecting hikers or campers little or no time to get out of the way. This was tragically demonstrated in the summer of 1997, when eleven people were killed in a flash flood in Antelope Canyon near Page, Arizona. The skies overhead were clear, and two unsuspecting groups entered this slot canyon, only to be overrun by a sudden wall of water produced by a storm more than twenty miles away. **When in doubt, use another route.** If storms are imminent, make sure you are not in harm's way; hike the rim of the canyon or wait out the storm in a safe place.

Another water-related hazard is that of **quicksand**, generally found in wash/river bottoms. Walking over quicksand is fairly simple; the most important thing is to keep moving, or you will slowly sink into the quagmire. The main danger is simply losing one's footwear, as you almost have to try to get fully stuck (at least in the stuff that we've encountered).

CANYON HAZARDS

The deep canyons of the Colorado Plateau can present their own unique problems. Navigation can be difficult; points separated on a map by a mere mile can require many, many miles of hiking to reach; a deep, inaccessible canyon can block a route; and sometimes you can't get out of the canyon where you want to. Climbing the walls of these canyons can be extremely dangerous, particularly to those inexperienced in this region. It is often fairly simple to climb a section of sandstone (slickrock), only to find that you can't go on, up or down, rendering you trapped on the wall. Always be certain when climbing that you can downclimb what you have ascended, and be aware of loose and crumbling rock above. You should also be aware of where you are placing your hands when climbing up the wall of a canyon; imagine unknowingly reaching into a rattler's nest!

Canyons can contain some major obstacles in the form of chockstones, which can block passage and be difficult to pass, and pouroffs, which are a sudden drop, or drop-off, of the canyon floor. Pour-offs can force one to climb out of the canyon and rim walk until another route is found back into the canyon (as in Young's Canyon in Section 3). Also, thick, thorny brush can create an annoying (and painful), but usually passable obstacle.

Being inside a canyon can make pinpointing your location difficult; all of the twisting and turning and lack of visible landmarks conspire to conceal your exact location. Deep and narrow canyon walls can also prevent one from using high-tech tools; you won't always be able to get GPS or cellular signals. Another major concern is related to the above discussion on flash flooding; in a deep canyon, it may be impossible to tell what the weather is like anywhere but directly above you.

NAVIGATION

The best way to safely navigate this region is by using map and compass and being *extremely* careful to always keep track of your exact location as you travel. We highly recommend using USGS 7.5 minute topographic maps; larger-scale maps, with their bigger contour intervals, can literally leave you hanging, since a fifty-foot cliff or pour-off might not even be noted.

ANIMALS

RATTLESNAKE

There are all kinds of living creatures in the Colorado Plateau; some are fairly common, such as mule deer, ravens, and rabbits; while others, such as desert bighorns and kit fox, aren't quite as evident. Traveling among these creatures can require some care but can also be quite rewarding. As with all elements of backcountry travel, some consideration should be given to sharing space with wild creatures. First, remember that you are visiting the creature's home, not the other way around. Wildlife should never be approached or fed. A good rule of thumb: **If an animal reacts to your presence, you are too close!**

Poisonous creatures. There are only a few venomous creatures that need consideration—rattlesnakes, scorpions (and vinegaroons), and brown recluse and black widow spiders. These are all fairly easy to avoid: check shoes before putting them on and check under the tent or sleeping bag before packing up for any critters that may have been attracted by the warmth of a sleeping body. Care should also be taken while climbing; be aware of where you are putting your hands. Statistics show rather conclusively that rattlesnakes bite only those who disturb or harass them, so leave them alone! Be aware that rattlesnakes don't always "rattle" as you approach, so you have to keep an eye out for them while hiking. Simply give them a little extra room as you pass to avoid a nasty encounter. We once found a faded pygmy rattler sleeping, coiled and quiet, inches away, while we were eating a snack. If you are bitten by any of these, medical attention should be sought. Immobilize the bitten extremity and head out immediately.

Insects and rodents. In the warmer months (midspring through early autumn), bug repellant and/or long sleeves and pants will be needed to fend off swarms of gnats, biting flies, mosquitoes, and "no-see-ums," particularly near riparian zones. Mosquito netting can be a very valuable (and lightweight) asset.

There is a large rodent population in the desert; you'll encounter the more bothersome ones in the night, particularly pack rats and mice. Care must be taken to prevent these pests from accessing your food supply; these critters will chew their way into most anything if given the opportunity. Pack rats have been known to take other small items besides food; a neat, clean campsite will help prevent such losses. In the course of establishing this route, we have had mice chew through plastic bags and containers and chew up pack and hiking pole webbing. We've awakened to mice scrambling over our sleeping bags, hands, and even faces. A squirrel searching for food chewed through the top of one of our packs. To avoid these situations, keep your food in the tent or secured pack and hang food bags (as in bear country); but keep in mind that these varmints can get just about anywhere they want. Ringtail cats, found throughout the region, but more prevalent in the Grand Canyon, can be a particular problem; with their larger size, they can devour enough of your food to end your trip!

Another concern with rodents is fairly recent: hantavirus. This virus, which has no known cure, can kill a person in as little as twenty-four hours. The illness is thought to be spread by airborne molecules that originate in rodent feces. The best we can tell you is not to disturb or stir up areas that have a high frequency of rodent traffic. These areas often include archaeological sites (granaries and ruins), pack rat middens or nests, and small caves.

There are a couple of birds that you may want to be aware of— ravens and scrub jays. These birds are relatively smart; they have been known to deprive folks of their food and gear, and they are reported even to have learned how to open pockets and pouches of packs. The recently released California condors along the Arizona Strip also have a reputation for disturbing camps; so keep a neat camp and don't ever leave food unattended.

Predators. While our so-called civilization has done its best to eradicate predators in this region at the behest of the ranchers and hunters, many still exist, and one should be aware of the risks involved (which are actually pretty minor). Fortunately, most area predators are extremely wary of human presence and are rarely even sighted. These include cougars (mountain lions), bobcats, coyotes, foxes, and the

**TRACKS FROM TWO-LEGGED AND
FOUR-LEGGED CREATURES**

very infrequent black bears (which are generally found in higher, wetter areas but are known to travel out of those areas during extended drought periods). While encounters with these creatures are very rare, they can happen. The best thing to do if you encounter one is to simply give the animal its space. If a violent encounter is inevitable, fight like hell. These animals want an easy meal and, unless they are defending their domain or families, they will generally back off from a battle. Keep in mind that cats kill their victims through strangulation, so protect your windpipe and back of neck at all costs. **Never run from a predator.** Running only prompts an instinctive pursuit, and they all can easily outrun a human. Slowly back away from a situation.

Livestock. Unfortunately, livestock still graze on much of the public land in this region and have left indelible marks on the land. Overgrazing has impacted many areas, changing the balance of the plant species, and nonnative plants have been introduced to the ecosystem. Many water sources have been rendered unusable, becoming filthy pools of stagnant and contaminated muck. Some cattle that have been left to fend for themselves in the range for extended periods can be quite ornery and will require that you keep a large distance between them and you.

CLIMATE

Preparing for an extended trek through this region requires careful thought and planning. Virtually all weather systems can potentially be encountered while traveling here, from freezing cold and blizzards to extended periods of heat and drought. One extreme can immediately follow the other, particularly when associated with elevation changes.

Wind is common. The dry desert air allows for huge shifts in the daily temperatures, from the heat of the midday sun to a clear and cool (even frosty) evening; a 40-degree (F) change is not unusual. Temperatures in the bottom of the Grand Canyon can reach 120 degrees, mountaintop temperatures can dip below zero. The bottom line: be prepared for anything. Always plan on using sunblock, even in the winter, as the dry desert air does not filter out much of the sun's harmful UV rays.

Traveling in this region in the summer months can be extremely hazardous and is not recommended. If you are traveling then, you should avoid strenuous activities, particularly under the heat and the intense rays of the midday sun. Sit out the hottest part of the day in the shade, and update your journal or treat yourself to a siesta if you must be out this time of year.

Winter travel also can be quite hazardous; ice can make passage dangerous or impossible. If you venture into any of the mountains, with their higher snowfall amounts, you should know how to determine snowpack stability and have good route-finding skills to avoid potential avalanche problems.

Monsoon season is another concern when traveling upon the Colorado Plateau. Mid-to-late-summer storms are responsible for many of the region's flash floods, so be sure to plan accordingly.

We recommend that those attempting to travel the length of the Hayduke Trail plan on a late winter or early spring departure from Arches National Park. While you will most likely encounter nasty weather at that time of year, it offers the best chances for easily finding water along the way without the hazards associated with summer squalls (i.e., flash floods). Fall weather can be very pleasant but, like the spring, any weather conditions could be encountered. A wet monsoon season can replenish springs and surface water sources that may be dry in midsummer.

GEAR

Here's a list of some essential gear that we carried with us as we hiked the trail.

- Water pump/filter (we always had an extra filter with us)

- 3-gallon water capacity per person

- Large collapsible water settling jug (to allow river water to settle before filtering and thus extend filter life). Another filter life extender is to use coffee filters wrapped around the wet end of the hose in silty water.

- Comprehensive first-aid kit and the knowledge of how to use it!

- Trekking poles (We do not consider these options; they are an incredible help.)

- Ropes (While there is no technical climbing on the route, we found it necessary to use ropes to haul our packs up and down on a few occasions. Try a 100-foot section of sturdy webbing.)

- Backpacking stove (Campfires are not recommended; in some areas they are not allowed.)

- Air mattresses with chair conversion kit (and repair kit)

- Sleeping bag (appropriate for the season)

- Tent (Helps keep out bugs, scorpions, snakes, and blowing sand.)

- Headlamps

- Multi-tool

- Binoculars (can help with route finding)

- Compass and the knowledge of how to use it!

- Clothing (Cotton kills, layering is vital! Always have a water/ windproof outer layer. Light-colored long pants and sleeves can help to keep insects and the hot sun off your skin.)

  — Footwear (hiking boots, river sandals, lightweight slippers)

  — Socks (Get decent hiking socks!)

  — Wide-brimmed hat (This often will be the only shade around.)

  — Sunglasses (good ones)

- Bug repellant/mosquito netting

- Sunblock

- Food (We used powdered bodybuilding mix, breakfast bars, Clif bars, homemade beef jerky, homemade trail mix, dried fruits, and freeze-dried backpacking dinners to sustain us on our adventures. Always carry at least one extra day's food. You never know when you could be delayed.)

CACHING FOOD AND WATER

Sometimes it will be logistically simpler to cache food and/or water than to meet with someone to resupply you. If you are going to cache supplies, make sure the area is going to be accessible when you plan on stashing them. This means caching in the fall, since places like the Kaibab Plateau area (North Rim of the Grand Canyon) probably will be snowed in—as may be almost any of the more remote dirt roads if you plan to cache things just before you start a through hike (if you start the Hayduke Trail in the early spring as recommended).

RETRIEVING FOOD CACHE ON HORSESHOE MESA, GRAND CANYON NATIONAL PARK

The following guidelines will help ensure that your supplies will be there when you show up to retrieve them:

- Use only sturdy weatherproof and critter-proof containers. (We used five-gallon pickle buckets with duct-tape-sealed lids. Cayenne pepper may help keep rodents from gnawing on the tape.)

- Make sure containers are well marked as to ownership and expected date of retrieval.

- Make sure containers are placed in a well-concealed location, preferably out of the elements.

- Always retrieve your cache containers after the trip is finished! Leaving them in place is nothing more than littering.

- **Don't ever move, or take anything from, any caches you may inadvertently stumble across! Someone's life may be dependent on those supplies!**

PETS AND PACK ANIMALS

Because of the nature of this route, neither pets nor pack animals are recommended on the Hayduke Trail. The national parks that the Hayduke Trail passes through do not allow pets in the backcountry, and the terrain will frequently prevent anything but an able human to pass. That said, there are trail sections that some of these animals could safely (and legally) manage. Read each section description carefully; any mention of large pour-offs, climbing, or roping packs is a sure sign that animals would not be able to continue.

Dogs should be in top hiking condition and should have boots for travel through this frequently hot land with its sharp plants and rocks to prevent damage to their pads. This is no place to train an animal; an ill-prepared pet will ruin your trip. Guaranteed. Make sure that all critters (human and otherwise) have adequate water; heat stroke should be your particular concern for pets in this region. Be sure to remove all dog waste from the trail; it is as unnatural as human waste is out there! Do not allow a dog to chase wildlife or to dig in archaeological sites, and, please, keep your animal under control at *all* times!

ARCHAEOLOGICAL SITES AND ARTIFACTS

The Colorado Plateau has been inhabited by humans at least sporadically for some ten thousand years or more. The various cultures include the big-game hunters of the last Ice Age, the "Basketmakers," the Fremont, and the Anasazi, as well as the more recent Paiute, Ute, Hopi, and Navajo people. All of these groups have left traces in the region, leaving behind markings on rock, shelters, tools, clothing items, pottery, and even human remains.

The Hayduke Trail passes near, or through, many of these archaeological sites. Under the U.S. Antiquities Act, it is **illegal** for any archaeological sites or artifacts to be disturbed. That means **no digging, no collecting, and no defacing** of any sites or items. You may find pottery sherds or stone tools on the ground; leave them there! Leave them for others to "discover" and enjoy. There is still much that is unknown about some of these civilizations, and we can only learn from these sites if they are left intact and unmolested. Artifacts are meaningless outside of the context of the site at which they are found; we urge you to resist the temptation to pocket any items. Please, take only pictures!

If you come upon a "ruin," do not attempt to excavate for lost treasures. You cannot camp on an archaeological site; you will disturb it, and that's illegal. And then there is one of the authors' pet peeves: **Never leave any type of mark on a pictograph** (painted) **or petroglyph** (carved) **panel.** Do not carve your initials, name, date, or anything else on the rock. Do not attempt to "outline" a preexisting image to see it better. In fact, don't even touch these panels (the oils of your skin can affect them). Although we encourage people to go out and explore this region, we also would like the remaining relics of past

ANCIENT DWELLING, BEEF BASIN

peoples left alone, so we have consciously left out directions to and descriptions of sensitive or lesser-known sites. (See How to Visit an Archaeological Site, in this volume.)

HISTORY

Indigenous people have been in the Colorado Plateau for at least 10,000 years, but Europeans have been in the area for less than 250 years (if one ignores the isolated instance of the Cardenas expedition that reached the south rim of the Grand Canyon in about 1540). Some of the first documented white men to travel to the Colorado Plateau were members of the Dominguez-Escalante expedition, which sought a route from Santa Fe (in present-day New Mexico) to Monterey, California, in 1776. They made their way to the Colorado River, which they crossed near Grand Junction, Colorado, and then headed north, crossing the Green River near the present-day town of Jensen, Utah. The Dominguez party members were the first of European descent to visit Utah Lake, coming off the Wasatch Plateau through Spanish Fork, where the indigenous "Timpanogos People" suggested that they would not make it across the western deserts alive. They headed south to return to Santa Fe, only to find their way obstructed by the canyons of the Colorado River. They finally found a ford across the river at a place that became known as the Crossing of the Fathers (now under the waters of Lake Powell). It wasn't until Mormon settlers arrived in the mid to late 1800s that Americans came to know the area. On the orders of Mormon leader Brigham Young, families and groups spread from the Salt Lake Valley and settled throughout the region. These settlers scratched a living from the soil, farming and grazing livestock where water allowed such activities, and founding towns such as Escalante, Boulder, St. George, and Kanab. U.S. Army Major John Wesley Powell was responsible for much of the early exploration of the area, and his expedition members also named many of the features. Another man who contributed much to the understanding of this region was the Mormon pioneer and explorer Jacob Hamblin.

The industrial age sparked a search for mineral and other resources, and many were found in this area, including coal, oil, iron, potash, salt, and uranium. These searches and subsequent mining operations have had huge impacts on the land. Uranium prospectors drove their jeeps everywhere they could in the hunt for the deadly element, and many of these old jeep tracks are still apparent today (and are often the source of what many Utah counties claim as established "roadways," despite the fact that many might not have been traveled on by vehicles in decades). Today, the primary use of this land is for recreation: hiking, biking, boating, sightseeing, photography, four-wheeling, and even base-jumping are some of the activities that you could expect to see folks involved in these days (though there is still grazing of livestock as well as mining and drilling for fuels).

GEOLOGY

The geology of the Colorado Plateau is rather complex and varied. The only layers of rock that will be specifically discussed here will be those of the inner gorge of the Grand Canyon, as these layers are used for trail descriptions and navigation.

The Colorado Plateau's physical history has in large part been exposed by the forces of wind and water. At various times in its long history this region has been under water, allowing the building of sediment and deposits. The deposition has then been acted upon by natural forces to become layer upon layer of rock. The layers are then eroded by winds, temperature cycles, and the action of running or falling water, with results as varied as Delicate Arch, Fairyland at Bryce Canyon, and the Grand Canyon.

Various upheavals, lifts, earthquakes, and volcanoes have been responsible for some of the area's more interesting features. The La Sal, Abajo, and Henry Mountain Ranges are all laccolithic (volcanic) in origin. The San Rafael Swell and features like the anticline near Moab are evidence of past localized uplifts. The Waterpocket Fold of Capitol Reef is simply a giant wrinkle in the earth's crust. Gold, silver, uranium, salt, oil, natural gas, coal, and even gemstones have been found in the region. Fossils from many eras have been found in this area, from dinosaur footprints to entire skeletons of long-extinct creatures. It would take an entire volume to discuss the geologic complexities here; we recommend you read one by a person with a formal background in geology!

The Grand Canyon's layering is easily remembered by this sentence: **K**now **T**he **C**anyon's **H**istory, **S**tudy **R**ocks **M**ade **B**y **T**ime, and is broken down as follows (from top to bottom):

> **K**aibab Limestone
> **T**oroweap Formation
> **C**oconino Sandstone
> **H**ermit Shale
> **S**upai Group
> **R**edwall Limestone
> **M**uav Limestone
> **B**right Angel Shale
> **T**apeats Sandstone
> Vishnu Schist

LEAVE NO TRACE!

We hope that visitors to the Colorado Plateau are respectful and responsible enough to adhere to the following backcountry practices (slightly modified by the authors to apply to the desert environment). They have been supplied by the National Outdoor Leadership School and Leave No Trace agencies; contact them at 1-800-332-4100 or www.lnt.org.

Plan Ahead and Prepare

- Know the regulations, inherent risks, and special concerns for the area you'll visit.

- Visit the backcountry in small groups.

- Use maps and compass to eliminate the need for tree scars, rock cairns, or ribbons.

- Choose equipment and clothing in subdued colors.

- Repackage food into reusable containers.

- Prepare for all types of weather.

Camp and Travel on Durable Surfaces

At Camp

▧ Good campsites are found, not made. Altering a site is unnecessary.

▧ Wherever possible, choose established legal campsites that won't be harmed by your stay.

▧ Restrict activities to areas where vegetation is compacted or absent.

▧ Keep pollutants out of water sources by camping at least 200 feet (70 adult steps) from lakes, streams, and potholes.

On the Trail

▧ Stay on designated trails. Walk in single file in the middle of the path.

▧ Do not shortcut switchbacks.

▧ When traveling cross-country, choose the most durable surface available: rock, gravel, dry grasses, or snow.

▧ Do not trample microbiotic/cryptobiotic crusts.

CRYPTOBIOTIC SOIL. FRAGILE.
STAY OFF!

Dispose of Waste Properly

▧ If you pack it in, pack it out. Inspect your campsites and rest areas for trash or spilled foods. Pack out all trash, both your's and others'.

▧ Deposit solid human waste in cat holes dug six to eight inches deep at least 200 feet from water, camp, and trails. Cover and disguise the cat hole when finished.

▧ Use toilet paper or wipes sparingly. Packing these items out is required at many places along the trail, so get in the habit of just taking them with you (a couple of Ziploc-style plastic bags will do the trick for safe transport).

■ To wash yourself or dishes, carry water 200 feet away from streams or lakes. We usually use sand to scrub dishes clean, and then use boiling water the next time the stove is set up to sanitize them. Scatter strained dishwater (try to remove larger pieces of food matter before dumping). Rodents can quickly establish themselves at a camp that has had food particles left behind, severely impacting future campers. Leave your camp at least as clean as you found it!

■ Pick up all spilled foods.

Leave What You Find

■ Preserve the past. Do not damage historical structures or remove artifacts.

■ Leave rocks, plants, and other natural objects where found.

■ Do not build structures or furniture or dig trenches.

Minimize Campfire Impacts

■ Campfires can create lasting impacts on the backcountry. Always carry a lightweight stove for cooking. Enjoy a candle lantern for light.

■ Where fires are permitted, use established fire rings or mound fires.

■ Keep fires small. Use dead, downed wood that can be broken by hand.

■ Burn all wood and coals to ash. Put out campfires completely, remove unburned trash, and then scatter the cool ashes.

Respect Wildlife

■ Observe wildlife from a distance. Do not follow or approach animals.

- Never feed wild animals. Feeding wildlife damages their health, alters natural behaviors, and exposes them to predators and other dangers.

- Protect wildlife and your food by storing rations and trash securely.

- Keep pets under control at all times.

- Leave young animals alone.

- Avoid nesting, feeding, or mating animals.

Be Considerate of Other Visitors

- Respect other visitors and protect the quality of their experience.

- Be courteous. Yield to other users on the trail.

- Step to the downhill side of trail when encountering pack stock.

- Take breaks on durable surfaces away from the trail.

- Let nature's sounds prevail. Keep noise levels to a minimum.

TRAIL ETHICS

To help ensure that all users of the Hayduke Trail will have a rewarding wilderness experience, there are practices beyond the Leave No Trace guidelines that are mostly a matter of common courtesy and consideration.

- Do not camp near another group (that means out of eyesight and out of earshot).

- Uphill travelers *always* have the right of way on a trail. Step aside to allow them to pass.

- Travel quietly.

- Wear subdued colors, so as not to stick out like the proverbial "sore thumb."

- Be aware that some people head to some places for the purpose of photography, do not camp in a place that would destroy a scene (such as under an arch).

- Do not camp in the middle of a trail! Not only will people passing through bother you, they will be bothered by having to walk through someone's camp.

- As far as wildlife is concerned, here is a good rule of thumb: if an animal reacts to your presence, you're too close!

PERMITS

All of the national parks that the Hayduke Trail passes through require permits for backcountry camping, as does the Grand Staircase–Escalante National Monument and the Glen Canyon National Recreation Area. Be sure to check where backcountry camping is or is not allowed. At the present time, no permits are needed to camp or travel on BLM or national forest land. Permits may be difficult to obtain for high-demand areas such as Canyonlands National Park (which is why we have the trail going overland instead of to the designated back-packing sites) and the Grand Canyon; you will need to plan well in advance. All of these federal agencies have websites that can be accessed through www.nps.gov.

Arches National Park
P.O. Box 907, Moab, Utah 84532-0907
435-719-2299
archinfo@nps.gov

Canyonlands National Park (Needles District)
2282 S. West Resource Blvd., Moab, Utah 84532-3298
435-719-2100
canyinfo@nps.gov

Capitol Reef National Park
HC 70 Box 15, Torrey, Utah 84775-9602
435-425-3791
CARE_interpretation@nps.gov

Bryce Canyon National Park
P.O. Box 170001, Bryce Canyon, Utah 84717-0001
435-834-5322
BRCA_superintendent@nps.gov

Zion National Park
SR 9, Springdale, Utah 84767-1099
435-772-3256
ZION_park_information@nps.gov

Grand Canyon National Park
P.O. Box 129, Grand Canyon, Arizona
520-638-7888 (recorded message)
GRCA_superintendent@nps.gov

Glen Canyon National Recreation Area
P.O. Box 1507, Page, Arizona 86040-1507
520-608-6200
GLCA_CHVC@nps.gov

Grand Staircase–Escalante National Monument
755 West Main, Escalante, Utah 84726
435-826-5499
escalant@ut.blm.gov

Paria Canyon/Vermillion Cliffs
(through Arizona Strip Interpretive Association)
345 E. Riverside Dr., St. George, Utah 84790
435-688-3246
ASFOWEB_AZ@blm.gov

MORE ABOUT THE ROUTE

The Hayduke Trail, as it is described in this book, is not exactly the same as the route that we traveled across this amazing region. There are various changes along the way, for a number of reasons, which include private property issues, very dangerous terrain, areas with hard-to-get permits, and our desire to protect sensitive archaeological areas.

For the curious, here is a brief description of some of the areas that we hiked through that are not on the Hayduke Trail but will provide more of an idea of the Colorado Plateau's character.

"Mitch and Mike's Misery." Three days after we began our second lengthy journey across the desert, we dropped more than 1,000 feet down "Fat Man's Misery," an extremely steep route into "The Barracks," a canyon of the East Fork of the Virgin River. Our intention was to travel four miles upriver to Rock Canyon (the route described in this guide), but after only three-quarters of a mile we came to a waterfall that we could not find a way around. Usually there is just a small amount of water coming through the canyon, but a large storm five days earlier had turned the small pour-off into an impassable obstacle. We were forced to find another way, which meant either turn around or climb out. We decided to climb out, through the most treacherous and difficult terrain we had ever encountered. For the next five hours we pushed, pulled, and carried our packs, with both bodies and ropes, up a ridiculously steep wall, all the while not even knowing whether or not our chosen route would take us to the top. We fought through thick scrub, loose soil, and rock faces complete with breakable holds and crumbling rock. Finally, an hour and a half after sunset, we collapsed, exhausted, bruised, scraped, and otherwise torn up, on the first level piece of ground that we encountered. Unfortunately, our battle with the Barracks didn't just beat us up, it also beat up most of our water containers, forcing us again off our planned route into the strange, polygamist town of Hildale, Utah, to replace those vital pieces of gear. We will forever refer to this route as Mitch and Mike's Misery, and we hope that no one else needs to escape the Barracks this way.

In the Grand Canyon we experienced what we refer to as our "three days of terror"—so named from going to bed scared and waking up scared, and generally being scared all day, often not sure we'd still be alive in an hour. We were going from Flint Creek to Crystal Creek. This particular route began with an insane forty-foot climb, with big exposure and rotten holds, before it got worse. After climbing a narrow chimney, we came to a particularly scary knife ridge, complete with about 800-foot drops on both sides. What made it even more interesting (besides, of course, the packs on our backs) was that it started as a hands-on climb and slowly broke over to horizontal, meaning somewhere in there you had to let go of the handholds and stand up. Coming off that narrow strip of rock onto the Sagittarius Ridge offered immense satisfaction—the feeling of survival is pretty sweet! This led us farther to the Flint/Tuna saddle, located below Point Sublime, where, exhausted and blown away by the scenery, we stopped for the night, despite the fact that we needed to get to the river, a few thousand feet below, to get water. That night, a cougar in heat serenaded us from way too close as we slept under the stars.

The next day began with a beautiful sunrise—one we hoped would not be our last. The descent to the river was unbelievably steep and hot; both of us took serious falls that day, resulting in torn flesh and shed blood (we discussed whether or not we were getting enough iron in our diet to replace all the blood we kept leaving around the place). We found an absolutely disgusting-looking pool of water on the way that we managed to extract a couple of liters of water from. Parched from the hot spring sun, navigating a route down into the schist layer was one of the most difficult things either of us had done. But the next day would bring us to the hardest part—a span of the schist had to be traversed to Crystal Creek. Schist in the depths of the Grand Canyon is slick, steep rock. Traveling across this rock above the icy water of the dam-choked river was treacherous at best. We worked our way across the rock, often using mere finger- and toeholds, again with backpacks and no roped protection. Any slip would have been fatal; either blunt trauma or drowning (there was nowhere to get out of the river) was the guaranteed result. The roar of Crystal Rapids also helped keep the river constantly on our minds. It literally took hours to go a fraction of a mile, and that travel was only possible because of a very low river flow. Terror at its best; we felt that the canyon kept trying to kill us. Such things can change one's perspective. We have opted to remove this section from the route for safety reasons.

The Paria River. After leaving the Grand Canyon and spending five days traveling across the hot Arizona Strip (with no water except at the lodges on the highway), we reached the Paria—an absolutely amazing canyon of spectacular color, changing from a fairly wide-open river drainage to a thousand-foot-deep, narrow canyon with sheer rock walls. There are numerous petroglyph panels, particularly in the lower section of the river, and cottonwood trees line the watercourse in all but the narrowest places. This canyon is truly a scenic marvel. We traveled up the river from Lee's Ferry (where most people go downriver), leaving Arizona at the confluence with Buckskin Gulch. A group of hikers we encountered reminded us that we needed to change our watches to Utah time there. We responded by saying that we didn't think that our watches could be set back that far! The numerous water crossings helped keep us cool and even offered the opportunity for some "swimming" in some of the pools that we encountered. We ended up leaving the river drainage a day earlier than planned because of a heavy cloud cover and concern over flooding. Due to limited permits and the extreme flash-flood hazard, we have omitted this section.

The Escalante Mountains and the Aquarius Plateau. Hiking through this area was a big surprise for us: we were out of the desert and in an alpine setting for a change. We started out of the Grand Staircase–Escalante National Monument and into the Escalante Mountains by way of Horse Canyon, a lovely little drainage that has been senselessly bladed by spiteful commissioners of Garfield County. Horse Canyon led us to Canaan Peak, the first place on our second long journey across the state to give us a sense of the alpine environment that we'd be in for quite some time. After crossing Highway 12, we followed a pack trail up onto Barney Top, an elevation of more than 10,000 feet. An incoming cold front dropped both snow and nearby trees. This was quite a change for us, considering that we so recently had been in the heat of the Grand Canyon's inner gorge. Following a generally northerly course, we stayed at high elevation over Barney Top, Griffith Top, and finally onto Boulder Top, reaching heights as great as 11,000 feet. These plateaus felt like big mountains, the only thing missing was the peaks. Alpine lakes dotted the aspen forests; evidence of elk, deer, and cougars abounded. Pleasant Creek took us from the top of Boulder Mountain at 11,000 feet all the way down to the Fremont River, in the heat of Capitol Reef's desert, at a mere 4,000 feet above sea level. It was absolutely fascinating to walk through the changing vegetative zones between the high alpine environment and the desert.

TRAIL RATINGS

Days for completion or trail sections that are listed are only for planning purposes; there are too many factors involved to allow us to tell you exactly how long each section will take *you* to complete. If you are traveling the length of the Hayduke Trail, make sure to give yourself "down" days for exploration, relaxation, and unforeseen delays. We have broken down each section into separate groupings that affect the overall degree of difficulty:

level of exertion: These listings are all relative; this is an undeveloped desert route, no travel out here is truly "easy." **Do not take these classifications lightly; if it says a route is difficult, it will be quite hard to travel through that area!**

easy	Relatively simple travel, little if any scrambling or bushwhacking; there will be minor vertical change.
moderate	May include deep sand, boulder hopping, or scrambling through steep, loose talus. Using hands on climbs/descents may be necessary. Some water crossings could be hazardous. There could be large vertical change.
difficult	May include very steep faces with a high degree of exposure, tight bushwhacking, hauling packs with ropes, dangerous water crossings, etc. Loss of life is not out of the question.
extreme	The name says it all; at times it may seem easier to die than to survive.

navigation: Always carry a detailed map and compass (and know how to use it), even when employing a GPS unit (which won't always work in deep canyons or whose batteries might run out, etc.).

easy	Fairly straightforward navigation; there may be marked trails, roads, obvious drainages, or ridges, and may have cairns or blazed portions.
moderate	The route may not always be obvious; careful following of terrain features, drainages, and map will be necessary. There may or may not be cairns or

blazes to follow. Trails may become faint or hard to follow.

difficult   Confusing terrain, with few landmark features; will most likely not have any cairns, blazes, or even a distinguishable path. **Getting lost is easily accomplished.**

water availability:

wet   Daily water sources, but may include dry camps (camping away from any water sources).

damp   Will involve carrying two days' worth of water at times; will have dry camps.

dry   Will involve carrying up to three days' worth of water; there will be dry camps, often two in a row. Careful planning will be needed to avoid a dangerous situation.

"desolation factor": based on the probable proximity to the nearest people (or help).

local   People will be close by (within a couple of hours hiking).

backcountry   The nearest folks could be as much as a day away.

out there!   You are on your own. Little chance of outside contact for at least a full day.

Short of a satellite phone or hiking out, the recommended method of attracting attention for the purpose of rescue is to employ a signal mirror (commercial airlines personnel must report any sighted signal attempt to the authorities).

While there are a couple of places on the route that may be considered "climbing," we have chosen not to rate these in the standard Yosemite decimal system. Each "climb" is fairly straightforward; none requires any special moves or skills (besides an ability to handle exposure!). They do require using hands, but there are no reaches that only tall folks can make. Packs will sometimes have to be passed with ropes in these areas.

MAPS

The maps in this guide are for reference only. Under no circumstances should they be used alone as a navigational tool. Although these maps show incredible detail and are shaded to show relief, their scope is just too narrow to adequately show distant landmarks and other important orienteering handrails. The purpose of these maps is to show the course of the trail, water sources, mileage, etc., and to allow you to copy this information to full-sheet 1:24,000 scale, 7.5 minute quad maps to be used for navigation in the field. The 7.5 minute quads are available directly from the United States Geological Survey by visiting their Web site at www.usgs.gov or calling them at 1-888-275-8747.

The detailed maps for this guidebook were masterfully created by Mark Silver at iGage Mapping Corporation, producers of the powerful All Topo Maps software series. These CD-ROM sets allow you to view and manipulate on your home computer all of the 1:24,000, 1:100,000 and 1:250,000 scale topographic maps you'll ever need for the Hayduke Trail. This software was absolutely invaluable to us in plotting the course of the trail. Full coverage map sets are available for all fifty states and can be purchased by visiting their Web site at www.igage.com. Because our maps were created by seamlessly marrying adjoining 7.5 minute quad maps (another useful feature of the All Topo Maps software), you need to be aware that the contour intervals will vary on some maps and sometimes change within the maps themselves.

The maps are labeled by section number, lettered according to sequence, and show the section mileage within the scope of each map. For example, the first map of Section 1 is labeled S01A M 0.0-8.1 and the next is labeled S01B M 7.6-16.8. Each map overlaps both the previous and the following map to make it a little easier keeping track of the trail while flipping pages. The maps in this guide were made using NAD 83 datum Lat/Lon and UTM grids, which are fully interchangeable with WGS 84.

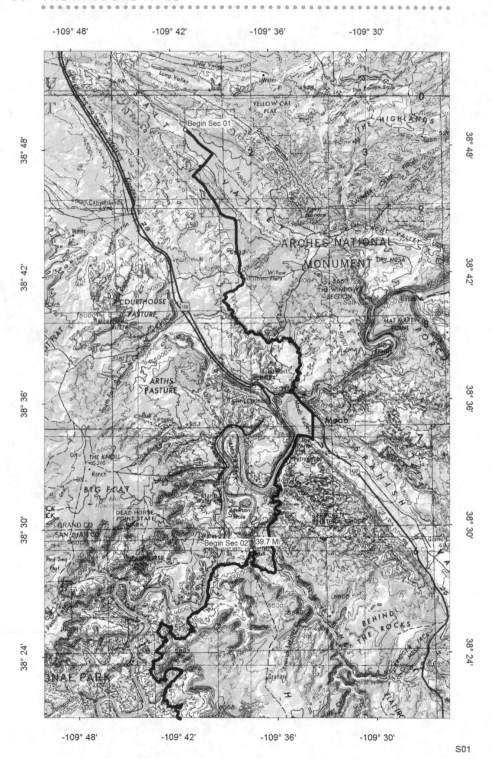

SECTION 1: OVERVIEW

■ SECTION 1
Arches National Park to Hurrah Pass
•••

APPROXIMATE TIME: 5 days

DISTANCE: 39.7 miles

EXERTION: easy

NAVIGATION: easy with a moderate section

WATER: wet

DESOLATION FACTOR: local

SPECIFIC HAZARDS: potential flash floods in Courthouse Wash and Kane Creek Canyon.

PERMITS: Arches National Park requires permits for overnight back-country use.

"I'm sitting against my pack, on an absurdly small green grass patch in an otherwise rolling, cactus and crypto [cryptobiotic soil] covered hill, twenty-five feet above Courthouse Wash. Behind me are a pair of huge amphitheaters in a 400 ft. high red rock wall. Across from me is a long, unbroken wall, with an amphitheater, or an arch-to-be, catching the setting sun. A mile or so down the wash is the once mighty Colorado River.

"Tonight we're in ornithological heaven. Two towhees are jumping around in the brush below us. They both are black with white markings on the wings, and an orange belly. I'm guessing they're eating all the grasshoppers and spiders we saw down there. There is a flycatcher perched in a dead tree just across the wash, jumping upward or sideways to snag his dinner. A canyon wren is serenading us from up the canyon, his lyrical song echoing off the red rock walls. Down the wash an owl offers the first tentative hoots of the evening. Something must be having a hard time out there somewhere; there are eight vultures circling over-head, none of them flapping a wing as long as I watched. Now a bat chases mosquitoes above us."

MARCH 22, 1998 [DAY 3 OF 94], COURTHOUSE WASH,
ARCHES NATIONAL PARK

This section begins at the Salt Valley entry to Arches National Park, on the park's northern boundary. Salt Valley is a graben valley, one where the walls are faulted and the floor drops out; it opens into Arches with outstanding views of the Sierra La Sal to the southeast.

Known for its fantastic amount of natural arches and unusual stone formations, Arches National Park was first created as a national monument in 1929. Ed Abbey called Arches home for a while. As a ranger while it was still a national monument (it received national park designation in 1971), he was increasingly frustrated by the ever-increasing development to provide easy access to the formations for the motorized traveler. A direct result of his time at Arches were his subsequent writings about industrial tourism and his condemnation of development for the sake of the so-called wilderness experience. He was of the belief (and the authors concur) that to experience the wilderness, you need to get out in it, not just pass through in a motor-driven capsule.

Camping outside of the park entrance before we began our first long journey across the desert was a remarkable experience, and, to us at least, offered the best possible setting for our embarking on a Colorado Plateau trek. Surrounded by good friends on a beautiful late winter day, overlooking Arches, we watched the light of the setting sun turning the snow-capped La Sals into a fountain of color, all the while being serenaded by a chorus of coyotes. We took it as a sign of good things to come.

You'll start your journey upon entering the park by following a dirt road for a short distance before heading overland, near the towering columns of the Marching Men, towards the park's western border (there is no camping in the northern section of Arches NP). As soon as we headed off the road, we immediately encountered a set of deer antlers, apparently still attached to an unseen skull, protruding from the sand at the bottom of a small pour-off. A series of small wonderfully patterned drainages is followed to Courthouse Wash, which you will follow the rest of the way through Arches NP. Plan on getting your feet wet in Courthouse; you will be splashing through the wash numerous times and will most likely find some quicksand in there as well.

RING ARCH, ARCHES NATIONAL PARK

As Courthouse Wash exits Arches, near its confluence with the Colorado River, you'll hop on the road surface and head over the Colorado River to Moab (be careful; there are no shoulders or sidewalks on the bridge). Look for the large restored pictograph panel high on the wall between the wash and river.

Moab was originally settled by Mormons in 1855 as part of their expansion into the Colorado Plateau's more desolate areas; but hostile Native Americans soon forced the abandonment of the settlement. Two decades passed before the area was resettled, this time permanently; but the town was really "put on the map," so to speak, when Charlie Steen discovered a massive uranium lode in the area in 1952. After numerous boom-and-bust industrial cycles, Moab now seems to have settled into the role of a tourist and recreational mecca.

KANE CREEK ROAD

The route follows along the outskirts of Moab and into the "Portal," where the Colorado River cuts into the redrock upthrust that makes up the Moab Rim. After heading through the Portal, you follow the road (which quickly turns to dirt) along Kane Creek, passing Moonflower Canyon and an Indian ladder and petroglyph panel along the way. There are BLM pay campsites along the road, but hiking a couple more miles will take you back to free camping. Look for a large boulder just off the road with a "birthing scene" petroglyph. The road can be followed all the way to Hurrah Pass, but we went overland, cutting off a good distance. The view from the pass is nothing short of breathtaking, looking over the Colorado River gorge, the anticline (notice the changing aspect of the strata), potash evaporation tanks, much of Canyonlands National Park, and the La Sal Mountains.

Some interesting side trips in this section could include hiking up to the top of the Moab Rim or investigating the Behind the Rocks Wilderness Study Area.

▪ **Trailhead at Salt Valley, Arches National Park:** Driving north, 27 miles from Moab (or 4 miles south of Interstate 70) on Utah Highway 191, turn east near mile marker 154 onto the Salt Valley Road. Drive northeast on this good dirt road for 1.3 miles to a junction and turn south. Head east-southeast, then east, and then southeast along the road for 2.7 miles to another junction. Turn south again and follow the road generally southeast for 6.7 miles to the Arches National Park boundary. The mileage for the entire Hayduke Trail, as well as this first section, will be measured from this boundary.

▪ **Resupply/Trailhead at Hurrah Pass:** From Main Street in Moab, go south on 500 West Street for 1.4 miles to the junction with Kane Springs Boulevard. Turn right and follow Kane Springs Boulevard for 3.9 miles along the Colorado River to the mouth of Kane Springs Canyon and the end of the pavement. The road turns to dirt here and you continue generally south along it as it winds its way up Kane Springs Canyon. At one point you must cross Kane Creek, which usually has running water. A Caddy is probably not going to make it across this one; **a high-clearance vehicle is strongly recommended**. Though the creek may be passable on the way in, due to the potential of flash floods, water may be over the hood on the way out. After 6.6 miles you will reach another junction. Turn south onto this high-clearance dirt road and follow it around to the west, then north, for 2.9 miles as it climbs up to Hurrah Pass.

▪ **Topos:** Klondike Bluffs, UT; Merrimac Butte, UT; The Windows Section, UT; Moab, UT; Trough Springs Canyon, UT; Shafer Basin, UT.

ROUTE DESCRIPTION AND MILEAGE

2.0 ▪ From the boundary fence, walk southeast down the sandy Salt Valley road for 2 miles to the second junction.

3.8 ▪ Take the small 4x4 road to the southwest for 1.8 miles. You will be going across the valley, over a pass, and down the other side to a road junction to the south of Klondike Bluffs.

7.5 ▪ Turn southeast onto this double track and go through the cliffs and down the forming wash. After about 2 miles, according to the most recent quads, you will notice that the map shows the road going south down the wash. However, when you flip to the Merrimac Butte quad you will see that this road actually goes southeast and parallels the cliffs to the northeast. Go southeast down this track for 1.7 miles until you cross a small wash. From here you will be able to see the park boundary fence to the southwest. **Be nice to this fence!** It keeps cattle out of the park and its barbless bottom wire allows jackrabbits and coyotes to slip through unscathed. Since you will still be within one linear mile of the dirt road, it is only legal to camp on the far side of this fence on BLM land (Arches National Park backcountry regulations prohibit camping within one mile of any road, dirt or paved). This is the most logical place from which to get to the fenceline. Take care to follow the wash bottom to the fence and back to the trail so you don't trample the cryptobiotic soil. The base of the white-capped formation provides a good place to spend the night.

9.0 ▨ Mileage figures resume where you left the track. If you spent the night outside the park, simply follow the fenceline due east to intersect the route. If not, leave the track where it crosses the wash and head due south for 0.1 miles, carefully following game trails, to the corner of the boundary fence. Follow the fence due south for 1.4 miles until you reach a set of sandstone fins.

10.3 ▨ *Now is the time to use those route-finding skills you had better have!* You must find your way down the myriad of small ledges and into the large, unnamed drainage below you to the southeast. *You are absolutely on your own here, there's no one to ask for directions.* There are likely several ways to get to the bottom of the drainage, and to some the route will be obvious. To those others, the best way to go down is generally in a south-southeasterly direction. **Make sure you don't jump down anything you can't climb back up!** If you do, make sure you leave a person with a rope on top while you scout ahead! Once you reach the bottom of the drainage, simply follow it south until you reach a double track crossing the drainage. This track is 1.3 miles from the fins.

10.6 ▨ Continue south-southeast down the wash for another 0.3 miles to where Willow Spring Wash comes in from the north. *If you* *are lucky, there may be a small trickle of water coming out of the wash. If not, you can try hiking a short distance up the wash toward the spring to get water.*

12.2 ■ Keep going down the drainage for 1.6 miles as it winds its way to the southwest, eventually spilling out into Courthouse Wash. *There is usually a small flow of water in this wash during most seasons.*

17.5 ■ Now turn southeast and go down Courthouse Wash for 5.3 miles to the bridge bearing the main park road over the wash. Look for Sevenmile Canyon and Ring Arch along the way and don't forget that you cannot camp within one linear mile of any road in Arches National Park.

23.1 ■ After going under the bridge, continue winding down Courthouse Wash generally east, then south, for 5.6 miles until you exit the canyon, leave the park, and then intersect Utah Highway 191. As you are nearing the mouth of the canyon you will probably encounter backwater of the Colorado River, depending on the river level. Here you will find a footpath on the east side of the slough. This path will lead you to a crossing through the boundary fence and then to the road.

For those of you looking only for a memorable three- or four-day excursion into the Arches backcountry, it would be best to end your trip here. Although the remainder of this section of the Hayduke Trail is very scenic, the walk through town may not be so enjoyable. But it is very practical for the through-hiker. Those of you out for multiple weeks or months will appreciate the chance to replace forgotten gear in the town of Moab and grab one last milkshake before you really dive in deep. You won't get this opportunity again.

24.9 ■ There are a couple of stops you should make before heading into town. Start by going east down the roadside. Before you cross the bridge over the Colorado River, take time to hike up to the recently restored Barrier Canyon–style pictographs north of the road. Once on the other side of the bridge, you will come to the junction with River Road. *Going 0.3 miles north up this road will lead you to Matrimony Spring, some of the best water around.* Return to the highway and follow it southeast to 500 West Street in Moab. This is 1.8 miles from where you left Courthouse Wash.

26.3 ■ Now turn south on 500 West and follow it for 1.4 miles to the intersection with Kane Springs Boulevard.

30.2 ■ Continue on Kane Springs Boulevard for 3.9 miles as it first goes west-northwest to the Colorado, then southwest along its banks and down the gorge. There are many interesting petroglyphs to see along the way, but please respect private property. The road turns to dirt where it leaves the river and enters Kane Springs Canyon.

36.8 ■ Continue along the dirt road as it swings southeast, and follow it up Kane Springs Canyon. *At the bottom of a long switchback in 2.2 miles is the small, dripping Kane Springs. You would be wise to take enough water from this source to last you to the end of this section. Although you will probably find more water in Kane Creek, you will have to treat it and possibly settle it first.* **There are some enticing campsites down by the creek, but don't be fooled into thinking they are safe!** Kane Creek originates far away, high in the La Sal Mountains. Violent thunderstorms often rage on the mountain while the skies remain perfectly innocent-looking overhead. You would never know if a torrent was racing down the creek to gobble you up! Continue up the road to the next junction. It is 6.6 miles from the mouth of Kane Springs Canyon.

39.7 ■ Go south down the dirt road and follow it as it swings its way around to the north and gradually climbs the cliffs to the west. After 2.9 miles you will come to Hurrah Pass, the end of this section.

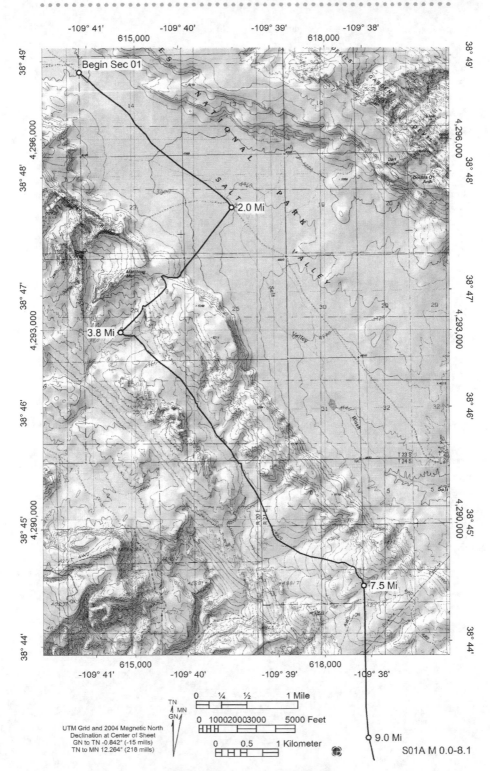

UTM Grid and 2004 Magnetic North
Declination at Center of Sheet
GN to TN -0.842° (-15 mills)
TN to MN 12.264° (218 mills)

S01A M 0.0-8.1

SECTION 1: 0.0–8.1 MILES

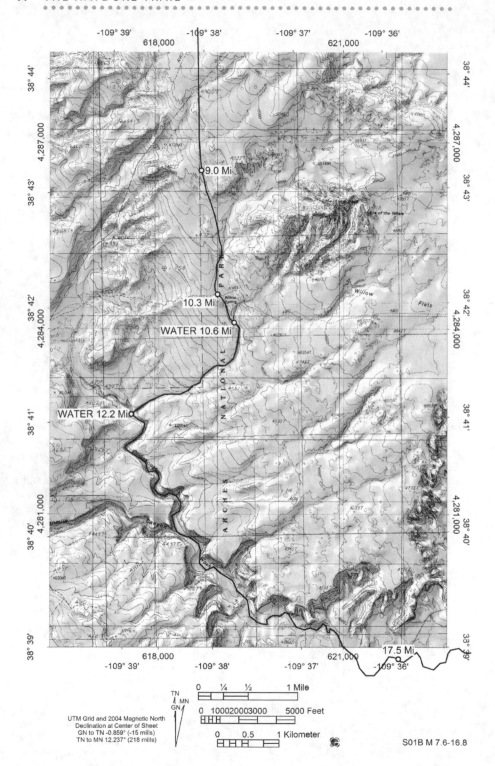

-109° 39'   -109° 38'   -109° 37'   -109° 36'

618,000   621,000

38° 44'   38° 44'

4,287,000   4,287,000

38° 43'   9.0 Mi   38° 43'

38° 42'   10.3 Mi   38° 42'

4,284,000   WATER 10.6 Mi   4,284,000

38° 41'   WATER 12.2 Mi   38° 41'

4,281,000   4,281,000

38° 40'   38° 40'

38° 39'   17.5 Mi   33° 39'

618,000   621,000

-109° 39'   -109° 38'   -109° 37'   -109° 36'

UTM Grid and 2004 Magnetic North
Declination at Center of Sheet
GN to TN -0.859° (-15 mils)
TN to MN 12.237° (218 mills)

TN
MN
GN

0   ¼   ½   1 Mile

0   1000 2000 3000   5000 Feet

0   0.5   1 Kilometer

S01B M 7.6-16.8

SECTION 1: 7.6–16.8 MILES

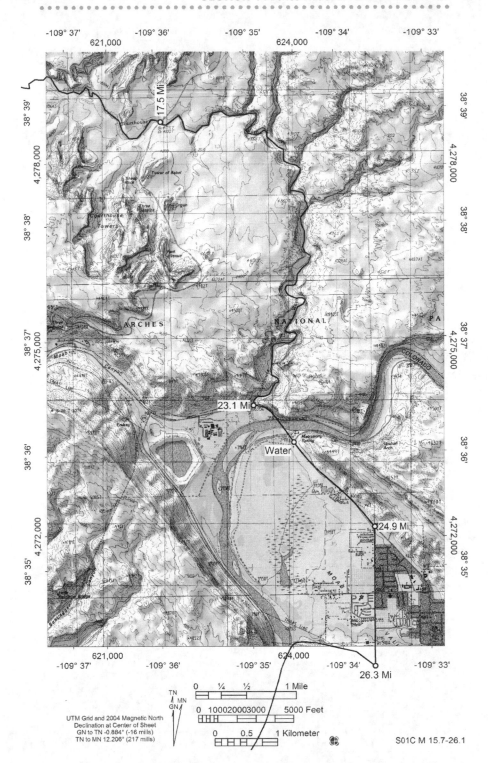

-109° 37'   -109° 36'   -109° 35'   -109° 34'   -109° 33'

621,000   624,000

38° 39'   38° 39'

4,278,000   4,278,000

17.5 Mi.

38° 38'   38° 38'

4,275,000   4,275,000

38° 37'   38° 37'

ARCHES   NATIONAL   PA

COLORADO

23.1 Mi.

Water

38° 36'   38° 36'

4,272,000   4,272,000

24.9 Mi.

38° 35'   38° 35'

621,000   624,000

-109° 37'   -109° 36'   -109° 35'   -109° 34'   -109° 33'

26.3 Mi

TN
MN
GN

0   ¼   ½   1 Mile

0   1000 2000 3000   5000 Feet

UTM Grid and 2004 Magnetic North
Declination at Center of Sheet
GN to TN -0.884° (-16 mills)
TN to MN 12.206° (217 mills)

0   0.5   1 Kilometer

S01C M 15.7-26.1

SECTION 1: 15.7–26.1 MILES

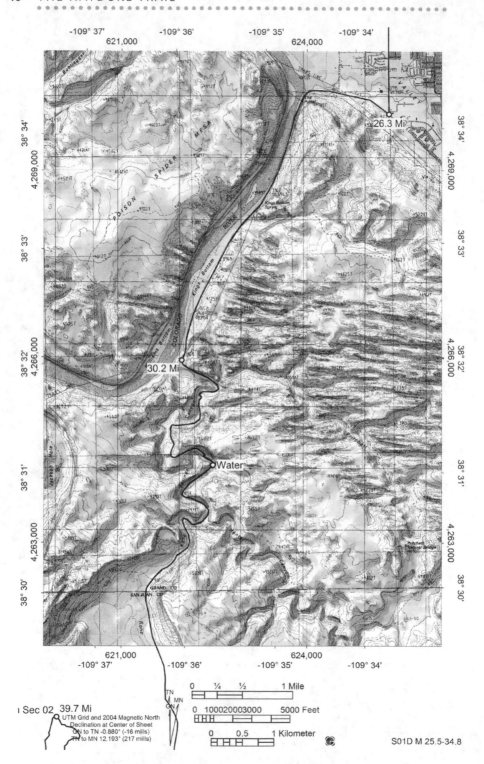

SECTION 1: 25.5–34.8 MILES

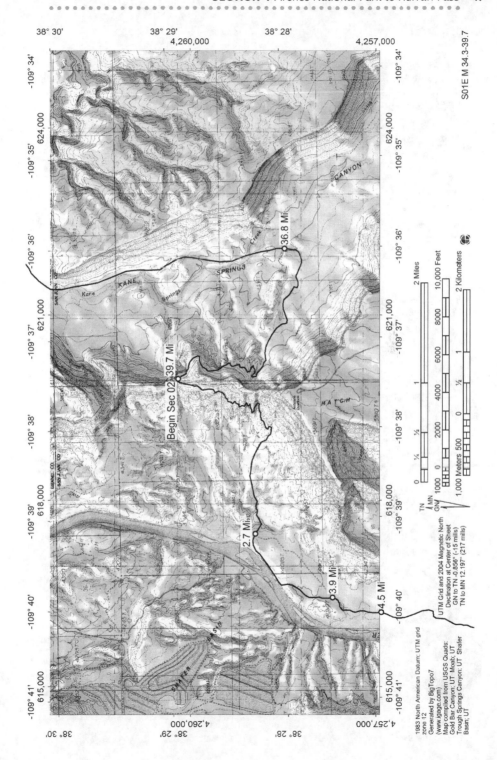

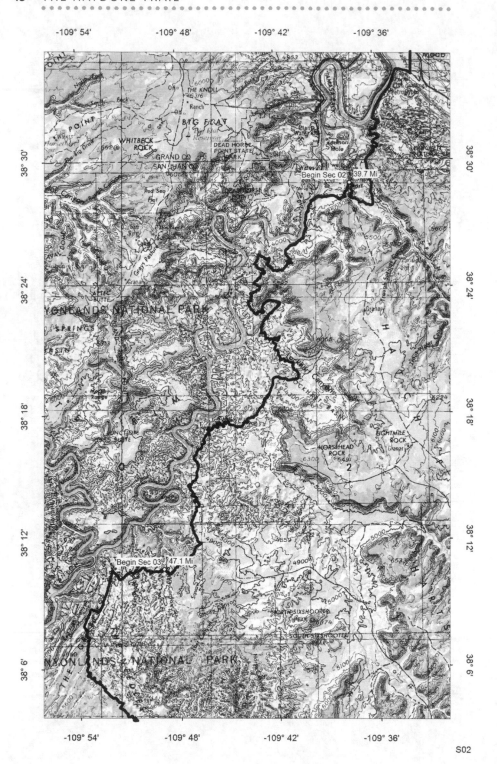

SECTION 2: OVERVIEW

■ SECTION 2

Hurrah Pass to Big Spring Trailhead, Canyonlands National Park

APPROXIMATE TIME: 7 days

DISTANCE: 47.1 miles

EXERTION: moderate

NAVIGATION: moderate

WATER: damp

DESOLATION FACTOR: backcountry

SPECIFIC HAZARDS: flash floods in any of the drainages.

PERMITS: Needles District of Canyonlands National Park requires permits for overnight backcountry use.

"Wow. What a night. Again, there was rain. We had spent the evening under some rocks, kind of a cave. We knew there wasn't enough space for us to keep our packs dry and sleep under the rocks also, so we set up the tent. We were pretty tired from the day's hike and were ready to turn in by dark. By this time it had been raining for a couple of hours, a steady, soft rain. The rate seemed to pick up when we hit the inside of the tent. It was actually pretty loud inside. It got interesting when it got loud outside. You gotta keep in mind that we're in a drainage—a straight walled, no-way-out place. We were perched on a high spot, shielded by a huge boulder (our cave), on the inside of a meander. First we heard what we thought sounded like bass drums, a steady thumping—but where are there bass drums in the middle of a nighttime desert deluge? I poked my head out of the tent, with a light, to see if there was water running in the drainage, but could see none. OK. A while later (still pouring out) I heard the distinct sound of a boulder rolling in water. It scared me half out of my sleeping bag. I'm thinking flash flood; we're going to die. But there's still not much running water. I keep thinking it's been raining long enough, where's the run-off? At this point we're both awake, and a bit apprehensive. Are we out of the way if a wall of

water comes? Is there an escape? Can we get out of the canyon if there's running water?

"We fall asleep again, rain pounding on the tent still. Suddenly Mitch is waking me up. It's not raining, but our little canyon has gotten loud. Really loud. I jump up; we put on raincoats and shoes and jump outside. The watercourse is raging. Foamy chocolate milk. We could hear rocks crashing into each other in the flow. We determined, to our relief, that we were in a safe spot, though the water was really a little too close for comfort."

MARCH 27, 1998 [DAY 8 OF 94], IN A DRAINAGE OF LOCKHART CANYON

"We walked up canyon, though we were only a mile or so from the Colorado River, to seek a good campsite, maybe for a couple of days' stay. After a mile or so up the canyon we found a rock overhang, which offered shelter for cooking, eating, writing, whatever. Just above was a good place for the tent. The site came complete with pottery sherds. Cool. We were eating lunch when it started snowing. Ah, the good life.

"The snow squalls stopped, so we decided to go for a walk/ exploring session. We decided to go up. Not up canyon, but up. Higher up. We worked our way from layer to layer, shelf to shelf, sometimes scrambling over steep, loose rock, other times squeezing through narrow gaps in the rocks. A ways up we found some 'calico' rock, as in calico cat. Weird. Lots of holes in it too. As we continued upward, a new level was always becoming visible. We found ourselves on a peninsula of rock, which we simply walked off onto 'the mainland.' Now more up. So up we went. We made it to some huge vertical protrusions, which were the only visible landmarks for miles—if you can get above all of the canyons. We were on top. One could see a long way.

"Everyday it seems I'm saying, 'this is the most incredible view I've ever seen.' This was one of those views. We peeked our heads through a notch in the vertical formations and—WOW!— we were right above the Colorado. Way above it. Yee haa, what a view! Through the notch—Island in the Sky. The Island is right there. White Rim Trail, the Needles, and their bizarre profile, Elk Ridge. On the side we started from is the whole canyon rim sys-

tem, Hart and Hatch Points, with all of their overlooks, the Six-Shooters, the Abajo's Shay Mountain, the La Sals, and all the crazy canyons below, all with indescribable, and unexplainable, formations....

"The level we were walking on up top was covered with chert. Every imaginable color was represented. Some had crystals attached. It seemed we were the only ones to have ever gone there. There was absolutely no sign of man, ancient or present. The only prints we saw were those of desert bighorn sheep. I like that."

MARCH 29, 1998 [DAY 10 OF 94], INDIAN CREEK WSA

This section gave us the first idea of what real backcountry travel on the Colorado Plateau is like; we began to feel that we were in quite a remote place, that we were truly on our own out there.

Leaving Hurrah Pass, you immediately drop down towards the Colorado River. The dirt road that goes towards Lockhart Basin is followed for a few miles before you drop into a small drainage that you follow until a large pour-off is reached. We saw a group of desert bighorns in this area, including a pregnant ewe. All seemed to vanish

ALONGSIDE THE COLORADO RIVER

POUR-OFF INTO LOCKHART CANYON

into the rocks before our very eyes, prompting us ever since to refer to these graceful desert creatures as "ghosts." Hiking around the pour-off leads to the edge of Lockhart Canyon, and following the rim will lead you to an access point into Lockhart Canyon. We found a large section of the canyon wall lying at the canyon bottom; it had fallen so recently that we could still tell where the sand had splashed out from the impact. You'll hike up Lockhart back to the road, which you'll follow until you can drop into Rustler Canyon. Lockhart Basin unfortunately is one of those amazing places that are under constant assault by those in the extractive industries who are more than willing to sacrifice a planetary gem for a short-term profit and a drop of oil; so you may want to visit it before the misnamed "wise use movement" allows this land to be forever degraded.

When we first hiked through Rustler Canyon, we hadn't been able to find anyone who could tell us whether or not we could hike through it from end to end. We found that you can. We also found almost an entire tree lying on the ground, looking as if it had fallen over only a

ABOVE THE ROUTE OUT OF INDIAN CREEK

short few years earlier but was in fact entirely petrified. It's the many things like this that have us wondering why the entire area was not included within the borders of Canyonlands National Park when it was established in 1964.

Rustler drains into Indian Creek, which you follow up, including a fairly simple climb to the rim, which once again offers incredible views of the canyon rim system. The only recent footprints we found up there were that of a cougar and bighorn sheep; not even cattle have impacted this place. You'll follow the ridge above the Colorado to a small drainage, which in turn leads to a dirt road, which then brings you into the Needles District of Canyonlands.

Any or all of the side canyons and drainages in this area are worth checking out, and archaeological sites are abundant out here. You may also want to follow Indian Creek to its confluence with the Colorado River.

■ **Resupply/Trailhead at Hurrah Pass:** See previous description.

■ **Resupply/Trailhead at Big Spring:** Simply drive into the Needles District of Canyonlands National Park on Highway 211 and follow the signs to the Big Spring Trailhead.

**ANTLERS IN WASH, NEEDLES DISTRICT,
CANYONLANDS NATIONAL PARK**

■ **Topos:** Shafer Basin, UT; Lockhart Basin, UT; Monument Basin, UT; The Loop, UT.

ROUTE DESCRIPTION AND MILEAGE

2.7 ■ From Hurrah Pass, go west along the road and follow it down the other side toward the Colorado River. The road runs to the south-southwest then west for 2.7 miles before it comes to a junction.

3.9 ■ Go straight, or west-northwest, through this junction and then follow the dirt road generally southwest for 1 mile into a shallow basin on a bench above the Colorado. *You can access the river here by way of a short down-climb if you need water.* From the shallow basin, continue south on the dirt road for 0.2 miles to a road junction.

4.5 ■ Continue generally south on this road for 0.6 miles to another junction.

6.8 ▪ Take the dirt road to the right, or southwest, and follow it generally south, then around to the southwest, for 2.3 miles to another junction.

11.3 ▪ Turn south onto this dirt road and follow it up the drainage to the southeast. Continue up the road as it switches back to the northwest and climbs out of the drainage and onto the upper bench. Follow the road across the bench as it traverses around the heads of the drainages below, and beneath Hatch Point above, to a pass overlooking the Colorado River. This point is 4.5 miles from the last junction.

16.8 ▪ Stay on the dirt road as it follows the bench generally south. You will pass right below Canyonlands Overlook, and after 5.5 miles the road will turn east and head into a cove beneath Hatch Point.

19.1 ▪ Follow the road generally east into the cove, then north and east as it swings around the large drainage below. After 2.3 miles you will cross a small feeder streambed. *There is an unreliable little seep in the sandy bottom of this feeder, less than one-half mile down it from the road.*

20.9 ▪ Leave the road here. Go 1.8 miles southwest down this wash from the dirt road until you come to a huge pour-off. **Don't go down!**

23.1 ▪ Instead, go south onto the bench that runs just beneath the 4,200-foot contour line and follow this level bench for 2.2 miles. You will swing around to the east and come to a cattle trail leading into a drainage to the south.

23.8 ▪ Take the cattle trail down into this canyon below you and go south, then east, down its bed. *In less than half a mile, back in an alcove on the north wall, there is a dripping spring. It is piped and falls into a trough.* After going 0.7 miles down the canyon from the bench above you will come out into Lockhart Canyon and intersect the dirt road there. *If you have the time or need the water, the Colorado River is only 2 miles down Lockhart Canyon from here.*

26.8 ▪ Follow the dirt road up Lockhart Canyon generally southeast for 3 miles to a road junction. We were unable to locate the spring shown on the topo as being in the wash, so we cannot vouch for its existence.

29.9 ▣ From the junction, continue on the dirt road that goes west across the lower end of Lockhart Basin, then south-southwest along the divide between Lockhart Canyon and Horsethief Canyon, for 3.1 miles to a drill hole.

32.3 ▣ Follow your compass overland from the drill hole generally southwest down into the drainage before you. Most of the many small gullies will lead you down into the wash. Once there, go southwest down the wash bottom. About 2.4 miles from the drill hole, depending on which gully you chose, you will reach the bed of Rustler Canyon.

35.1 ▣ Go 2.8 miles, generally west, down Rustler Canyon to its confluence with Indian Creek. *You should find flowing water here during most seasons.* On the way to Indian Creek you will encounter a large pour-off. Climb down the broken layers on the south side of the plunge. The route down is easy once you find it, and you should be able to spare your rope by handing down your packs.

36.9 ▣ **Your route finding and navigational skills must be impeccable in order to proceed! If you have any doubt about exactly where you are at all times, then follow Indian Creek upstream to the paved road and then follow that road west into the park. Not too many people are going to want to try looking for you out here!** If you've been to the middle of nowhere before and liked it, go 1.2 miles south up Indian Creek to the point where the canyon turns to the east. Right in the middle of this sharp turn in the canyon you will see a small side canyon coming in from the southwest. Just to the east of this drainage is a shoulder that comes almost all the way down to the creek. *Make sure you take enough water from the creek to see you to the end of this section.* Climb up onto this shoulder and make your way southwest up the ridge, over a series of small ledges, and out of Indian Creek. After 0.6 miles from the floor of Indian Creek you will come to the unmarked boundary of Canyonlands National Park on a bench at the base of a "chocolate layer cake"-type formation. Welcome to no-man's-land.

38.4 ▣ Contour south-southwest along the east side of the formation, but don't let yourself be drawn down into any of the drainages. The

goal for now is to stay on top. From the southern end of this formation, head south to the pyramid marked 4795T on the map. Contour
along its eastern side and then head to a second pyramid, which you
can see to the southeast. Skirt around that and head south-southwest
to the third pyramid. It is 1.5 miles from the last waypoint at the park
boundary.

39.3 ■ Go south-southeast across the divide between the drainage
that's below you to the southwest and the tributary of Indian Creek to
the northeast. Turn southwest here and go toward the point. Head
down the draw between the two fingers and into the drainage below
you to the south. We named it We-hope-so Wash because at the time
we weren't exactly sure we wanted to be there. **You will have to find
your own way down the many ledges to the bottom of this wash.
Remember, don't jump down anything you can't climb back up!** The
best way to go about "dropping ledges" is to send your strongest
climber down while the rest wait on top with the rope. Now make the
climber come back up unassisted to prove that at least one of you can
get back up without a rope. It's funny how a ledge can look a lot easier
to climb when viewed from above. The bottom of this wash is about
0.9 miles from the last pyramid, depending on where you find your
way into it.

42.5 ■ Turn south and, always staying in the main wash, go generally
south-southeast up it for 1.9 miles to a fork. Go up the southwest arm
and follow it south-southwest for 1.3 more miles, up and out of the
drainage to a dirt road.

42.9 ■ Head south-southeast down the dirt road for 0.4 miles to the
hamburger rock formations.

44.3 ■ Take the dirt road south-southeast and then southwest for 1.4
miles to where it crosses Salt Creek, just above the Lower Jump.

45.1 ■ Leave the road here and cross Salt Creek, going 0.8 miles
southwest up the little drainage and out its head.

45.6 ■ Continue southwest across the divide and into the next drainage. Then follow it northwest 0.5 miles until you reach the bottom of
Little Spring Canyon.

46.7 ◼ Turn southwest and go up Little Spring Canyon 0.4 miles to a fork. *The spring you pass may or may not be flowing, depending on the water year, but you are within a quarter mile of help if you need it.* Continue up the southwest arm for 0.7 miles to the park road.

47.1 ◼ Go northwest for 0.4 miles on the park road to the parking area at Big Spring Trailhead and the end of this section.

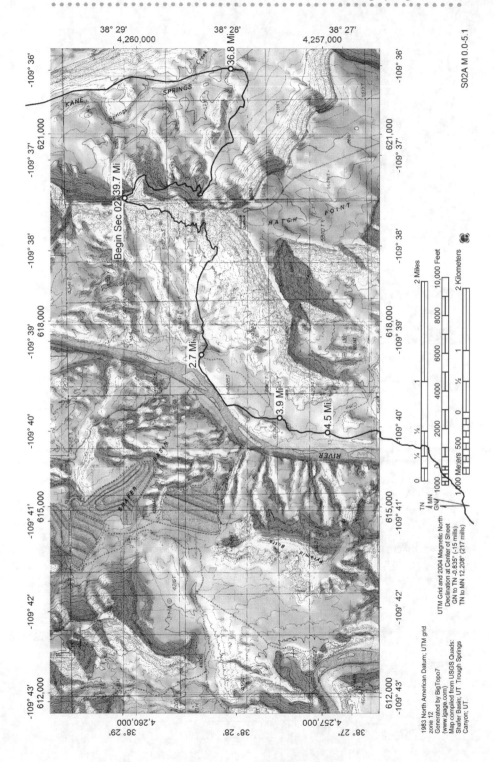

1983 North American Datum; UTM grid
zone 12
Generated by BigTopo7
(www.igage.com)
Map compiled from USGS Quads:
Shafer Basin; UT Trough Springs
Canyon; UT

UTM Grid and 2004 Magnetic North
Declination at Center of Sheet
GN to TN -0.835° (-15 mills)
TN to MN 12.208° (217 mills)

S02A M 0.0-5.1

SECTION 2: 0.0–5.1 MILES

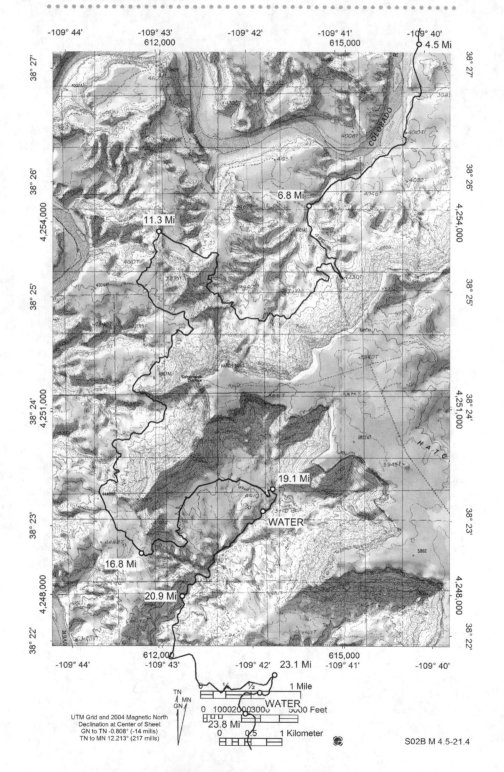

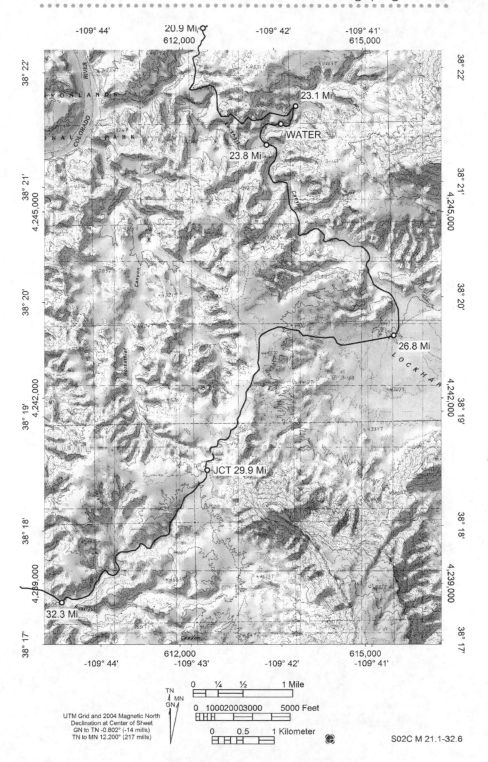

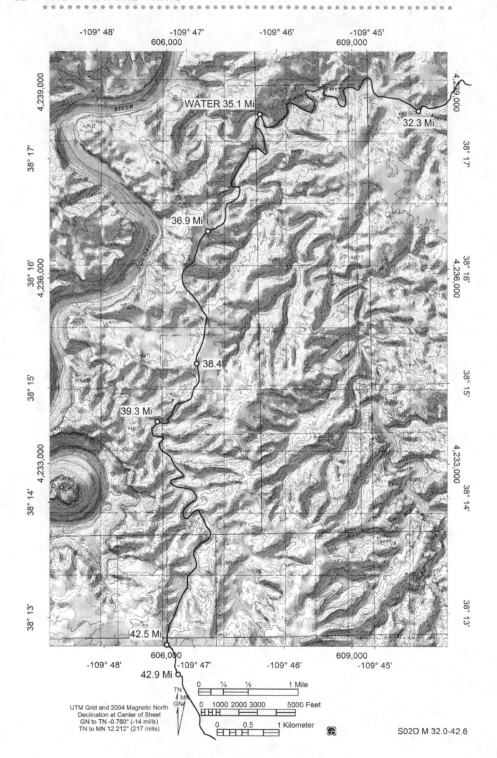

SECTION 2: 32.0–42.6 MILES

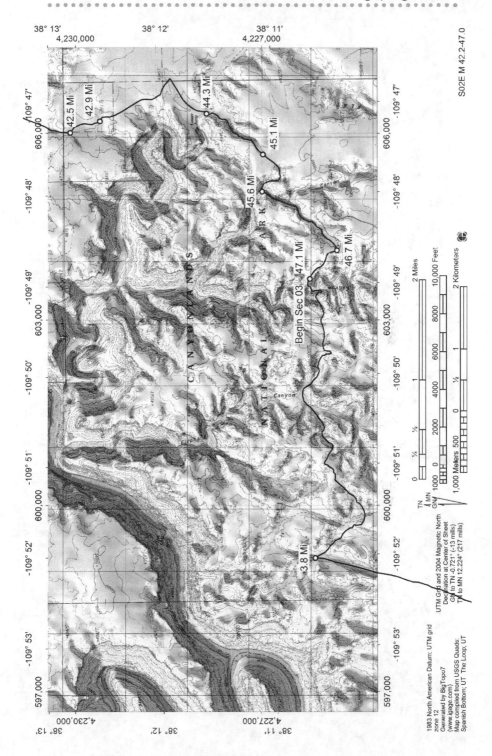

S02E M 42.2-47.0

38° 13'
4,230,000

38° 12'

38° 11'
4,227,000

-109° 47'

42.5 Mi
42.9 Mi

44.3 Mi

45.1 Mi

45.6 Mi

46.7 Mi

-109° 48'

Begin Sec 03 47.1 Mi

-109° 49'

43.8 Mi

1983 North American Datum: UTM grid
zone 12
Generated by BigTopo7
(www.igage.com)
Map compiled from USGS Quads:
Spanish Bottom, UT The Loop, UT

UTM Grid and 2004 Magnetic North
Declination at Center of Sheet
GN to TN -0.721° (-13 mils)
TN to MN 12.224° (217 mils)

TN
MN
GN

0   ½   1   2 Miles

0   ½   1   2 Kilometers

1000   0   2000   4000   6000   8000   10,000 Feet

1,000 Meters 500   0   ½   1

SECTION 2: 42.2–47.0 MILES

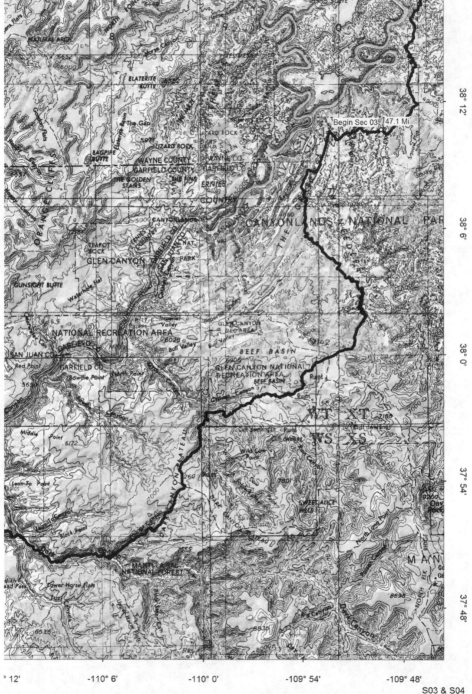

SECTION 3: OVERVIEW

■ SECTION 3
Big Spring Trailhead, Canyonlands National Park to Hite
∙∙∙

APPROXIMATE TIME: 11 days

DISTANCE: 67.9 miles

EXERTION: difficult

NAVIGATION: moderate, with some difficult sections

WATER: dry (a water cache or some very long days carrying 3 days' supply of water are necessary)

DESOLATION FACTOR: out there!

SPECIFIC HAZARDS: running out of water! Flash floods in Dark Canyon; tough climbing with exposure in Young's Canyon.

PERMITS: Needles District of Canyonlands National Park and Glen Canyon National Recreation Area require permits for overnight backcountry use.

"Walking in a wash, in the desert, is fascinating. It is the main thoroughfare through the land, generally the path of least resistance, though not always the shortest, because of all the meanders. The sand records who passed—footprints left to tell the story. We've followed bobcat tracks, fox and coyote tracks, cougar tracks. We've seen rabbit tracks, raven tracks, skunk tracks, and mouse tracks, though the small rodents only cross the wash in specific, high-rodent-traffic areas. There are lizard tracks, snake tracks, even insect tracks. We've found bones in washes and rocks enough to make a rock collector go wild. Log jams, dried up holes, where there'd be pools if there was any water. We've found garbage, probably from the road, ten miles upstream. Antlers. Pine cones of all types. Arrowheads. Crazy patterns in the sand...."

APRIL 6, 1998 [DAY 18 OF 94], BUTLER WASH WSA

"OK, words to describe my feeling walking down Dark Canyon today: awestruck, amazed, dumbfounded, blown away, delighted, giddy.

"This place is soooo beautiful. Everything where we are is flowering. White flowers. Purple flowers. Red flowers. Yellow flowers. Purple, white, and yellow flowers. And so on! But you have to look close; a lot of them are small. I am surrounded by huge red rock (well, that's the predominant color you see, anyway) walls, gouged by wind and water, leaving layer upon layer exposed, sometimes broken, sometimes one solid wall, the formations always spectacular. Large cumulus clouds cruise by in the bluest of skies. Water gurgling, green trees rocking in the sometimes chilly breeze. I may be in heaven. This place just takes your breath away.

"We walked six miles down a canyon that could completely change character at every bend. One moment you're walking on sand, through thick willow chutes, right at water level, the next you're walking a narrow ledge over a twenty-foot-deep, ten-foot-wide gorge, and then you're cruising through fossils embedded in every rock you see. Wow. It's even full-blown spring here, weeks ahead of what we've seen before."

APRIL 14, 1998 [DAY 26 OF 94], DARK CANYON PRIMITIVE AREA

This is a beautiful but long section. We originally had planned this as two sections (and you may want to split this, conditions permitting). We had planned on meeting with our resupply team in Beef Basin, but the roads were snowbound when we were passing through, so we settled for a meeting after just a few days at the Horsehoof Arch campsite (4WD access only) in Needles, leaving a 12-day jaunt ahead. You will need to plan on either caching water or

HORSEHOOF ARCH, NEEDLES DISTRICT, CANYONLANDS NATIONAL PARK, 1998 (THIS ARCH HAS SINCE FALLEN)

meeting with someone, perhaps at Horsehoof Arch, to avoid the need to push through Needles and Butler Wash while loaded with two

CONFLUENCE OF THE GREEN AND COLORADO RIVERS AS SEEN
FROM NEEDLES DISTRICT, CANYONLANDS NATIONAL PARK

weeks' worth of food and three or more days' worth of water. (Note: Horsehoof Arch has fallen since our visit there in 1998.)

From the Big Spring Trailhead you follow a park trail into Elephant Canyon (home of Elephant Hill, a popular 4WD excursion area) and on towards the Grabens, a series of sandy-bottomed canyons. Make sure to check out the confluence of the Green and Colorado Rivers. (If you enjoy listening to the sound of your own voice, give a shout off the edge over the confluence; the echoing goes off in three distinct directions, seemingly forever.). A double-track road through Cyclone Canyon takes you into Red Lake Canyon, and then into Butler Wash, which you'll follow most of the way up into Beef Basin. (Red Lake Canyon can also lead to the Colorado River across from Spanish Bottom and just above "Brown Betty," the first of Cataract Canyon's rapids.) Horsehoof Arch is only a couple of hundred yards from Butler Wash. All of the Needles District is worth exploring if you have the time; Chesler Park, Devils Kitchen, and the Joint Trail are among the stand-outs. Again, there is no water out there; this area has sand hundreds of feet deep, so plan accordingly.

**INSPECTING FOSSILS IN BUTLER WASH, NEEDLES DISTRICT,
CANYONLANDS NATIONAL PARK**

You will take a small side drainage from Butler Wash to Beef Basin, which contains a natural bridge that was undocumented until we encountered it on our 1998 trek. We have named it Seldom Seen Bridge. When climbing out of the drainage that contains Seldom Seen Bridge, you'll be following a game trail (at least we first thought it was a game trail until we realized that we only saw cougar tracks on the trail). Watch for a large arch on the ridge above to the south. Once in Beef Basin, known for its large concentration of archaeological sites and wildlife, you head overland towards this section's first permanent natural water source. The Fable Valley pack trail will then lead you into, not surprisingly, Fable Valley! There is a perennial stream in Fable Valley, which leads you to Dark Canyon Plateau, where you can encounter some of the route's most sweeping views (we also experienced gale-force winds and blowing sand).

Young's Canyon is then descended, until a huge pour-off is reached, at which point it becomes necessary to climb back out of the canyon and then follow the rim for a while until an access point to a very steep descent back into the canyon is reached. We were able to follow footprints that had been left by a National Outdoor Leadership

SELDOM SEEN BRIDGE

School group the previous autumn (yes, even footprints leave long-lasting evidence of your visit), but the route up is otherwise not very obvious. Young's will then lead to Dark Canyon, an exceptional place with many ancient relics. Look for the faint petroglyph panel in Dark Canyon, just above the confluence. (Hiking up the canyon a ways would make for a great day trip.)

Dark Canyon will be followed until you reach the Sundance Trail, a very steep scramble up 1200 feet of loose rock (you could only go a short distance farther before you reach the waters of Lake Powell in the Dark Canyon drainage). Passing the Squaw and Papoose Rock, dirt roads will then be followed for several miles to Hite.

■ **Resupply/Trailhead at Big Spring:** See previous description.

■ **Resupply/Trailhead at Hite:** From Utah Highway 95 between the bridge over the Dirty Devil River and the bridge over the Colorado River, turn northeast onto a dirt road marked as the Flint Trail or Road #663. Arrange for your resupply to meet you at the information kiosk at the top of the rise just down the dirt road.

■ **Topos:** The Loop, UT; Spanish Bottom, UT; Cross Canyon, UT; Druid Arch, UT; House Park Butte, UT; Fable Valley, UT; Bowdie Canyon, UT; Black Steer Canyon, UT; Indian Head Pass, UT; Copper Point, UT; Sewing Machine, UT; Hite North, UT.

ROUTE DESCRIPTION AND MILEAGE

3.8 ■ **Unless it happens to be pouring rain, or you have wisely cached a lot of water somewhere in between, you won't find a single source of water on this route until you reach a good spring in Beef Basin, 25 miles away!** That may not seem far, but don't forget you will be teetering off with about two weeks' worth of food and hauling it around in deep sand. Follow the pack trail from the parking area generally west for 3.8 miles to the dirt road in Cyclone Canyon. You will descend into and climb back out of Big Spring Canyon, then Elephant Canyon, along the way. You should take the time to hike the 1.3 miles northwest on the spur road out to the Confluence Overlook.

6.2 ■ Follow the dirt road south-southeast down Cyclone Canyon for 2.4 miles to the Red Lake Canyon Trail.

7.7 ■ Take this trail west-northwest for 0.5 miles down the drainage and into lower Red Lake Canyon. *If you really need water, this trail continues another 3.2 miles down to the Colorado River across from Spanish Bottom.* Leave the trail here and head south-southwest up this graben for 1 mile to the mouth of Butler Wash.

11.8 ■ Travel generally south-southeast up Butler Wash for 0.8 miles to its junction with Chesler Canyon. Stay in Butler Wash by taking the south fork and continue up it, generally south, then southeast, through a series of pour-offs for 3.3 miles until you come out of the canyon and then intersect the dirt road that leads to Horsehoof Arch and the Joint Trail.

19.7 ■ Continue generally southeast, then south, up Butler Wash for 7.9 miles to a fork in the canyon marked by a small spire.

21.1 ■ Go south-southwest up this side canyon for 1.4 miles to a fork.

21.7 ■ Continue south up the left fork for 0.6 miles, through Seldom

Seen Bridge, then climb south-southwest out of the canyon and onto the divide between this drainage and the one to the south.

22.2 ■ Now go west-southwest down into the drainage to the south and contour generally west along game trails to the head of this drainage. Climb the steep, loose-dirt ascent west out of this drainage and onto the divide between it and Middle Park of Beef Basin. You will have gone 0.5 miles from the last divide between the drainages.

23.8 ■ Head southwest across the sage flat in front of you. After 1 mile you will intersect a dirt road that runs north-south. Cross this dirt road and continue overland west- southwest for 0.6 more miles until you come to a second dirt road.

24.7 ■ Follow this road northwest, then southwest, for 0.7 miles until the road starts turning to the northwest again. Leave the road at that point and go 0.2 miles west down into the bottom of the drainage below you. *If the spring shown here on the quad maps is not running, Homewater Spring is reliable and is only 0.5 miles away.*

27.0 ■ Continue generally southwest, then south, down the wash for 2.3 miles as it swings around to the west and crosses a dirt road.

29.0 ■ Keep following the wash generally west for 2 more miles until you intersect Beef Basin Wash and the dirt road that crosses it. *Along the way are some overgrown, rather permanent-looking waterholes. These may be dry by late summer, but we found them full of water and being guarded by a pair of ducks the day we walked by in the spring. If you need water, South Spring is a reliable producer and is only 1 mile south down the dirt road.*

30.4 ■ Get on this road and follow it 0.7 miles southwest to a road junction. Follow this dirt track generally west-southwest for 0.7 more miles to the Fable Valley pack trail.

34.1 ■ Follow the pack trail for 3.7 miles as you contour generally southwest, then west, high above Gypsum Canyon, and then turn south-southwest and descend onto the floor of Fable Valley. *You should find water running down the wash here. If not, try searching some of the deeper holes in the wash bottom farther up the valley.*

POUR-OFF IN YOUNG'S CANYON

35.1 ■ Turn and go west, then generally south, up Fable Valley for 1 mile to a side canyon that comes in from the south. *A worthwhile excursion would be to explore the rest of Fable Valley and its ruins, rock art, and spring.*

38.3 ■ Go south, then southwest, up this brushy tributary canyon for 2.6 miles, climbing up or around numerous pour-offs, until you exit the head of this drainage and come out onto the Dark Canyon Plateau. *You may find some dank water along the way.* Walk south across the flat for 0.6 miles to the dirt road.

38.5 ■ Get on the road and go 0.2 miles southeast, past a junction and then a stock pond, to a double track that joins from the southwest.

39.0 ■ Take this track generally southwest for 0.5 miles down into Horse Pasture.

40.2 ■ Leave the road and continue south-southwest down the wash through Horse Pasture for 1.2 miles, and use the wash to guide yourself down to the floor of Young's Canyon.

DARK CANYON BOTTOM

40.7 ■ Now go west-southwest down Young's Canyon for 0.5 miles to the brink of a huge pour-off over a gaping abyss. **Stop!** Seriously. The canyon floor is suddenly way down below you.

41.8 ■ Turn around and go back a little way to a point where you can climb south out of the canyon. Although there may be better ways to get there, using the pour-off as a landmark is a good way not to get lost. The goal here is to get up to the rim of the canyon. There is no trail to speak of and the route shown is merely the one that we found. It actually wasn't too miserable. Once you reach the rim, follow it generally southwest to a point overlooking the very impressive Young's Canyon. Depending on how side-tracked you get, you will have gone about 1.1 miles since you left the bottom of the canyon.

42.2 ■ On the south side of this point is a very faint trail. If you try hard to stay on this seldom-used path, and have a little luck, it will lead you generally south down through the rubble below. You will land on a bench just above the pour-off of the hanging tributary south of the

CLIMBING OUT OF DARK CANYON ON THE SUNDANCE TRAIL

point. *You remembered to pack that rope, didn't you?* To the west, towards Young's Canyon, is a sandstone tower on the same platform as you. For some reason, we went toward it, then through the gap between it and the point above. We then scrambled and fell our way northwest the rest of the way down the suicidal scree to the bottom of Young's Canyon. At one place it was necessary to lower the packs. The canyon floor is 0.4 miles from the canyon rim. *There may be a better way to finish the descent into the canyon, but we didn't spend the time to find out. Gravity had a strong hold of us by the time we started down and it seemed a lot easier to just go with it. You will have worked pretty hard to get down into Young's Canyon, but life just got a whole lot better!*

45.0 ■ Once in Young's Canyon again, the going is relatively straight-forward, short of a few easy-to-manage pour-offs. Go 2.8 miles southwest down the floor of Young's Canyon to its confluence with Dark Canyon. *We found beautiful, running water all the way to Dark Canyon.*

51.9 ■ Go generally west, then northwest, down Dark Canyon for 6.9 miles until you reach the bottom of the Sundance Trail between Lost

ROUTE BACK INTO YOUNG'S CANYON

Canyon and Lean-To Canyon. *There should be flowing water all the way down.* You will generally be walking on ledges right above the creek and could easily get temporarily stranded. This is more of a nuisance than a real danger. It is normally a simple matter of backtracking, then crossing the creek to get back on track. **However, if Dark Canyon is in high run-off or flooding, you may not make it down!** We did notice, however, a faint trail in the talus above the creek bed that may serve as a high-water alternative. Due to the easy going on the canyon floor, we did not explore this high trail, so we won't speculate where it goes. But don't forget, you will be starting on the north side of the creek at Young's Canyon and will need to be on the south side at the Sundance Trail. **If you can't safely cross the creek in Dark Canyon at the mouth of Young's, you definitely won't be able to cross it 6.9 miles farther down after it has picked up the flows of several side canyons! Go back the way you came or wait for the water to recede.**

52.8 ■ Now take the Sundance Trail generally west, then northwest, for 0.9 miles as it switches back and forth, up through the talus, out of Dark Canyon and finally to the rim. This is a grueling ascent of 1,200 feet, but at least the trail is pretty obvious. As is the case with most punishing ascents, you will be well rewarded by the views.

54.1 ■ Once you reach the rim, continue generally west, then south, on the trail for 1.3 miles to the dirt road.

55.1 ■ Cross the road and go overland south-southwest for 1 mile, dodging the head of Sheep Canyon, through the pinyon-juniper forest to intersect the Squaw and Papoose Road.

57.5 ■ Follow the Squaw and Papoose Road, first northwest, then southwest, for 2.4 miles. You will pass an intersection coming in from the northwest and then come to a T-intersection.

58.8 ■ Turn right and continue generally northwest on the dirt road for 1.3 miles, past an intersection on the left, to another T-intersection. *You may find water in the large pothole shown on the map. It is just to the west of where the road crosses a wash before the T-intersection.*

66.1 ■ Go left here and west, then northwest, then generally west again for 7.3 miles on the dirt road to its junction with Highway 95. You will pass a couple more intersections and an airstrip along the way.

67.5 ■ Go northwest on Highway 95 for 1.4 miles, crossing the bridge over the Colorado River.

67.9 ■ Continue northwest on the road for 0.3 miles to a point where you can leave the road and find your way up the short slope to the north. After another 0.1 miles you will intersect the dirt road known as the Flint Trail or #663. This is the end of this section. You can stage your resupply, shuttle, or car drop anywhere you see fit along the first mile or so of this road, but the information kiosk near the highway seems to be a most logical landmark for everyone to find.

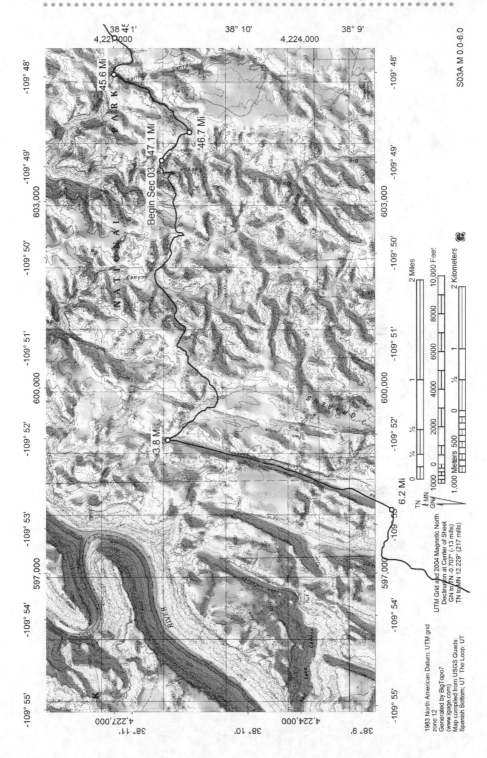

38° 11'
38° 10'
38° 9'
4,222,000
4,224,000

-109° 48'
-109° 49'

603,000

45.6 Mi

Begin Sec 03 - 47.1 Mi

46.7 Mi

Big

Canyon

Canyon

3.8 Mi

6.2 Mi

600,000

597,000

-109° 48'
-109° 49'
-109° 50'
-109° 51'
-109° 52'
-109° 53'
-109° 54'
-109° 55'

RIVER

N A T I O N A L   P A R K

S03A M 0.0-6.0

2 Miles
10,000 Feet
2 Kilometers

1,000
500
Meters

0
1000
2000
4000
6000
8000

TN
MN
GN

UTM Grid and 2004 Magnetic North
Declination at Center of Sheet
GN to TN -0.707° (-13 mils)
TN to MN 12.229° (217 mils)

1983 North American Datum; UTM grid
zone 12
Generated by BigTopo7
(www.igage.com)
Map compiled from USGS Quads:
Spanish Bottom; UT The Loop; UT

38° 11'
38° 10'
38° 9'
4,227,000
4,224,000

SECTION 3: 0.0–6.0 MILES

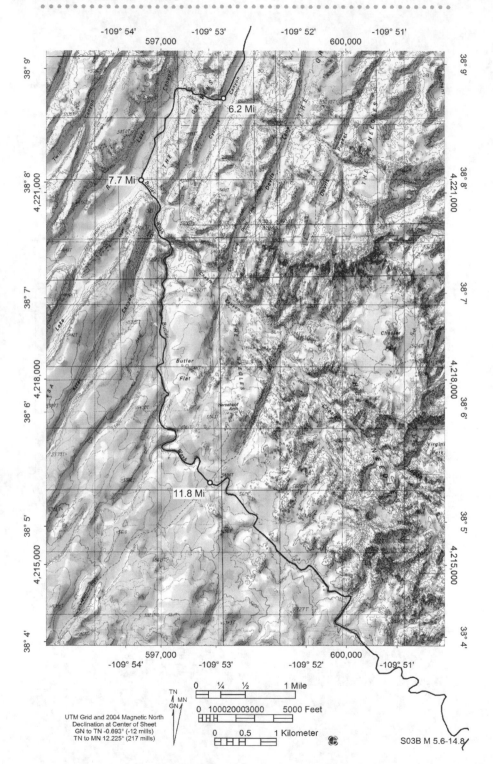

SECTION 3: 5.6–14.8 MILES

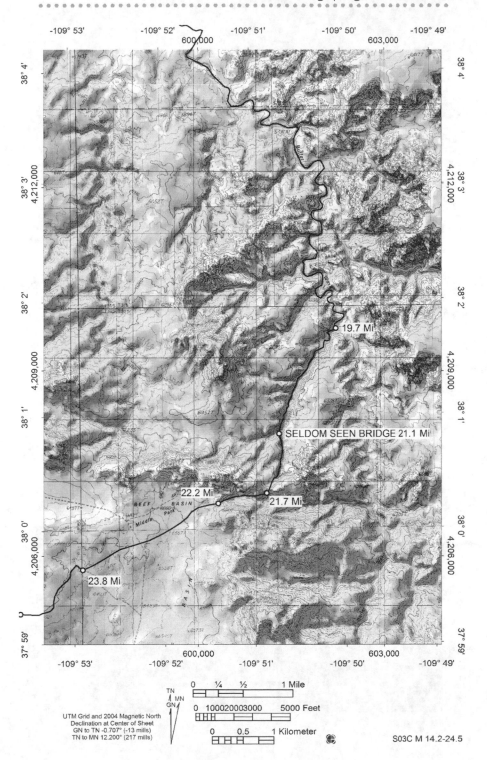

19.7 Mi

SELDOM SEEN BRIDGE 21.1 Mi

22.2 Mi

21.7 Mi

23.8 Mi

TN
MN
GN

UTM Grid and 2004 Magnetic North
Declination at Center of Sheet
GN to TN -0.707° (-13 mils)
TN to MN 12.200° (217 mils)

0   ¼   ½   1 Mile

0   100020003000   5000 Feet

0   0.5   1 Kilometer

S03C M 14.2-24.5

SECTION 3: 14.2–24.5 MILES

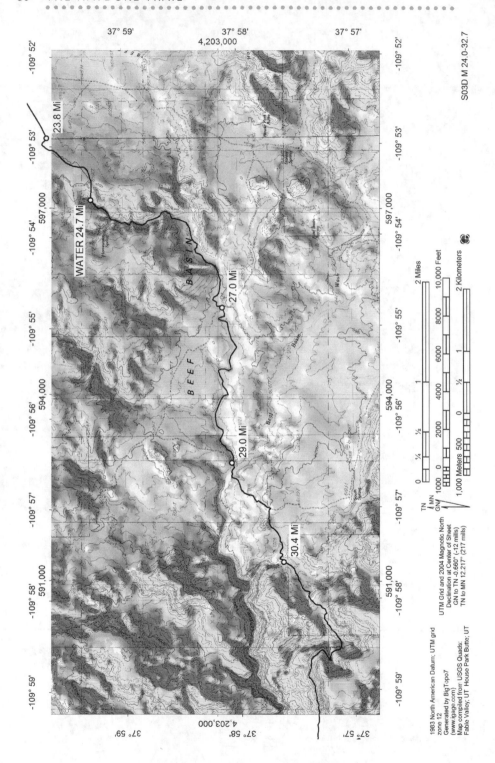

37° 59'   37° 58'   37° 57'
4,203,000

23.8 Mi

WATER 24.7 Mi

B A S I N

27.0 Mi

B E E F

29.0 Mi

30.4 Mi

S03D M 24.0-32.7

TN
MN
GN

UTM Grid and 2004 Magnetic North
Declination at Center of Sheet
GN to TN -0.660° (-12 mils)
TN to MN 12.217° (217 mils)

2 Miles
10,000 Feet
2 Kilometers

1000   0   2000   4000   6000   8000
1,000 Meters   500   0   1

1/4   1/2   1
0   1/2

1983 North American Datum, UTM grid
zone 12
Generated by BigTopo7
(www.igage.com)
Map compiled from: USGS Quads:
Fable Valley, UT; House Park Butte, UT

SECTION 3: 24.0–32.7 MILES

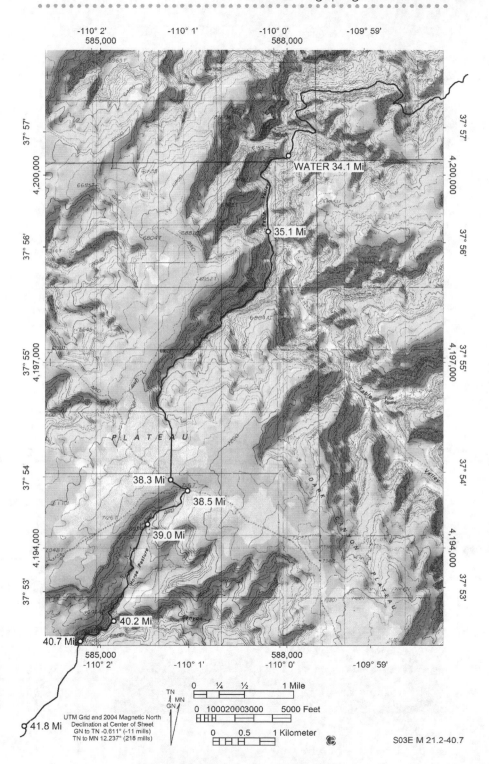

WATER 34.1 Mi

35.1 Mi

P L A T E A U

38.3 Mi
38.5 Mi

39.0 Mi

40.2 Mi

40.7 Mi

41.8 Mi

TN
MN
GN

UTM Grid and 2004 Magnetic North
Declination at Center of Sheet
GN to TN -0.611° (-11 mils)
TN to MN 12.237° (218 mils)

0   ¼   ½   1 Mile

0 1000 2000 3000   5000 Feet

0   0.5   1 Kilometer

S03E M 21.2-40.7

SECTION 3: 21.2–40.7 MILES

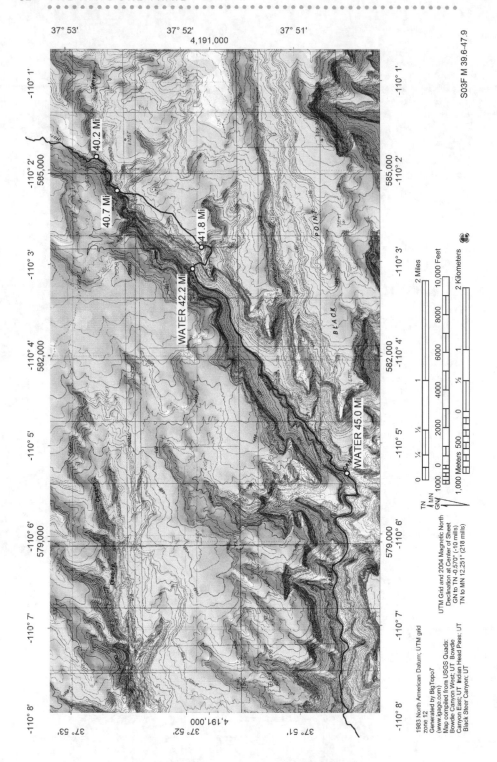

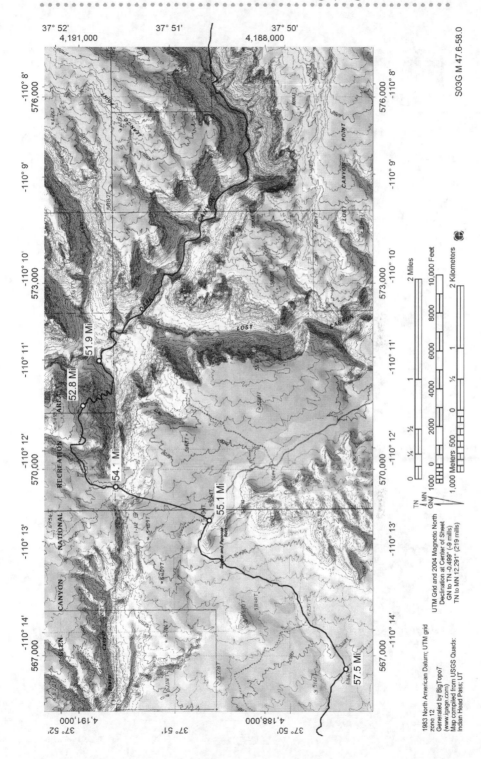

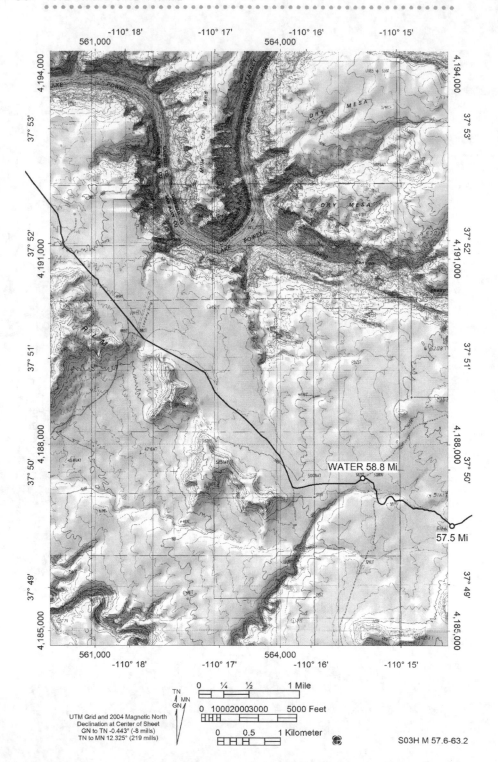

SECTION 3: 57.6–63.2 MILES

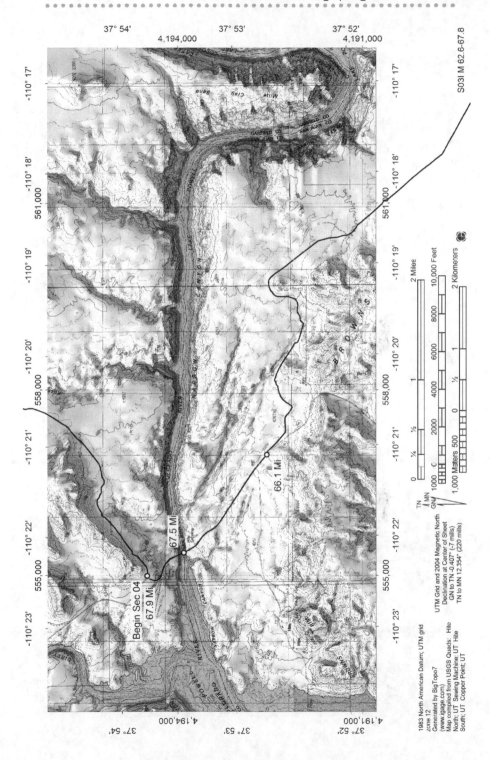

SECTION 3: 62.6–67.8 MILES

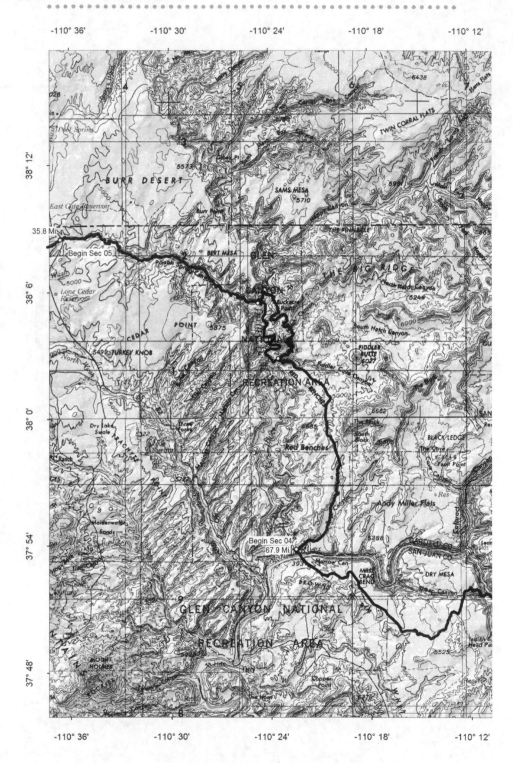

SECTION 4: OVERVIEW

■ SECTION 4
Hite to Poison Spring Canyon

••

APPROXIMATE TIME: 7 days

DISTANCE: 35.8 miles

EXERTION: moderate

NAVIGATION: mostly easy, but part is difficult

WATER: damp

DESOLATION FACTOR: deep backcountry (parts are very remote)

SPECIFIC HAZARDS: quicksand and large water flow in the Dirty Devil River corridor; watch for poison ivy.

PERMITS: Glen Canyon National Recreation Area requires permits for backcountry use.

"Mitch was up first. I found him around the corner, so to speak, looking at names engraved in a flat panel of rock. Names like Ezra Huntsman, Ferron, Utah, Feb. 7 1922. Albert Weber, Hanksville, Wayne Co., Utah, Feb. 17 1920. Clive Cheshire, Jan. 1 1939. Leo Madsen, Jan. 7 1927. N.L. Chaffin, Green River, Utah, Feb. 22nd 1935. Leland Bohleen, Ferron, Utah, Mar. 4 1932. Clyde Olsen. Mont Caldwell, 1930. Less Wareham, March 17, 1938. Back in 1954 again to the Ledges, Mont Caldwell. Hans Larsen, Ferron, Utah, Jan. 28, 1933. Slats. Louie Hitchcock Dec. 25 1919. J. Jeffs.

"Apparently we're at an old cowboy camp. Further inspection of the area yielded some interesting remnants: several horseshoes, some whole, some broken, all different sizes. Boot heels, a buckle, a metal button. Some old bottles, requiring stoppers or corks. . . .

"So when does this stuff become historic artifacts? When is it just litter, or junk? How about the rock register? The name added in 1988 bothered me. It was out of place. . . ."

APRIL 19, 1998 [DAY 31 OF 94], RED BENCHES (LEDGES)

"After a very warm and windy night, we packed up early and headed up Poison Spring Canyon. It is a stunning canyon indeed.

COWBOY RELICS, RED LEDGES

It starts as a deep narrow canyon, inside of huge red rock walls. As we followed the road, it slowly ascends, our start in the 7,700' vertical climb to the top on Mt. Ellen.

"The day turned out to be a perfect one for walking, not too hot, puffy clouds, and a light breeze. We saw a lot of people on the road today; we spoke with quite a few, including some people we knew from Solitude [ski area]. I guess the mountain closed last weekend. We missed out on five weeks of skiing! Bummer, huh?

"We saw a couple of rock faces with petroglyphs, both of them had cowboy names that we've seen before: Mont Caldwell, A. Weber, and Jess Larsen. The boys got around. Pottery sherds were found around the bases of the rock faces. There's a spring in the canyon, it's got a small masonry "reservoir," with a pipe pouring clear, cool water out of it. We dumped our river water and filled up with the spring water."

APRIL 24, 1998 [DAY 36 OF 94], POISON SPRING CANYON

After leaving Hite and the bridge across the Colorado River, you travel a couple of miles along the Flint Trail (dirt road) until you reach the west fork of Rock Canyon, where there is a short but very steep climb out of the canyon to the rim level, which is known as the Red Ledges (hauling packs up on ropes is required).

On the Ledges (also known as the Red Benches), you go overland until you reach the access into Fiddler Cove Canyon; but you are also loosely following what is known as "the Chinese Trail," so named because of its huge, pagodalike rock cairns (there's at least one that's nine feet tall). There are a good deal of remains left by cowboys of old in the area; we found some names engraved in a rock that we would see repeatedly over the next few weeks. Here on the Ledges navigation can be tricky, and the drop-off point into Fiddler Cove, named for a fiddle-playing sheepherder, can be difficult to find. Once in Fiddler Cove Canyon, navigation becomes simple; it's all about following large drainages all the way to the end of the section. Hiking down Fiddler Cove leads to Hatch Canyon, which in turn leads to the Dirty Devil River. You may want to take a hike *up* Fiddler Cove Canyon before leaving the area; it's rather scenic (there are also a lot of interesting rocks to be found in there; geodes and other wildly colored ones abound). Once at the Dirty Devil, you head up river until you reach Poison Spring Canyon. Plan on getting wet feet in the river, and

CAIRN ON "CHINESE TRAIL"

FIDDLER COVE CANYON

beware of quicksand (we found the carcass of a stuck bovine in the middle of the riverbed)! If you are visiting this area in the warmer months, be prepared for an onslaught of biting insects.

Poison Spring Canyon has a dirt road running its length, and has become a popular place to visit because of its outstanding scenery, so plan on seeing other folks there. Leaving the Dirty Devil River begins an ascent of more than 7000 feet as you work your way to the top of Mt. Ellen. Keep an eye out for the many petroglyph panels along both the canyon walls and on freestanding rocks. This section ends at the canyon's junction with Utah Highway 95.

■ **Resupply/Trailhead at Hite:** See previous description.

■ **Resupply/Trailhead at Poison Spring Benches:** About 17 miles south of Hanksville on Highway 95 is a break in the guardrail where the road crosses Poison Spring Wash. There is a sign here and to the east is the dirt road that goes down Poison Spring Canyon all the way to the Dirty Devil River. It is the same dirt road that you will eventually be following on foot.

■ **Topos:** Sewing Machine, UT; Fiddler Butte, UT; Stair Canyon, UT; Burr Point, UT; Baking Skillet Knoll, UT; Turkey Knob, UT.

SHEEP PETROGLYPH, POISON SPRING CANYON

ROUTE DESCRIPTION AND MILEAGE

It is 15 miles to the first water you might possibly find in the Dirty Devil River. *If there is water in the river (in late summer or during dry years there may be none at all), use it sparingly! This was some of the nastiest water we have sampled. It is highly alkaline, probably full of heavy metals, definitely bearing the accumulated agricultural waste of the Fremont River, and who knows what else. If you can settle it out overnight, you may not immediately destroy your water filter; but what you will get is a foul-tasting chemical soup that at least is mostly H_2O. Here's the catch: the water gives you the runs, so you drink more to fight the ensuing dehydration caused by the runs, which naturally makes your diarrhea even worse, so you drink more water. . . . It is a vicious cycle, but you have to appreciate the irony in it. In short, if at all possible, carry enough good water to see you all the way to Poison Spring Canyon.*

4.0 ■ Go generally northeast, then north-northeast, up the dirt road for 4 miles until you cross the west fork of Rock Canyon just beyond a corral.

6.0 ◼ Leave the dirt road here and go north up the wash. After 2 miles the canyon narrows and turns hard to the west. This is where we exited this canyon, but there may be other ways. Since this is the only way we have been, it is the way we will describe in detail. However, there is an old mining track clinging to the west wall about halfway up the canyon. Since there also is an old track on top of the canyon, the two are possibly linked.

6.1 ◼ Up in the cove, on the northeast side of the bend, is a chimney route that will quickly get you out of the canyon and where you need to be. You will need to do a short, dead-lift, pack haul to get your stuff up. *As you scramble up the talus into the corner of the cove, the chimney will become obvious. If it's not, you're going to have problems later on in this section finding the route down into Fiddler Cove Canyon, and you should consider bagging it. After all, it's an easy 6 miles back to the car from here rather than wandering across the blistering Red Benches and back after you become stymied by the route into Fiddler Cove.* From the bottom of Rock Canyon to the rim is another 0.1 miles.

13.1 ◼ If you are confident in your route-finding ability and can accept the real possibility of never being heard from again, follow your compass north-northwest, then north, then northwest across the Red Benches. If you pay attention, you may catch a glimpse of one of the giant stone cairns that mark the way of the forgotten Chinese Trail. This ghost of a trail does not take you where you want to go today. You must find your way around dozens of small ravines to cross the Red Benches and past the Block. Unfortunately, you will generally be going against the grain across the ravines, and few of them go in the direction you want. After about 7 miles, depending on how many drainages you have to weave in and out of, you will find yourself high on the rim of Fiddler Cove Canyon.

13.2 ◼ **Make sure you know exactly where you are before you start the descent into Fiddler Cove Canyon!** *There are several spots that may seem to be "likely places" for the route down, but the actual route down may be less likely looking than the other traps are. Don't be fooled! There is only ONE route down here and it is right where it is* *shown on the map. If you have any doubts, go back!* Once you find the route down, the rest should be fairly straightforward. Just follow gravity! It is a steep descent, 750 feet in 0.1 miles, down and around numerous ledges, through the boulders and debris.

15.0 ▪ When you get to the bottom, simply follow this deep and winding canyon generally west for 1.8 miles to the Dirty Devil River. You will pass Hatch Canyon on the way, a very interesting diversion and a high-water route.

20.5 ▪ Now go generally north-northwest up the Dirty Devil for about 5.5 miles to the mouth of Poison Spring Canyon. You will have to cross the river repeatedly, so if it is flowing be prepared for deep holes and a lot of quicksand! **Be wary of this seemingly gentle river!** *The Dirty Devil River is capable of carrying as much water as does the Colorado River in the Grand Canyon, and it has! Although that would be rare, this normally quiet river does flood in the spring and after hard rains, making foot travel in its corridor impossible. Its flow is prone to fluctuate wildly and unpredictably. We have hiked in its bone-dry bed and canoed down its length in the same year!*

If you find the Dirty Devil River to be running too high, there is an alternate route. Go up Hatch Canyon generally northeast, then north, for 4.0 miles. Now ascend the sloping, western wall of the canyon and follow the route as shown, generally northwest, for 0.4 miles to intersect a dirt road. Now follow this dirt road generally northwest for 5.0 miles until it runs into the Dirty Devil River. If it is safe to do so, cross the river here. (Since you've probably taken this alternate route due to high water, this last part probably means "swim across the river here.") Now follow the dirt road again, generally southwest, for 0.8 miles to return to the Hayduke Trail in Poison Spring Canyon.

21.0 ▪ Go generally west up Poison Spring Canyon for 0.5 miles until you intersect a dirt road. There is a panel of petroglyphs on the north wall between the road and the river. This is the first of many panels to be found in the canyon, with most of them being on the north side. **Remember, just look! Simply touching rock art will eventually lead to its demise.**

25.4 ■ Follow the dirt road generally west-northwest, then northwest, as it winds its way up Poison Spring Canyon. After 4.4 miles you will have come up from the lower canyon into the upper canyon above Black Jump. *There is normally a small flow of water in the bottom of the canyon above the jump. Because there are quite a few cows typically grazing alongside the stream in Poison Spring Canyon, this water is not always very appealing. If you can wait to take water, there is a great little spring on the north wall another 1.7 miles up the canyon.*

27.1 ■ Continue generally west-northwest along the dirt road for 1.7 miles to the spring. *This spring has been piped and a masonry wall built around it to contain it and keep the cows at bay.*

32.8 ■ Keep following the dirt road generally west, then northwest, up Poison Spring Canyon for another 5.7 miles. Here the road leaves the canyon and starts going up Butler Wash.

35.5 ■ Leave the road and continue following Poison Spring Canyon northwest, then generally west. After 2.7 miles you will come back to the dirt road.

35.8 ■ Follow the dirt road west-southwest for another 0.3 miles up the wash to its junction with Highway 95. This is the end of this section. You could stage your resupply/car drop either here or anywhere on the dirt road within a mile or so of the highway.

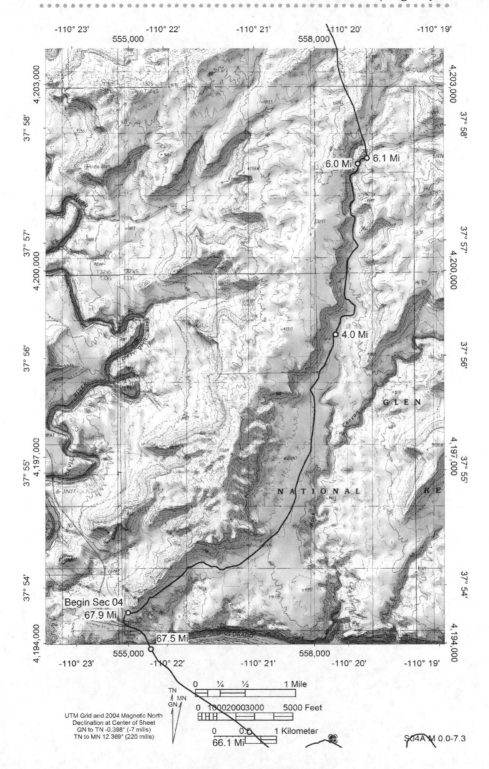

-110° 23'   -110° 22'   -110° 21'   -110° 20'   -110° 19'

555,000   558,000

4,203,000   4,203,000

37° 58'   37° 58'

6.0 Mi ○ 6.1 Mi

37° 57'   37° 57'

4,200,000   4,200,000

○ 4.0 Mi

37° 56'   37° 56'

G L E N

4,197,000   37° 55'

37° 55'

N A T I O N A L   R E

4,194,000

37° 54'   37° 54'

Begin Sec 04
67.9 Mi ○

67.5 Mi ○

555,000   558,000

4,194,000

-110° 23'   -110° 22'   -110° 21'   -110° 20'   -110° 19'

0   ¼   ½   1 Mile

TN
MN
GN

0   1000 2000 3000   5000 Feet

UTM Grid and 2004 Magnetic North
Declination at Center of Sheet
GN to TN -0.398° (-7 mils)
TN to MN 12.369° (220 mils)

0   0.5   1 Kilometer

66.1 Mi

S04A M 0.0-7.3

SECTION 4: 0.0–7.3 MILES

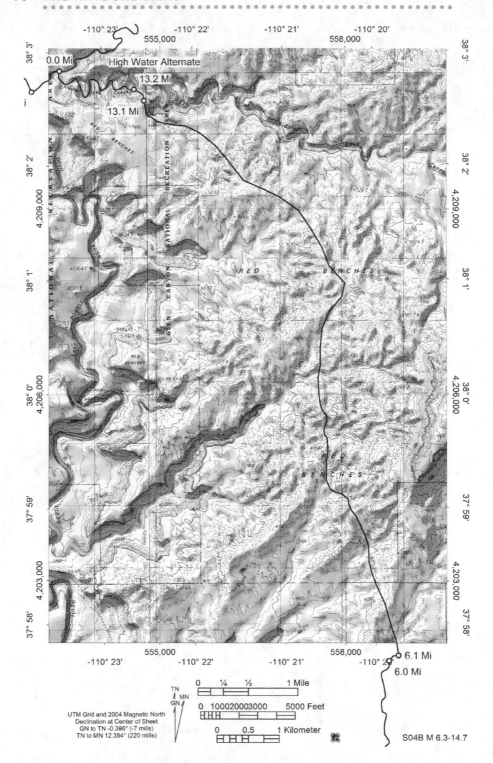

SECTION 4: 6.3–14.7 MILES

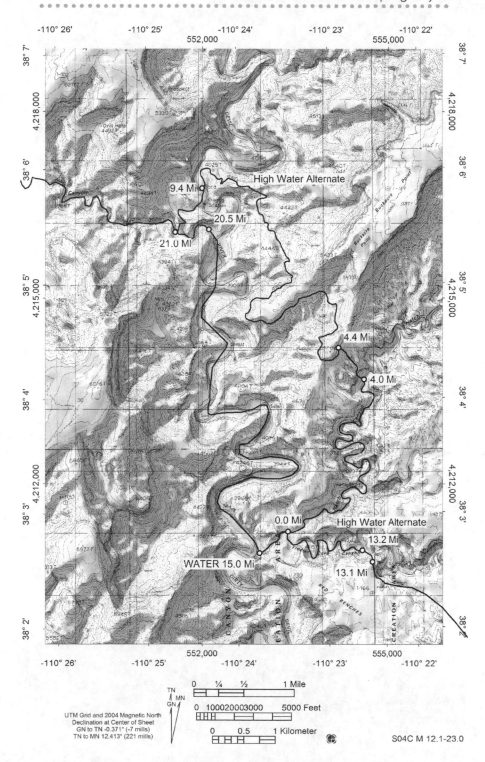

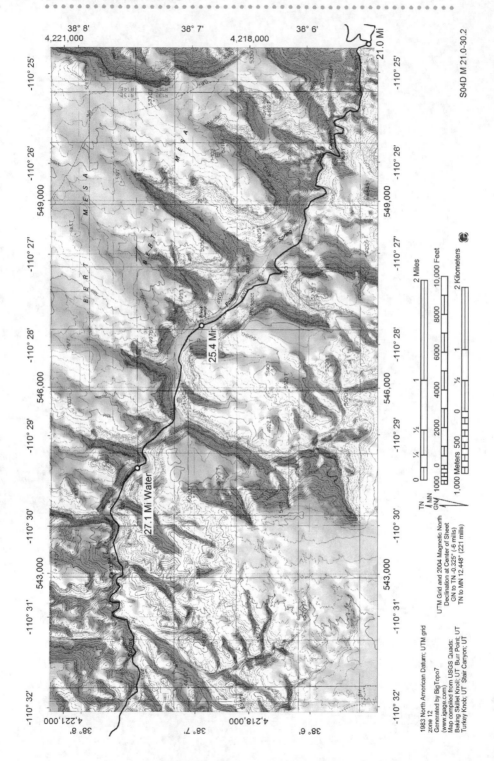

SECTION 4: 21.0–30.2 MILES

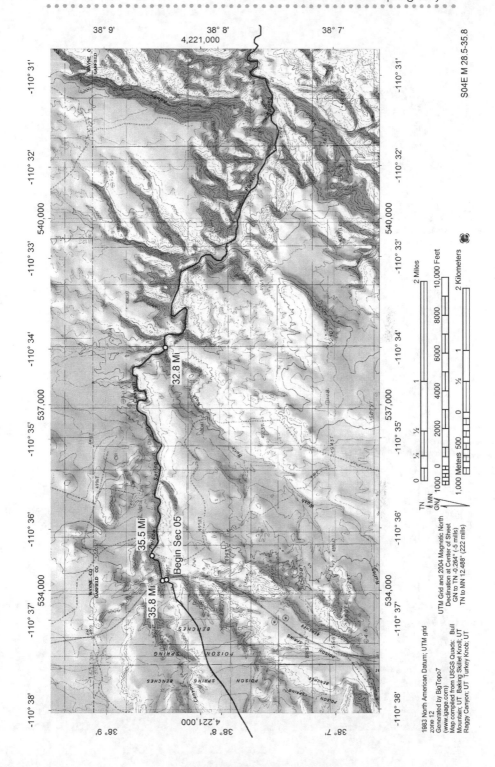

38° 9'   38° 8'   38° 7'
4,221,000

-110° 31'   -110° 31'

S04E M 28.5-35.8

-110° 32'   -110° 32'

540,000   540,000

-110° 33'   -110° 33'

-110° 34'   -110° 34'

32.8 Mi

537,000   537,000

-110° 35'   -110° 35'

-110° 36'   -110° 36'

35.5 Mi

Begin Sec 05

534,000   534,000

35.8 Mi

-110° 37'   -110° 37'

-110° 38'   -110° 38'

4,221,000

38° 9'   38° 8'   38° 7'

2 Miles

1000   0   2000   4000   6000   8000   10,000 Feet

1,000 Meters 500   0   1   2 Kilometers

1983 North American Datum; UTM grid
zone 12
(Generated by BigTopo7
(www.igage.com)
Map compiled from USGS Quads: Bull
Mountain, UT Baking Skillet Knoll, UT
Ragsy Canyon, UT Turkey Knob; UT

UTM Grid and 2004 Magnetic North
Declination at Center of Sheet
GN to TN -0.264° (-.5 mills)
TN to MN 12.488° (222 mills)

TN
GN MN

SECTION 4: 28.5–35.8 MILES

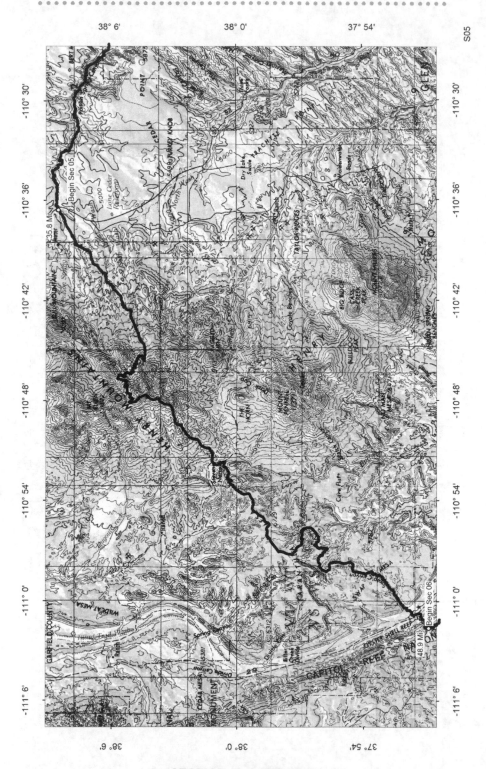

SECTION 5: OVERVIEW

Poison Spring Canyon to the Burr Trail, Capitol Reef National Park

●●●

APPROXIMATE TIME: 8 days

DISTANCE: 48.9 miles

EXERTION: moderate to difficult (mostly because of large vertical ascents and descents)

NAVIGATION: moderate

WATER: damp

DESOLATION FACTOR: backcountry

SPECIFIC HAZARDS: possible snow avalanche danger (seasonal); exposure on route off of Tarantula Mesa.

PERMITS: Capitol Reef National Park requires permits for overnight backcountry use.

"A superlative day already! And it's only noon!

"We started the day before sun up, heading up the little knob by our camp to watch the sun rise. What an incredible sunrise it was. The night's clear sky had two advantages for us: the sunrise was so sweet, watching the sun peek out from behind the distant La Sals. It also allowed for a nice cold night (yes, we actually were hoping it would be cold). The cold allowed the snow to freeze, making it supportable, with less post-holing for us.

"The view from the knob also showed another sight besides the sunrise: a bison, hobbling around up the ridge. I say hobbling because this guy (definitely a bull) was limping hard. His front right leg didn't seem to work. I wonder whose dinner he'll end up being.

"We walked to the ridge on mostly supportable snow, then I skinned up, Mitch set a boot track. The snow seemed good, the view constantly getting better. I kept below the ridge itself until the very summit, staying on snow, keeping myself in suspense as to the view to the west. Until now, we mostly only had been able to see the places we'd recently traveled. Finally I could see where

SNOWBOARDING ON MOUNT ELLEN

we'd be going. Wow! The Waterpocket Fold was visible for its entire length. There was Boulder Mountain, Thousand Lake Mountain, Fifty Mile Mountain, Navajo Mountain, the Abajo Mountains, the La Sal Mountains, and finally the rest of the Henry Mountains. Nice view! It's so surreal to be in such an alpine environment, with such a crazy desert landscape below. While the haze prevents us from seeing far-off details, we can still see almost our entire route! And then to be up here, so high above it all. Exhilarating!

"We skied/boarded first in a higher bowl than the one we'd been looking at from our camp, the ridge was about 11,325'. We skied about 1,500' vertical, ending in a halfpipe-like drainage. The second run was in the bowl we had been looking at. The sun had gotten to it first; the skiing was great, but the fresh snow from the last couple of storms was rollerballing, obliterating our tracks. And we had wanted to be able to gloat over them from camp! The things we put up with!

"After the second run, which we knew would be the last because of the hot sun, we headed down the head of the Granite Creek drainage, hoping to intersect the road. The way soon proved to be too much for a snowboard; it was too flat, too deep *(rotten snow), and too thick (trees). Mitch headed up the side, hoping to find a better way. I kept going, and slowly pushed through to the road, finally seeing our tracks from yesterday. Mitch was nowhere in sight. I took off my skis when the sun melted the pack off the roadway, knowing that I'd be putting them back on once the road turned another bend. I had only walked a short way up the hill when I looked up the road and saw the cat. A large, wooly looking, no-tailed bobcat. I had finally seen a wild cat in Utah! And a wild bison. In one day! And I skied. And the view. Alpine. Desert. Sometimes I think my head might explode!"*

APRIL 29, 1998 [DAY 41 OF 94], IN THE HENRY MOUNTAINS

Because of a steep descent from Tarantula Mesa into Muley Canyon, we recommend following this section in the direction described. This section offers some amazing scenery: the view from the top of the Henry Mountains is sublime, and hiking down into the Waterpocket Fold through Tarantula and Swap Mesas, with their unique colors and formations, is a beautifully impressive experience.

The Waterpocket Fold, which is the prominent feature of Capitol Reef National Park, is basically a giant wrinkle in the earth's crust, running in a north/south orientation, for almost one hundred miles. Named for its rock domes that are suggestive of the U.S. capitol, Capitol Reef, originally a state park, achieved national monument status in 1937, and was expanded and designated a national park in 1971.

Departing Highway 95, you begin by following a little-used dirt road into the Henry Mountains, which happen to have been the very last mountain range in the "lower 48" to be explored. They can still be quite desolate. Depending on the season (and the snowpack), there may be water running down various drainages. Keep an eye out for the occasional bison (the Henry's have one of America's last free-roaming herds. They generally will be found on the northern and western flanks of the range. Originally reintroduced into the Burr Desert in 1941 from Yellowstone, they quickly absconded for the cooler and wetter mountains, where they have stayed. We saw deer and even a bobcat up there as well. If there is an adequate snowpack, skiing/boarding can offer a fun break from hauling packs around.

VIEW FROM THE NORTH SUMMIT OF MOUNT ELLEN (11,522 FEET)

We skied off both the north and south summit ridges of Mount
Ellen and were absolutely astounded by the contrast of playing on a
high alpine, snow-covered slope, while at the same time looking down
on the sprawling red rock world around us. We could see as far to the
east as the Sierra La Sal, therefore over the entire route that we had
just come, and west over the Waterpocket Fold, to the Kaiparowits
Plateau, where we would be heading.

The route travels over the south summit of Mount Ellen (11,419
feet above sea level) and along the south summit ridge as it descends
towards Tarantula Mesa. Once you leave the mountain ridges, you'll
follow Sweetwater Canyon as the vegetation changes from ponderosa
and aspen to pinyon and juniper. You will then leave the drainage for a
few miles of road walking through the pinyon and juniper across
Tarantula Mesa before you turn into the trees and head to the rim. A
very steep route drops through the cap rock and down into a Muley
Canyon drainage. An old stock route is followed in and out of a number of drainages of Swap Mesa until you come to the rim above Swap
Canyon. A relatively easy route leads down into the canyon, which is
followed out to the base of the Burr Trail.

**VIEW FROM THE TOP OF THE BURR TRAIL,
CAPITOL REEF NATIONAL PARK**

This section ends at the top of the Burr Trail switchbacks, at the junction with Muley Twist Canyon, where you'll find a sign-in register and trailhead. It's also worthwhile to look for the large petroglyph panel on the rock face that wraps around from the Burr Trail into upper Muley Twist, just a little farther to the west.

■ **Resupply/Trailhead at Poison Spring Benches:** See previous description.

■ **Resupply/Trailhead at Burr Trail:** This one is located at the Lower Muley Twist Trailhead in Capitol Reef National Park. You will have to go outside of the park if you want to camp next to your vehicle without a permit. There are a couple of ways to get to the trailhead. Either drive 36 miles south down the dirt Notom to Bullfrog Road from Highway 24 (or north up this same road from Bullfrog) to the well-marked Burr Trail. Turn west and take the road to the top of the switchbacks. Or you can get there from the other end of the Burr Trail in the town of Boulder. Simply get on the Burr Trail in town and follow it 40 miles east to the trailhead.

▨ **Topos:** Baking Skillet Knoll, UT; Bull Mountain, UT; Raggy Canyon, UT; Mount Ellen, UT; Steele Butte, UT; Cave Flat, UT; The Post, UT; Wagon Box Mesa, UT.

ROUTE DESCRIPTION AND MILEAGE

2.2 ▨ Walk west-southwest for 2.2 miles on the dirt road on the west side of the highway. It turns to the northwest just before coming to a junction.

4.7 ▨ Turn southwest at the junction and follow the dirt road, generally southwest, for 2.5 miles to a T-junction.

4.9 ▨ Leave the road here and follow your compass south-southwest for 0.2 miles until you find yourself in the bottom of the upper reaches of Butler Wash.

5.3 ▨ Go generally west up the wash for 0.4 miles to a feeder coming in from the southwest.

6.1 ▨ Now follow this feeder generally southwest for 0.8 miles to where it splits.

7.3 ▨ Take the southwest arm and follow it southwest, then west-southwest, for 1.2 miles to a dirt road.

8.0 ▨ Follow the dirt road east, then around to the west, and then generally south-southwest for 0.7 miles to its junction with the dirt road coming out of Crescent Creek.

10.9 ▨ Follow this dirt road first west-northwest, then west-southwest, and finally west for 2.9 miles to another junction. *After 2 miles you will be closely paralleling Crescent Creek, a good source of cold, clear water.*

14.1 ▨ Turn northeast at the junction and follow this dirt road northeast, then north, and then generally northwest for 3.2 miles. *You will be cutting a traverse across the Granite Ridges and in and out of several drainages, some with running water.* You will end up at Wickiup Pass, elevation 9240 feet.

16.7 ▥ At the road junction at Wickiup Pass, go generally southwest for 2.6 miles up the dirt road to Bull Creek Pass, elevation 10,485 feet.

17.8 ▥ Turn south at the pass, leave the dirt road, and follow a faint trail generally southeast onto the south summit ridge. This trail is directly across the road from the north summit trail. Continue going southeast up the ridge to Mount Ellen's south summit, elevation 11,419 feet. The summit is 1.1 miles from Bull Creek Pass.

18.3 ▥ Now go southwest down the ridge for 0.5 miles to the saddle between Bromide Basin and the North Fork of South Creek.

18.6 ▥ Contour around the small peak to the south by staying on the east, or Bromide Basin, side of it on a game trail. Follow this contour generally south for 0.3 miles to the pass between Bromide Basin and Slate Creek.

18.9 ▥ Go west-southwest, then southwest, back onto the south summit ridge. After 0.3 miles you will have dropped down to the saddle marked 10677-T.

19.2 ▥ Continue generally south-southwest along the ridge another 0.3 miles up to the top of a small summit.

20.2 ▥ Descend south-southwest, then southwest, off of this summit and down onto South Creek Ridge. Now follow this ridge west-southwest until you intersect a dirt road. It is 1.0 mile from the last summit.

20.5 ▥ Continue generally west-southwest for 0.3 miles down South Creek Ridge. You will pass an antenna configuration on the ridge.

20.8 ▥ Drop off of the ridge into the head of Sweetwater Creek by descending this sloping shoulder south for 0.3 miles to the wash bottom.

21.9 ▥ Now follow the floor of Sweetwater Creek generally southwest. You may encounter a small flow of water in the bottom of the canyon. In 1.1 miles you will intersect a dirt road. *If you are having water issues at this point, Birch Spring (a good and reliable water source, fenced-off from cattle) is only 1.5 miles away, generally west, then north, along this dirt road.*

22.6 ■ Cross the road and continue down Sweetwater Creek generally south, then southwest. In 0.7 miles you will come to a small pour-off.

22.7 ■ Bypass the pour-off by climbing southeast a short way off of the floor of the canyon and then contouring 0.1 miles generally southwest and back down to the streambed.

22.9 ■ Continue south-southwest down Sweetwater Creek for 0.2 miles to another, much larger, pour-off.

23.3 ■ Contour around this pour-off generally south, then southwest, for 0.4 miles until you can get back down to the canyon floor. Keep the canyon in view to your right as you traverse along and you will easily find the way.

23.7 ■ Follow Sweetwater Creek southwest, then west, for 0.4 miles to a side canyon that comes in from the north. If you haven't encountered any water in Sweetwater Creek yet, there is a reliable spring 0.3 miles north up this side canyon. *Wherever you find it, make sure you take enough water to carry you 13.4 miles to the next water in Muley Creek.*

23.9 ■ Continue generally west down Sweetwater Creek another 0.2 miles to the point where the canyon turns north after a short run to the south.

24.1 ■ Climb west out of the canyon and go west-southwest for 0.2 miles across the flat to intersect a dirt road.

24.8 ■ Follow this dirt road generally south-southeast for 0.7 miles to a junction.

31.9 ■ Turn right, or west, onto this dirt road and follow it generally southwest for 7.1 miles to another junction. You will be following a wide spit of land out onto Tarantula Mesa.

32.6 ■ Go left, or south, at this junction and follow this dirt road generally south for 0.7 miles.

33.1 ■ Leave the road here and go generally southeast, then east, for 0.5 miles along this flat hilltop to the point marked 6627T on the map.

33.4 ■ Continue on this flat-topped ridge generally south-southwest for another 0.3 miles. *Here begins your descent to Muley Creek. Pay attention!*

33.6 ■ Leave the ridge and set off due west for 0.2 miles until you come to the rim of the nearest side canyon of Muley Creek. **Take a long look around and make sure you know exactly where you are!** *If you have any doubt at all, walk along the rim until you figure it out. There is only one way down! If you still can't say with 100 percent certainty that you are on the route described, then this is the place to turn around. Do it now while your tracks leading you back to the dirt road are still fresh and you have enough water to get you back to Sweetwater Creek.*

33.8 ■ Leave the rim traveling east-southeast for 0.2 miles and descend onto the narrow bench. If you're lucky, cairns that we left will be there to show you the way, but don't count on it. Funny things happen to cairns out here.

33.9 ■ Follow this bench generally north-northwest for 0.1 miles until you come out onto a steeply sloping shoulder.

34.0 ■ Now carefully pick your way northeast for 0.1 mile down this loose-dirt-and-boulder-filled shoulder to the floor of this Muley Creek side canyon. You will probably want to hand down your packs at least once through this stretch.

34.4 ■ Go generally southeast, then east, down this wash for 0.4 miles to intersect Muley Creek.

34.6 ■ Now follow the floor of Muley Creek generally southeast for 0.2 miles to where another wash joins in from the north.

35.3 ■ Leave the wash bottom here and follow this flat bench, contouring generally south, then southwest, along the base of the talus. In 0.7 miles you will cross a small drainage.

36.2 ■ By now you should have picked up the stock trail that traverses the base of the cliffs that separate Swap Mesa from Tarantula

Mesa above. Follow this trail generally southwest, then northwest, for 0.9 miles along the base of the talus to the point shown.

36.4 ■ Leave the stock trail here and head west-southwest for 0.2 miles into the drainage below you.

37.1 ■ Follow this drainage generally south for 0.7 miles to the good springs at the junction of this drainage with another drainage coming in from the northwest.

37.9 ■ Turn up the drainage coming in from the northwest and follow it generally northwest for 0.8 miles to intersect another stock trail.

38.2 ■ Follow this stock trail west out of the drainage for 0.3 miles onto the bench above. Here the stock trail becomes the remnant of an old mining track.

39.0 ■ Take the mining track as it winds along at the base of the talus generally southwest for 0.8 miles. The feature marked 5959T on the map will be directly to the south.

40.4 ■ Stay on the track and follow it another 1.4 miles generally southeast, then south, to a point just north of the head of a south-trending Swap Canyon tributary. The mining track will come and go, but just be sure to stick to the route shown. Stick to the high ground and follow along carefully with your map.

41.1 ■ Now go generally south-southeast, then southwest, and then west for 0.7 miles, again sticking to the high ground, out onto the spit of land separating the south-trending and west-trending tributaries of Swap Canyon.

41.3 ■ Turn to the northwest and find the break in the rim. You may get lucky and find some cairns leading the way. If not, don't worry. The route down is obvious, even if you have to poke around a bit before you find it. Trust your mapmaker. Follow the break northwest, then west-southwest, for 0.2 miles down to the floor of Swap Canyon.

41.6 ■ Go generally south down Swap Canyon for 0.3 miles to the springs. *This will be your last chance to fill up your water bottles.*

46.5 ▪ Now just follow Swap Canyon generally southwest for 4.9 miles to intersect the Notom to Bullfrog Road out in the bottom of the Waterpocket Fold.

46.8 ▪ Follow this dirt road south-southeast for 0.3 miles to its junction with the Burr Trail.

48.9 ▪ Take the Burr Trail to the southwest and follow it generally southwest for 2.1 miles, up the massive switchbacks to the Lower Muley Twist Trailhead. This is the end of this section.

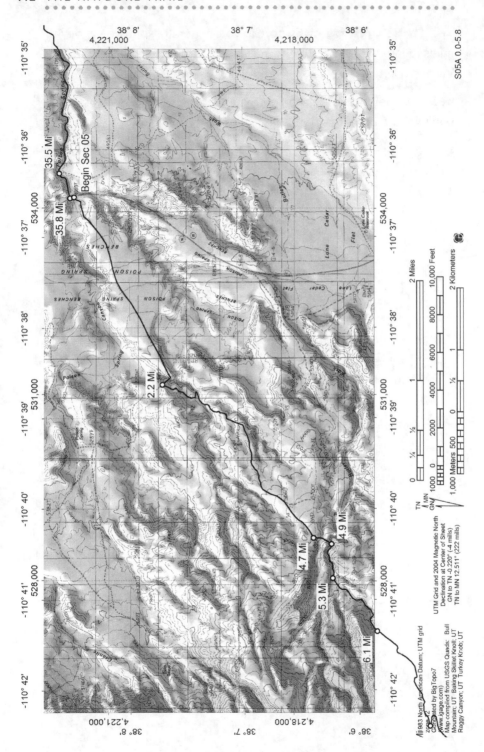

SECTION 5: 0.0–5.8 MILES

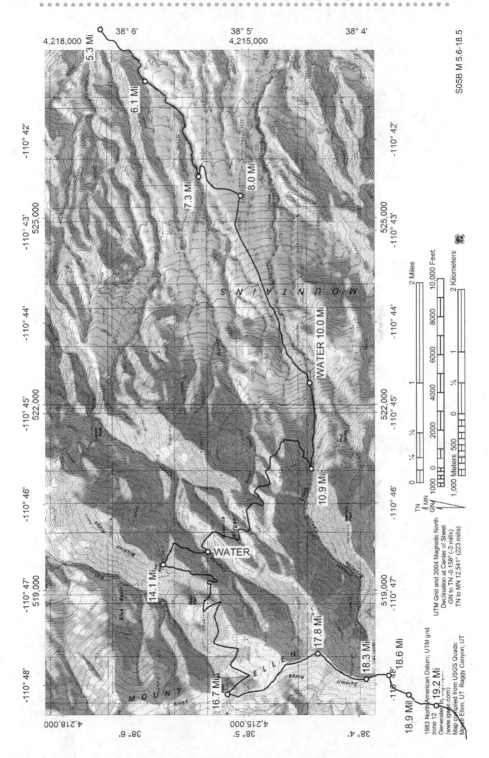

S05B M 5.6-18.5

1983 North American Datum; UTM grid
zone 12
Generated by Topo! ©2006
(www.topo.com)
Map compiled from USGS Quads:
Mount Ellen, UT Ragay Canyon, UT

UTM Grid and 2004 Magnetic North
Declination at Center of Sheet
GN to TN -0.158° (-3 mils)
TN to MN 12.541° (223 mils)

SECTION 5: 5.6–18.5 MILES

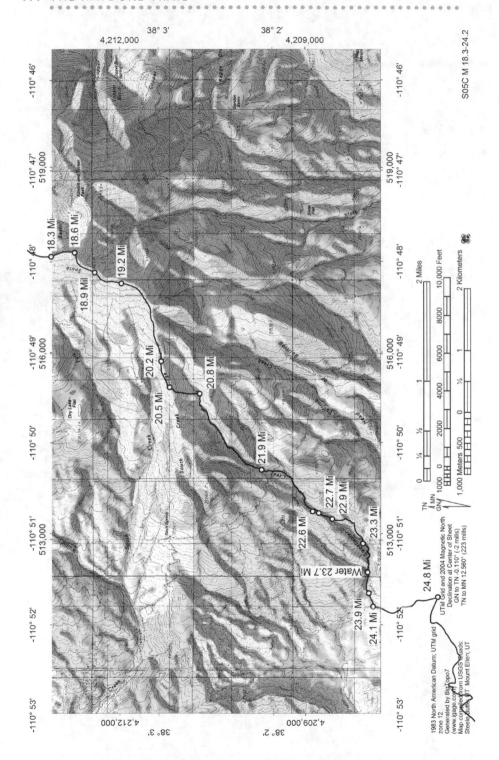

SECTION 5: 18.3–24.2 MILES

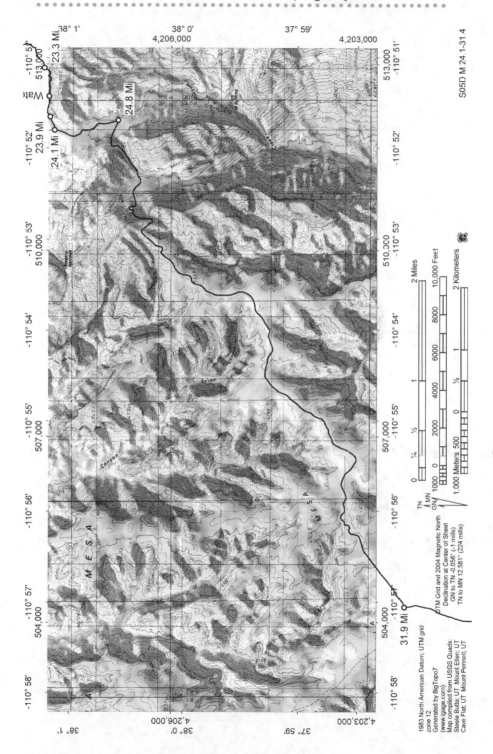

S05D M 24.1-31.4

1983 North American Datum; UTM grid
zone 12
Generated by BigTopo7
(www.igage.com)
Map compiled from USGS Quads:
Steele Butte; UT Mount Ellen; UT
Cave Flat; UT Mount Pennel; UT

UTM Grid and 2004 Magnetic North
Declination at Center of Sheet
GN to TN -0.056° (-1 mills)
TN to MN 12.581° (224 mills)

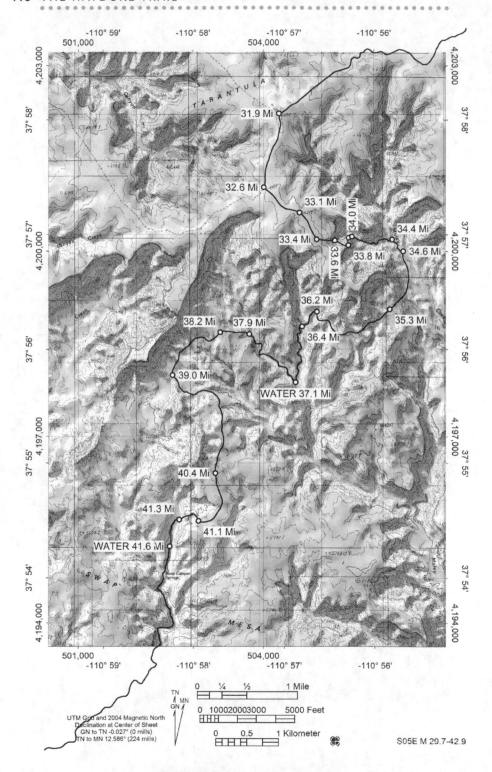

SECTION 5: 29.7–42.9 MILES

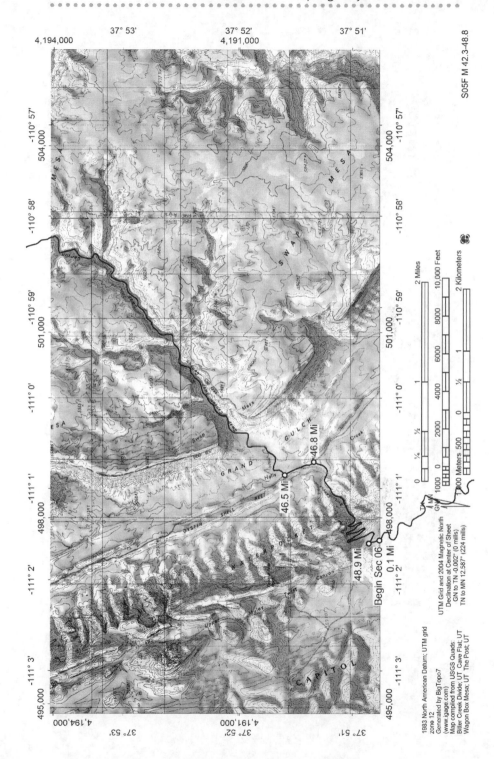

37° 53'
4,194,000
37° 52'
4,191,000
37° 51'

S05F M 42.3-48.8

46.8 Mi

46.5 Mi

48.9 Mi

0.1 Mi

Begin Sec 06

2 Miles

10,000 Feet

8000

6000

4000

2000

1000 Meters 500

2 Kilometers

1

½

0

¼

½

1

½

0

1983 North American Datum; UTM grid
zone 12
Generated by BigTopo7
(www.igage.com)
Map compiled from USGS Quads:
Bitter Creek Divide, UT Cave Flat, UT
Wagon Box Mesa, UT The Post, UT

UTM Grid and 2004 Magnetic North
Declination at Center of Sheet
GN to TN -0.002° (0 mills)
TN to MN 12.587° (224 mills)

37° 53'
4,194,000
37° 52'
4,191,000
37° 51'

SECTION 5: 42.3–48.8 MILES

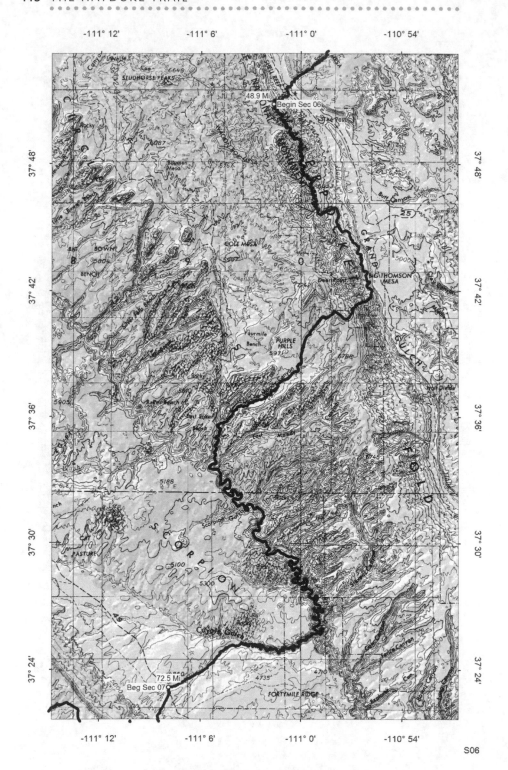

SECTION 6: OVERVIEW

SECTION 6
Burr Trail, Capitol Reef National Park to Hole-in-the-Rock Road

· ·

APPROXIMATE TIME: 11 days

DISTANCE: 72.5 miles

EXERTION: difficult to extreme

NAVIGATION: moderate

WATER: first dry, then wet

DESOLATION FACTOR: out there!

SPECIFIC HAZARDS: poison ivy, rattlesnakes, scorpions, quicksand (all in the Escalante River corridor). Flash floods are also a real danger in this section.

PERMITS: Capitol Reef National Park, Glen Canyon National Recreation Area, and Grand Staircase–Escalante National Monument require permits for overnight backcountry use.

"A tough day, but not without reward. Leaving the last turns of Lower Muley Twist Canyon behind, we started looking for the Muley Tanks to replenish our water supplies. The old double track led us to an obvious archaeological site, so we dropped packs and combed the ground. A BYU group had left a marker of an earlier study, and we also found a large number of broken stone tools and a couple of bits of ceramic remains. Around the next bend was the Muley Tanks, freshly refilled by recent storms; we took water right from a pothole by the plunge pools that form the tanks. Another couple of miles along Halls Creek and we started a 2200' climb up the Red Slide to a pass that leads out of the Waterpocket Fold and into the Circle Cliffs. The old uranium miners' track was hard to follow, but the views were of the most surreal landscape that I think I've ever witnessed: the winding, twisted layers of strata snaking north toward the plateaus, colored fangs of rock dotting out of the canyon floor, through which Halls Creek meanders until it is engulfed in sandstone at the southern reaches of the Fold. Across to the east are the mesas, with their gray and

119

yellow layers. The peaks of the Henry Mountains dominate the skyline above, while bits of the distant La Sals and other landmarks are visible behind them. And that was just on the way up; the view from the pass, to the west, showing virtually the entire Escalante River system, wasn't hard on the eyes either. Even the ground we walked upon was bizarre: at one point it was bright purple!"

OCTOBER 3, 2003, RED SLIDE, CAPITOL REEF NATIONAL PARK

"It was another beautiful night under the stars: warm, a light breeze, clear skies, and the bright moon. A mockingbird spent the night serenading us. I must say, I never had any idea how many birds there are in the desert. We even spent our time while eating dinner last night watching a young bald eagle soaring around the canyon, then being harassed by ravens and some smaller birds.

"Today's walk started immediately with a river crossing. There were lots of those today. The water seems a little higher, and a little faster, the farther we go downriver. I even got shut down on one crossing. The water, though only knee deep, was just moving too swiftly to move in. Moving down canyon has also revealed one other thing: the layer of rock underneath the huge red sandstone cliffs. A very rotten, broken, sandy layer that is invariably hard to get by. In fact, this whole canyon is like that: hard to travel in. Up, down, up (in deep sand), down (loose rocks), cross the river, look for a trail, bushwhack through more brush and trees and scrubs. We both are covered with scrapes, scratches, puncture holes, and blood at the end of the day's journey. Rugged canyon, rugged beauty."

MAY 12, 1998 [DAY 54 OF 94], ESCALANTE RIVER CORRIDOR

This section is rather strenuous, but it is one of the scenic highlights of the Hayduke Trail. You'll begin by descending lower Muley Twist Canyon, a beautiful canyon, which, as the name implies, does a bit of twisting around. It was said that the canyon was rough enough to "twist a mule," and it is also a historic route between Boulder and Halls Crossing (a Colorado River ferry site). Back and forth, you'll wind through this amazing drainage as it works through the layers of the

ESCALANTE RIVER

Waterpocket Fold. Not only is there one of the biggest walls around, but you may get lucky, as we did, and view some desert bighorns; we ran into five rams on the way down. There is a small petroglyph panel under an overhang a couple of miles down the canyon. Leaving the confines of the canyon as it empties into Halls Creek, keep an eye out for the Muley Tanks, likely the only water around.

After getting an adequate water supply, you'll continue down Halls Creek until you see an abandoned miners' road leading up a shoulder of the Red Slide, a huge mudslide that came down from the Circle Cliffs. It will lead you out of the Waterpocket Fold. Following the old route, and then heading off the drainages at the top of the slide will lead you through some incredible terrain as you work toward the pass at the top (it's a 2,200-foot vertical climb). Weather permitting, spending a night at the pass is highly recommended; the scenery is phenomenal. Dropping off the pass through the Circle Cliffs leads you into Middle Moody Canyon, which you will follow to Moody Canyon and then to the Escalante River.

The Escalante River is then followed, forded, waded, etc., for about 30 miles. This is *extremely* difficult travel. It is also beautiful. We found at times that it was much easier to hike in the river than to try and work our way down the thickly vegetated, steeply sloped talus

**35. STEVENS ARCH, AS SEEN FROM
THE ESCALANTE RIVER**

along the banks. Beware of quicksand in the river bottom; keep moving if it is encountered! There are many side canyons to explore along the way. Stevens Arch, high on the ridge to the east at Stevens Canyon, will signal that your Escalante River trek is nearing its end. The next drainage to the west will be Coyote Gulch, which is taken up to Hurricane Wash, which in turn leads to the Hole-in-the-Rock Road, where this section ends.

Coyote Gulch is so amazingly beautiful that you may need to spend a couple of days just taking it all in. There is plenty of water, and even a couple of excellent springs to draw water from. There are a couple of exit points in the canyon, but we strongly recommend following the full length of this wonderful desert oasis. Coyote Gulch was also the first place on our first trip that we saw other backpackers.

JACOB HAMBLIN ARCH, COYOTE GULCH

A beaten trail will show the way into Hurricane Wash, a short but pretty, sandy-bottomed wash that leads to the trailhead and Hole-in-the-Rock Road. We found it somewhat strange that much of this section is in the Glen Canyon National Recreation Area since there is no longer a Glen Canyon. You enter the Grand Staircase–Escalante National Monument *after* you leave the Escalante River drainages.

■ **Resupply/Trailhead at Burr Trail:** See previous description.

■ **Resupply/Trailhead at Hole-in-the-Rock Road:** 5 miles southeast of the town of Escalante on Highway 12 is the well-signed Hole-in-the-Rock Road. Turn on to this sometimes-rough dirt road and follow it southeast for 35.5 miles to the Coyote Gulch trailhead, where Hurricane Wash crosses the road.

AMPHITHEATER IN COYOTE GULCH

■ **Topos:** Wagon Box Mesa, UT; The Post, UT; Deer Point, UT; Horse Pasture Mesa, UT; Scorpion Gulch, UT; King Mesa, UT; Stevens Canyon South, UT; Big Hollow Wash, UT.

ROUTE DESCRIPTION AND MILEAGE

0.1 ■ From the Lower Muley Twist Trailhead follow the trail generally south for 0.1 miles to the wash bottom.

2.2 ■ Now follow the floor of Lower Muley Twist Canyon generally southeast for 2.1 miles. You will come to a place where a tributary comes into the wash through a break in the canyon wall to the west.

10.5 ■ Continue down Lower Muley Twist generally southeast, then south. In 8.3 miles the canyon makes a major swing to the east.

12.1 ■ Follow the canyon another 1.6 miles generally northeast as it spills out into the Waterpocket Fold, then south-southeast down the wash until you intersect an old wagon track.

12.5 ■ Take this wagon track south, then south-southwest, for 0.4 miles to the Muley Tanks. *Take enough water from this typically generous water source to see you through the next 18.8 miles to the* *spring in Middle Moody Canyon. If you find the tanks dry and need to bail out, follow Halls Creek generally north for 6.8 miles to the Notom to Bullfrog Road at the Post.*

13.1 ■ Continue generally southeast on the faint wagon track for 0.6 miles until you reach the bed of Halls Creek.

16.0 ■ Now follow Halls Creek generally southeast, then south, for 2.9 miles until you intersect the Halls Creek Overlook Trail. *Here's another place you can save your hide if you need to. You can take this trail generally northeast, then south-southeast, up through the cliffs for 1.2 miles to the Halls Creek Overlook (an excellent place to leave a water cache). It is another 2.8 miles on a dirt road, generally north, then northeast, out to the Notom to Bullfrog Road.*

17.9 ■ Keep following Halls Creek generally south-southeast for 1.9 miles. You will pass the trail to the Brimhall Double Arch, a worthwhile side trip. Leave the creek bed, as shown, at the base of the Red Slide and intersect the relic mining track.

19.5 ■ Follow this track generally southwest for 1.6 miles as it switches back and forth up the Red Slide. Stop at the point where the track descends into a steep draw.

20.4 ■ Leave the mining track here and pick your way south up to the base of the cliffs above. Find the path of least resistance and work your way around to the west onto a broad bench. It is 0.9 miles from where you left the track.

21.1 ■ Now travel generally northwest across this bench for 0.7 miles up to the pass.

21.8 ■ From the pass, go south-southwest, then southwest, then northwest, for 0.7 miles as you work your way down the steep talus to the floor of the drainage below. You will be passing from Capitol Reef National Park into the Glen Canyon National Recreation Area.

22.9 ■ Follow this drainage generally southwest for 1.1 miles to its junction with Middle Moody Canyon.

26.7 ■ Now follow Middle Moody Canyon generally southwest for 3.8 miles. On the south wall of the canyon there is a good shelter cave. On the north wall there is a rock fall leading up to the mouth of a small hanging canyon. On the western rim of this little side canyon is an unmarked dirt road. This road leads around to the dirt road in Moody Creek, and it can serve a dual purpose: it is a reasonable bailout point as well as a convenient place to cache food and water along the route.

31.3 ■ Continue generally southwest down Middle Moody Canyon another 4.6 miles. You should find good water in the bottom of the canyon here. *If you can, take enough to get you through another day and a half. The water in Middle Moody will be clear, while the water in the Escalante will be thin mud. You will find some beautiful springs as you work your way down the river and you should try to use them and not have to filter the river water.*

31.7 ■ The canyon turns to the west here. Follow it another 0.4 miles to the junction with Moody Creek.

34.2 ■ Now go generally south down Moody Creek for 2.5 miles to the Escalante River.

59.7 ■ Follow the Escalante River gorge downstream for 25.5 miles to the mouth of Coyote Gulch. You will generally be going southeast, but you will find yourself going in all directions as the canyon wiggles along. *Be prepared to cross the river a million times. Well, maybe just a thousand. Sometimes you will find it easier to walk right in the river itself, depending on its flow.* **But remember, the Escalante drains a large area, is prone to flooding, and moves a lot of snowmelt! High water would make foot travel in the gorge impossible, so endeavor to be there either before or after spring run-off and not during the monsoon season.**

67.2 ■ Leave the river here and go up Coyote Gulch, generally southwest, then west, for 7.5 miles to the mouth of Hurricane Wash. Coyote Gulch is an amazing canyon full of beautifully streaked amphitheaters, a clear running stream, and lush growth reminiscent of an eastern broadleaf forest, complete with plenty of poison ivy. And the walking is easy on a well-worn trail! Along the way you will pass Cliff Arch high on a wall, go right through Coyote Natural Bridge, and go around the imposing Jacob Hamblin Arch. **Coyote Gulch, like all desert canyons, is prone to flash flooding!** *If this seems redundant, listen to this. An acquaintance of mine (on his first backpacking trip in the desert) recently got flooded out of this canyon. In the middle of a starry night, with no warning at all, a flood came screaming down the canyon and he barely got out of his tent before the torrent carried it away with all his newly purchased gear. After spending the night in a tree, he had to walk back out, naked and with only one shoe. The shoe and his life were all he had time to save.*

72.5 ▩ The Coyote Gulch/Hurricane Wash junction is a critical intersection that some people miss. *Pay special attention to where you are. Believe it or not, this same acquaintance, on his nude retreat out of the canyon, missed the intersection and kept going up Coyote Gulch. Although the gulch does eventually reach the Hole-in-the-Rock Road, it adds about five additional miles. Every mile counts when you only have one shoe.* Go southwest up Hurricane Wash for 5.3 miles to the Hole-in-the-Rock Road. *If necessary, water can be found a short distance northwest up the Hole-in-the-Rock Road at Willow Tank.* This is the end of this section.

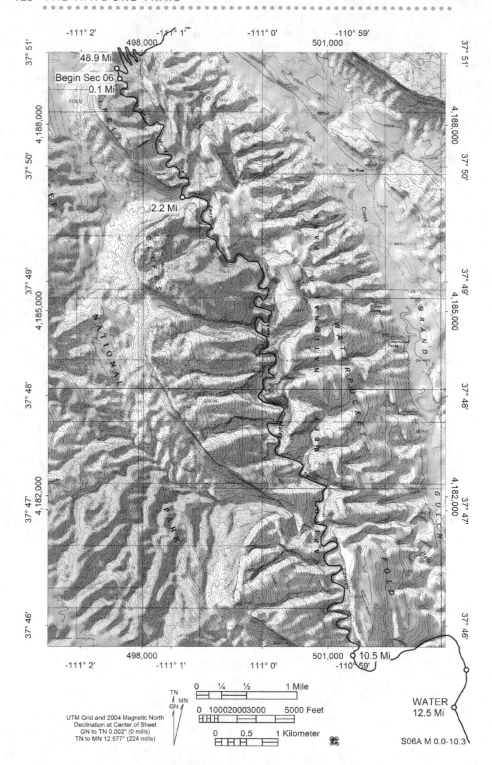

SECTION 6: 0.0–10.3 MILES

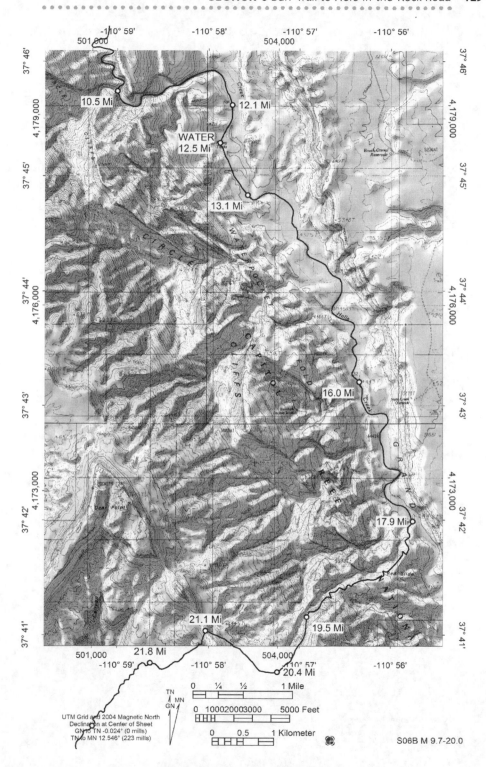

SECTION 6: 9.7–20.0 MILES

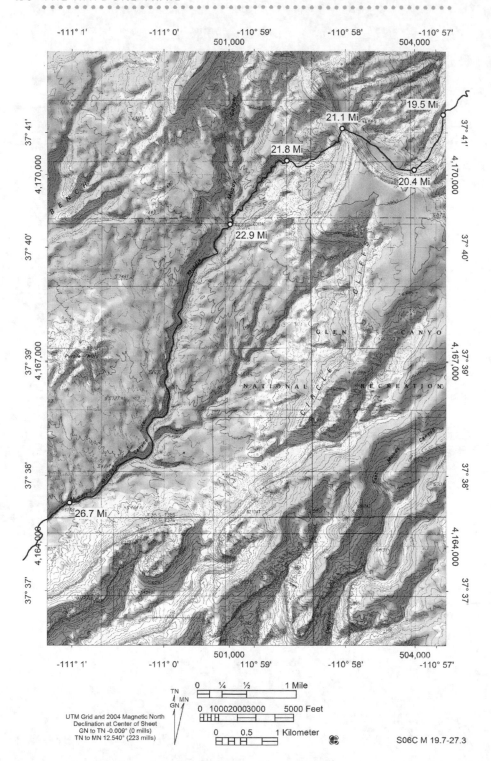

19.5 Mi
21.1 Mi
21.8 Mi
20.4 Mi
22.9 Mi
26.7 Mi

TN
MN
GN

UTM Grid and 2004 Magnetic North
Declination at Center of Sheet
GN to TN -0.009° (0 mills)
TN to MN 12.540° (223 mills)

0   ¼   ½   1 Mile

0 1000 2000 3000   5000 Feet

0   0.5   1 Kilometer

S06C M 19.7-27.3

SECTION 6: 19.7–27.3 MILES

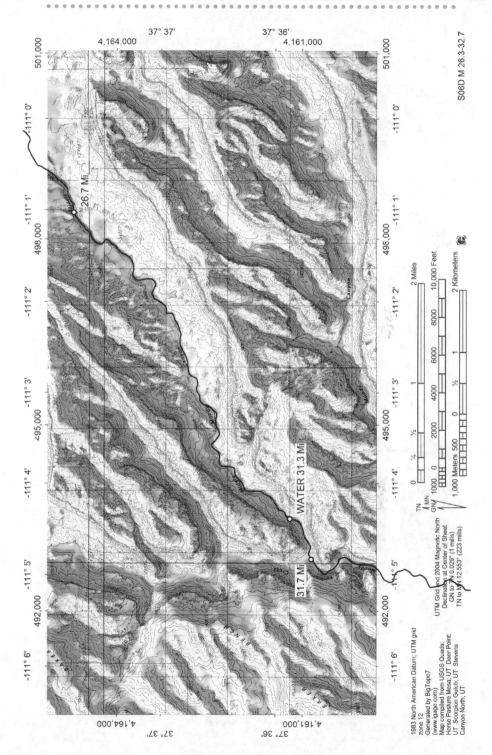

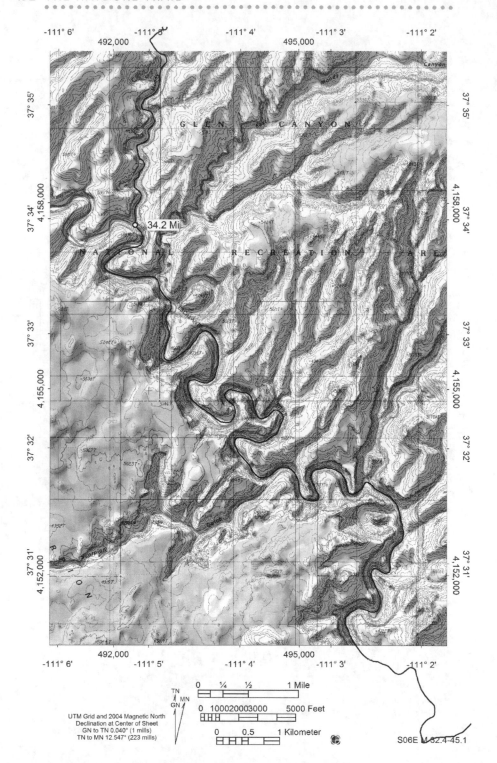

SECTION 6: 32.4–45.1 MILES

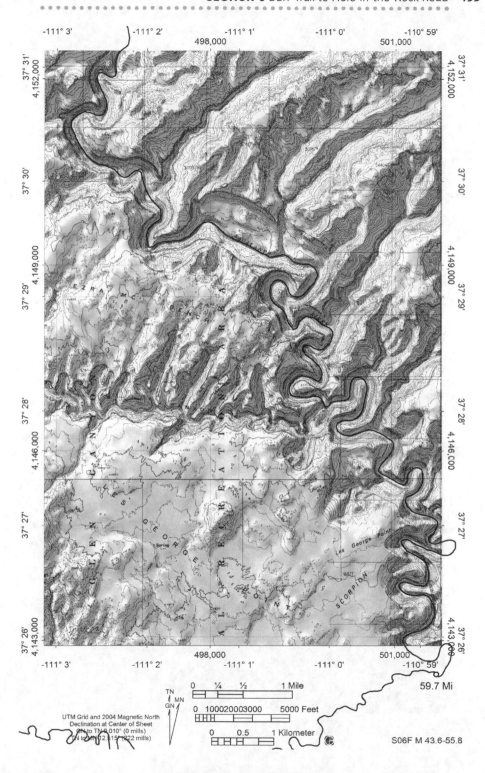

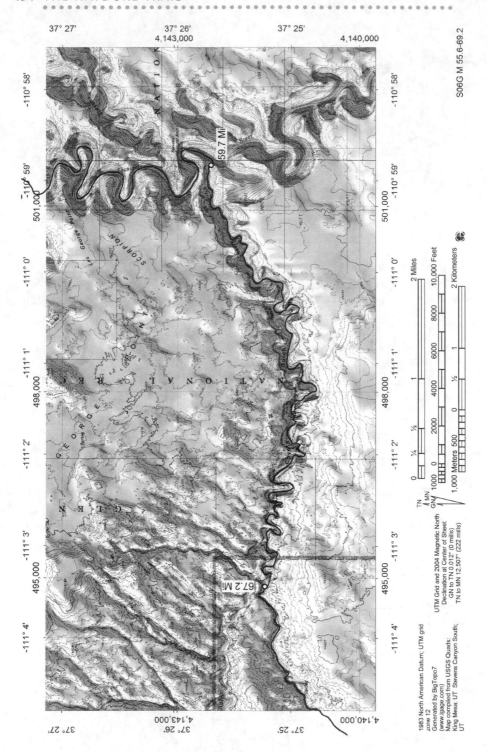

1983 North American Datum; UTM grid
zone 12
Generated by BigTopo7
(www.igage.com)
Map compiled from USGS Quads:
King Mesa; UT Stevens Canyon South;
UT

SECTION 6: 55.6–69.2 MILES

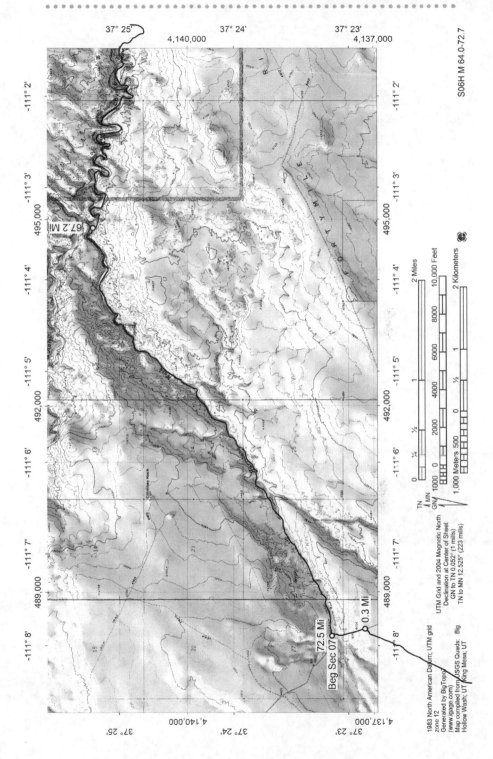

37° 25'   37° 24'   37° 23'   4,140,000   4,137,000

S06H M 64.0-72.7

67.2 Mi

72.5 Mi   0.3 Mi

Beg Sec 07

1983 North American Datum; UTM grid
zone 12
Generated by Big Topo
(www.igage.com)
Map compiled from USGS Quads: Big
Hollow Wash; UT King Mesa; UT

2 Miles

10,000 Feet

2 Kilometers

TN   MN   GN

UTM Grid and 2004 Magnetic North
Declination at Center of Sheet
GN to TN 0.052° (1 mills)
TN to MN 12.525° (223 mills)

SECTION 6: 64.0–72.7 MILES

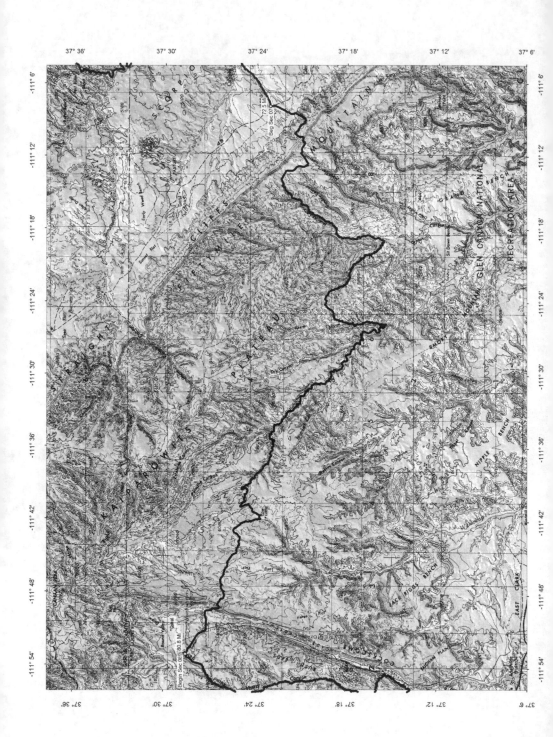

SECTION 7: OVERVIEW

■ SECTION 7
Hole-in-the-Rock Road to Round Valley Draw

. . . .

APPROXIMATE TIME: 12 days

DISTANCE: 80.8 miles

EXERTION: difficult

NAVIGATION: moderate

WATER: dry

DESOLATION FACTOR: out there!

SPECIFIC HAZARDS: running out of water

PERMITS: Grand Staircase–Escalante National Monument requires permits for overnight backcountry use.

"At the head of Monday Canyon we found a bunch of pottery shards and pieces of arrowheads. We walked down into the drainage through steep, scrub-covered slopes. The pines and oaks made travel pretty rough at times, but, as usual, we made it through. The next couple miles could be tough, too: the canyon drops and is at its narrowest. From where we are camped, in the middle of two small forks, the canyon looks pretty daunting. Steep, but not vertical, white walls, covered with pines mostly, along with some oak and other scratchy shrubs. And narrow. But what a frame for the sunset, with the brilliant magenta and pink clouds. Lower, the canyon opens up a bit, which usually offers better options for skirting tricky spots. I hope we don't need more options than we have tomorrow!

"Behind us, up on the hillside above the wash, is a series of ancient dwellings. Some of the walls still stand, but barely. One has a wooden roof, collapsed, but mostly intact. One has a metate in front; I found a mano lower down. The ruin with the roof had three things scattered throughout its perimeter: pottery sherds, maize husks, and (yikes!) cougar scat. I also found a piece of squash husk inside. Lower down on the slope we found some red pottery, painted, signifying a change in subcultures.

"It's now after dark, and we're finding lots of insects around here. Ants. Ants with wings. Scorpions. Big Ants. Scorpions. Even a Jerusalem Beetle. Nasty!"

MAY 19, 1998 [DAY 61 OF 94], KAIPAROWITS PLATEAU

"The canyon [Last Chance] changed a lot as we came up it. First there was almost no vegetation anywhere, just barren, sunbaked ground and rocks. Then there was some sage and cactus (which are currently in full bloom), and then we started seeing pinyons, junipers, and cottonwoods. It is a beautiful canyon. All the while, the creek was flowing, filled with tadpoles. We even saw coyote tracks again.

"Mitch just called me over to the other side of the creek, up on a rocky bench layer. There is all sorts of evidence of previous peoples. Cowboys and Indians. It's kind of strange to see their stuff mixed up together, considering the completely different approach to the land that they took. Either way, we found their refuse: horseshoes, cans, broken bottles of many colors, a button, part of a trap. Then chert flakes, broken arrowheads, pieces of broken pottery."

MAY 23, 1998 [DAY 65 OF 94], LAST CHANCE CREEK, GRAND STAIRCASE–ESCALANTE NATIONAL MONUMENT

This is a long and desolate section, traversing the heart of one of the largest remaining roadless areas in the lower forty-eight states. Water is very limited, so plan on carrying with you large amounts from each source that you come to.

Leaving from the Hurricane Wash parking lot on Hole-in-the-Rock Road, you immediately start climbing up the face of Fiftymile Mountain, or the Kaiparowits Plateau, via the Middle Pack Trail, which leads you all the way to the rim. The view from the top (elevation 7300 feet) is sensational. You follow the rim through beautiful aspen groves, an area where we saw a huge raven rookery, to Monday Canyon, which is followed with some difficulty (pour-offs and rock falls provide some pretty tough obstacles) through to Rogers Canyon. There are some archaeological sites in the area, and we also found a bobcat skull in

LOOKING DOWN MONDAY CANYON, KAIPAROWITS PLATEAU

NAVAJO CANYON

one of the drainages. Follow Rogers Canyon down to Navajo Canyon, which is followed up to Reese Canyon. These canyons are all sparsely vegetated; one gets the feeling of being on another planet out there. Reese Canyon is followed to Last Chance Creek, which should have available water (it's actually a very pretty drainage). Last Chance is climbed to Paradise Canyon, which is followed to a dirt road that will

LAST CHANCE CREEK

take you across Dog Flat, Fourmile Creek, Tommy Smith Creek, and Wahweap Creek and on to the Cockscomb and Grosvenor Arch. From Grosvenor Arch, you simply follow the Cottonwood Canyon Road to Round Valley and the end of this section.

■ **Resupply/Trailhead at Hole-in-the-Rock Road:** See previous description.

■ **Resupply/Trailhead at Round Valley Draw:** From Highway 12 in Cannonville, Utah, turn south onto the Cottonwood Canyon Road. There is a sign at this turn-off that directs you to Kodachrome Basin State Park. Follow this road for 7.6 miles to the turn-off for the state park. Continue east-southeast on the Cottonwood Canyon Road another 7.2 miles to Round Valley Draw.

■ **Topos:** Big Hollow Wash, UT; Blackburn Canyon, UT; East of the Navajo, UT; Needle Eye Point, UT; Ship Mountain Point, UT; Petes Cove, UT; Horse Mountain, UT; Butler Valley, UT; Slickrock Bench, UT.

ROUTE DESCRIPTION AND MILEAGE

0.3 ■ Head south-southeast down the Hole-in-the-Rock Road for 0.3 miles to a junction.

GROSVENOR ARCH

3.5 ▪ Take the dirt road to the southwest and follow it generally south-southwest across the flat and up Willow Tank Slide. After 3.2 miles you will come to the junction with a pack trail on the Fiftymile Bench.

5.2 ▪ Get on the pack trail and follow it generally west, then northwest, across the Fiftymile Bench for 1.7 miles to its junction with the Middle Pack Trail.

6.6 ▪ Take the Middle Pack Trail generally south-southwest, then west-southwest, for 1.4 miles, and 1,300 feet up, to the top of the Straight Cliffs and the junction with another pack trail.

7.5 ▪ Take the new pack trail northwest, then west, for 0.9 miles to the spring at the head of Llewellyn Canyon. *Although we found that this spring had water, it was so fouled by cattle that we took our chances and passed it up.*

8.7 ■ Here the trail turns to the southwest. Follow it for 1.2 miles to Mudholes Spring. There is a line shack here and the spring has been fenced to keep cattle out. *Please be respectful of the hard work that must have gone into building this little cabin and stay out of it. Obviously somebody depends on this shelter and its provisions, and disturbing it could seriously jeopardize their very existence in this remote place. Leave it alone!*

You should take as much water here as you can. *This is the last decent water for about 30 miles until you get to Last Chance Creek. Pocket Hollow Spring, just up the trail, is one of the worst-looking water sources either of us had ever seen. That was until we saw the water down in Rogers Canyon! The cows had rendered both sources utterly useless.*

9.6 ■ The trail turns again here. Follow it for 0.9 miles, generally north-northwest, to Pocket Hollow Spring.

10.5 ■ Continue northwest, then north, on the trail for another 0.9 miles.

11.0 ■ Leave the trail here and follow your compass west-northwest for 0.5 miles. You will cross the upper reaches of Gates Draw and find yourself on the rim of Monday Canyon at the head of one of its small side canyons.

11.3 ■ Go west-northwest down this side canyon for 0.3 miles to the floor of Monday Canyon.

18.3 ■ Follow the bed of Monday Canyon, generally southwest, for 7 miles to its junction with Rogers Canyon. The going is pretty easy at first, but about halfway down the canyon you will start to encounter a series of pour-offs. All of them can easily be skirted. In this section of pour-offs we found a small tank of good rainwater, but don't count on it always being there. If you do find water in it, take some. In fact, whenever you find good water out here, take it. If your bottles are already full, at least sit down and drink up.

21.3 ■ Now go generally south for 3 miles down Rogers Canyon to the junction with Sunday Canyon. This confluence is the beginning of Croton Canyon.

22.7 ■ Go south-southwest down Croton Canyon for 1.2 miles to the mouth of Navajo Canyon. You can leave the streambed in Croton Canyon when you can see the opening of Navajo Canyon on the right. Contour around 0.2 miles into Navajo Canyon and drop down into its dry bed. *If you are desperate for water here, continue south down Croton Canyon another 2.5 miles to a dirt road. Take this dirt road east for 3.0 miles across Croton Bench to a line shack in Little Valley. There are springs above and below the line shack.*

30.1 ■ Go up Navajo Canyon generally northwest for 7.4 miles to the junction with Surprise Valley. You will pass a small pour-off and dozens of side canyons on the way. **Make sure you carefully follow along on your map as you find your way up Navajo Canyon.** *Surprise Valley looks just like any other side canyon and you need to be able to recognize it, with no uncertainty, when you come to it.*

30.4 ■ Go west into Surprise Valley and follow it generally northwest for 0.3 miles to where a double track comes in from the northwest.

31.0 ■ Get on this dirt road and follow it generally northwest, then southwest, for 0.6 miles up and out of Surprise Valley to the dirt road that runs on the divide between Navajo Canyon and Reese Canyon.

31.3 ■ Go northwest for 0.3 miles on the dirt road to where you can see down the head of a drainage into Reese Canyon to the southwest.

32.9 ■ Leave the dirt road and follow this drainage generally southwest for 1.6 miles until you intersect a double track coming in from the north.

34.7 ■ Follow the dirt road the remaining 1.8 miles south-southwest down the drainage to its junction with Reese Canyon.

37.6 ■ Go generally south for 2.9 miles down the floor of Reese Canyon to the junction with Last Chance Creek. *You should find water here. Judging by the amount of aquatic life we found in and around* *the creek, we believe it to be perennial. If you don't find water here at the confluence, concentrate your search up Last Chance Creek. The higher you go up the canyon, the more likely you will be to find water.*

49.8 ■ Head into Last Chance Creek and go generally northwest up the canyon for 12.2 miles until you reach a dirt road crossing the drainage.

54.0 ■ Continue generally northwest up Last Chance Creek, sometimes on the double track you'll find down there, for an additional 4.2 miles to the junction with Paradise Canyon. *The stream may become intermittent as you get closer to Paradise Canyon. We found come-and-go running water most of the way up Paradise Canyon, but we wouldn't count on it; this is a time to camel some water. Whenever we do find water in an especially dry area of desert, we are in the habit of spending a little time and drinking as much as we dare. Much like a camel. We won't leave until we can't drink any more. The first step to staying hydrated in a place like this is to start off hydrated. After you drink your fill, take enough water from Last Chance Creek, or the farthest up-canyon water you deem wise, to get you to the end of this section. The funny thing about an intermittent stream is that it is hard to decide when you've seen it for the last time. As you watch it disappear into the sand again, you have to decide whether to load up the pack with water weight there or take your chances and hope the water will reappear in a half mile or so.*

59.6 ■ Go generally west, then northwest, up Paradise Canyon for 5.6 miles to a junction. *There are a lot of side canyons in this stretch and it is easy to lose track of them as you travel up the canyon. Pay close attention to the map and count off the side canyons as you pass them.*

61.4 ■ Go 1.8 miles, generally northwest, up this side canyon until you reach a dirt road that comes down to the wash from the southwest. Although you will be leaving Paradise Canyon, you will still be heading northwest.

63.8 ■ Get on this dirt road and follow it, first generally south, then west-northwest, for 2.4 miles out of the drainage and to its junction with another dirt road on a divide.

65.7 ▨ Take this dirt road for 1.9 miles, south-southeast along the divide and then southwest down the west side of the bench to another junction.

70.5 ▨ Follow the dirt road on the right and take it 4.8 miles to another junction near Tommy Water. The road goes generally west-southwest, then north-northwest, to Dog Flat. From there it turns southwest and finally west, crossing Tommy Smith Creek just before the junction. *There may be water in Tommy Smith Creek or at Tommy Water, but it is so alkaline that you would only want to drink it in an emergency.*

77.2 ▨ Stay on the dirt road and follow it generally northwest for 6.7 miles across Long Flat and Wahweap Creek, then through the Gut in the Cockscomb to Grosvenor Arch. *There is water at Headquarters Spring, 3.3 miles north up Wahweap Creek, if you really need it.*

78.2 ▨ Continue west on the dirt road for another mile to the junction with the Cottonwood Canyon Road in Butler Valley. *You should be able to find water 1.0 mile south on the Cottonwood Canyon Road at the marked well and corral.*

80.8 ▨ Now follow the Cottonwood Canyon Road generally north-west for 2.6 miles as it leads you up Butler Valley and down to a road junction in Round Valley Draw. This is the end of this section.

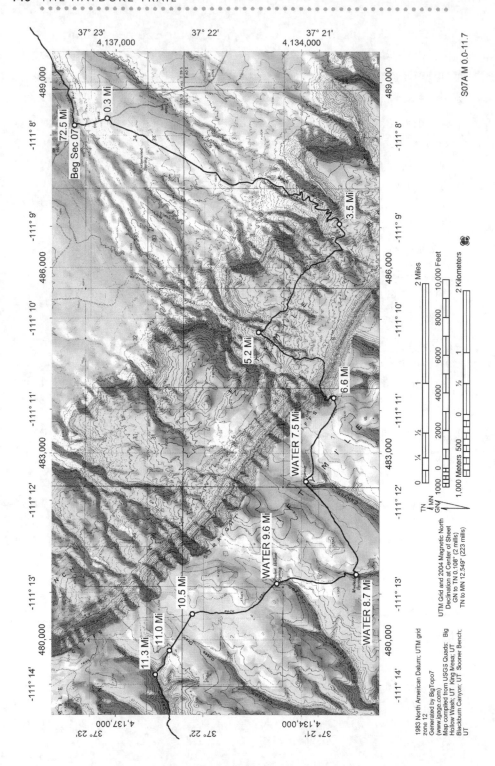

Beg Sec 07
72.5 Mi
0.3 Mi
3.5 Mi
5.2 Mi
6.6 Mi
WATER 7.5 Mi
WATER 9.6 Mi
10.5 Mi
11.0 Mi
11.3 Mi
WATER 8.7 Mi

S07A M 0.0-11.7

37° 23'   37° 22'   37° 21'
4,137,000   4,134,000

-111° 8'
-111° 9'
-111° 10'
-111° 11'
-111° 12'
-111° 13'
-111° 14'

489,000
486,000
483,000
480,000

2 Miles
2000   4000   6000   8000   10,000 Feet
0
1000
1,000 Meters 500   0   1   2 Kilometers

TN
MN
GN
UTM Grid and 2004 Magnetic North
Declination at Center of Sheet
GN to TN 0.108° (2 mills)
TN to MN 12.549° (223 mills)

1983 North American Datum; UTM grid
zone 12
Generated by BigTopo7
(www.igage.com)
Map compiled from USGS Quads: Big
Hollow Wash; UT King Mesa; UT
Blackburn Canyon; UT Sooner Bench;
UT

SECTION 7: 0.0–11.7 MILES

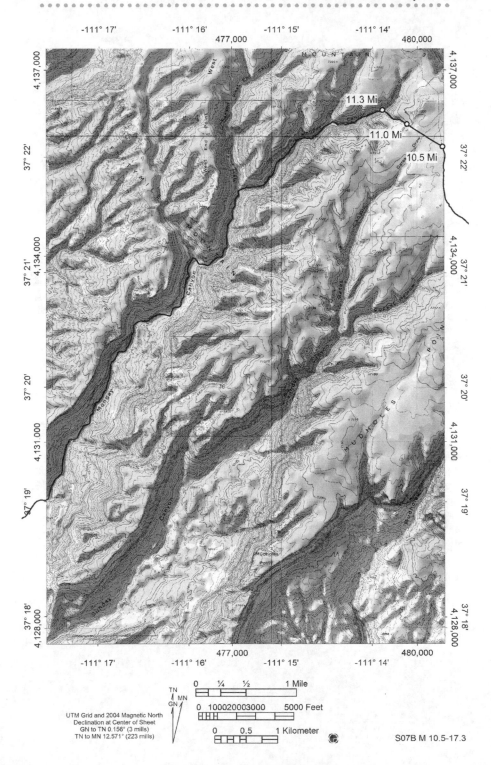

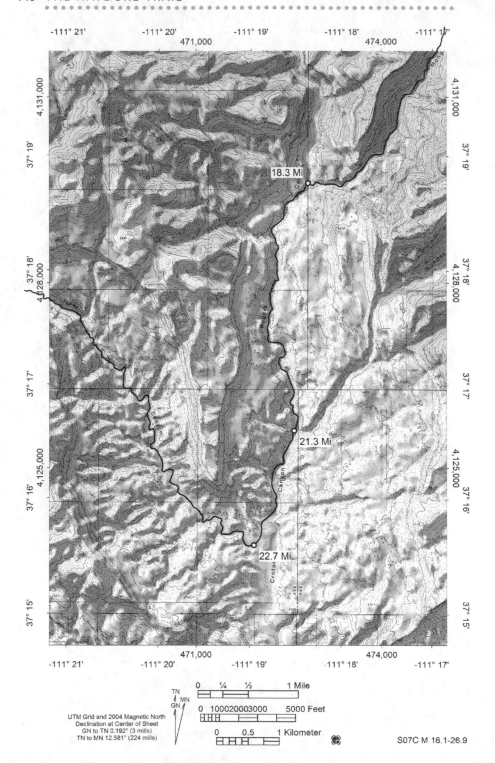

SECTION 7: 16.1–26.9 MILES

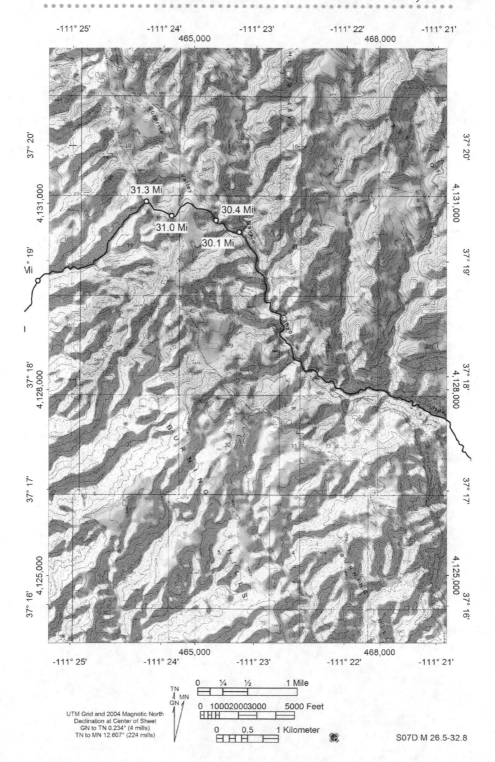

S07D M 26.5-32.8

SECTION 7: 26.5–32.8 MILES

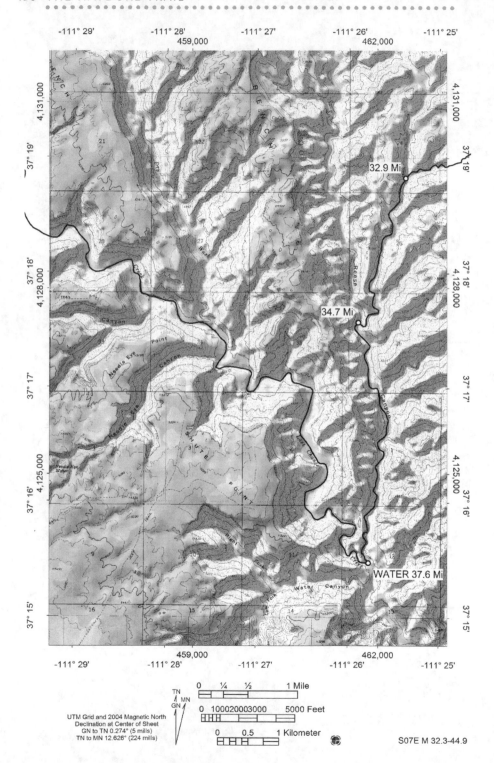

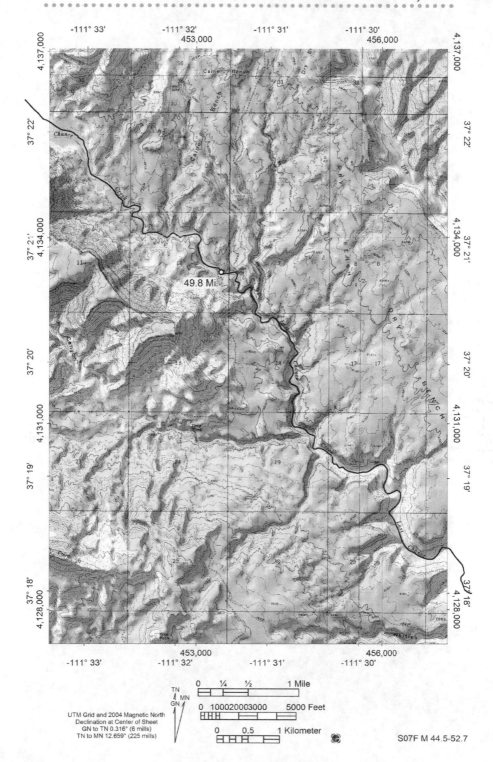

UTM Grid and 2004 Magnetic North
Declination at Center of Sheet
GN to TN 0.316° (6 mills)
TN to MN 12.659° (225 mills)

S07F M 44.5–52.7

SECTION 7: 44.5–52.7 MILES

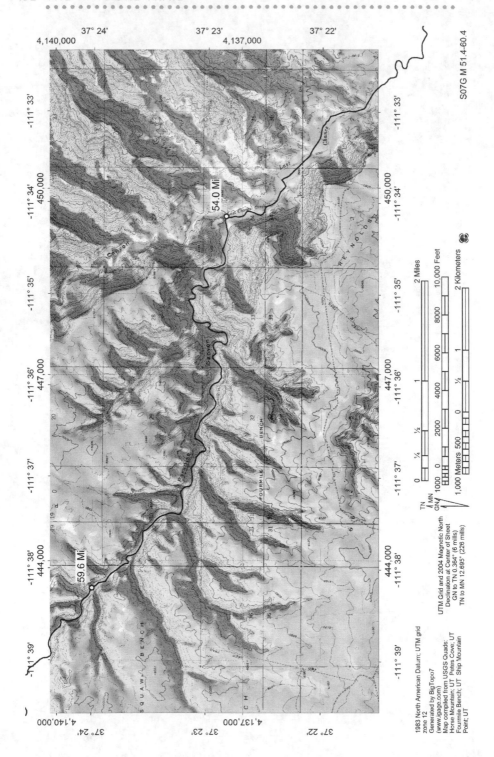

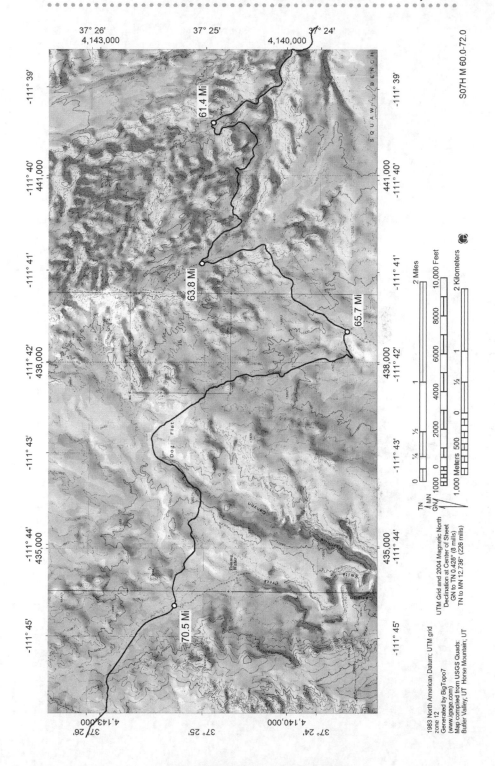

S07H M 60.0–72.0

1983 North American Datum; UTM grid
zone 12
Generated by BigTopo7
(www.sgege.com)
Map compiled from USGS Quads:
Butler Valley, UT Horse Mountain; UT

UTM Grid and 2004 Magnetic North
Declination at Center of Sheet
GN to TN 0.428° (8 mills)
TN to MN 12.736° (226 mills)

SECTION 7: 60.0–72.0 MILES

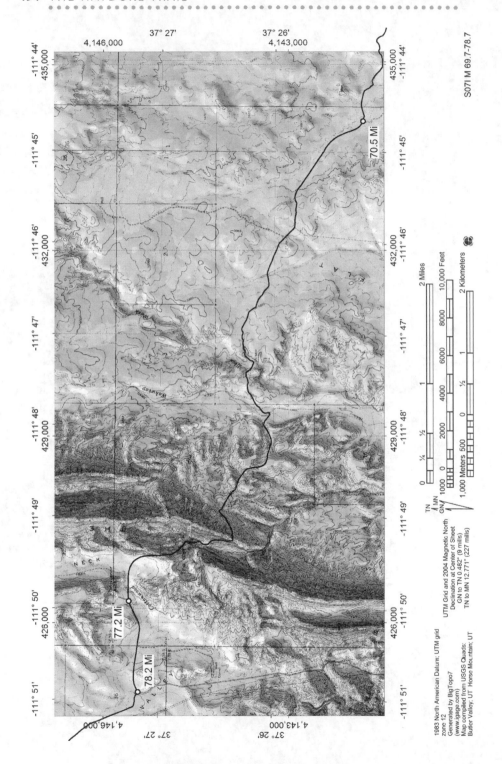

70.5 Mi

77.2 Mi

78.2 Mi

2 Miles

10,000 Feet

2 Kilometers

1,000 Meters 500

1983 North American Datum: UTM grid
zone 12
Generated by BigTopo7
(www.sgage.com)
Map compiled from USGS Quads:
Butler Valley, UT: Horse Mountain, UT

UTM Grid and 2004 Magnetic North
Declination at Center of Sheet
GN to TN 0.482° (9 mills)
TN to MN 12.771° (227 mills)

S07I M 69.7-78.7

SECTION 7: 69.7–78.7 MILES

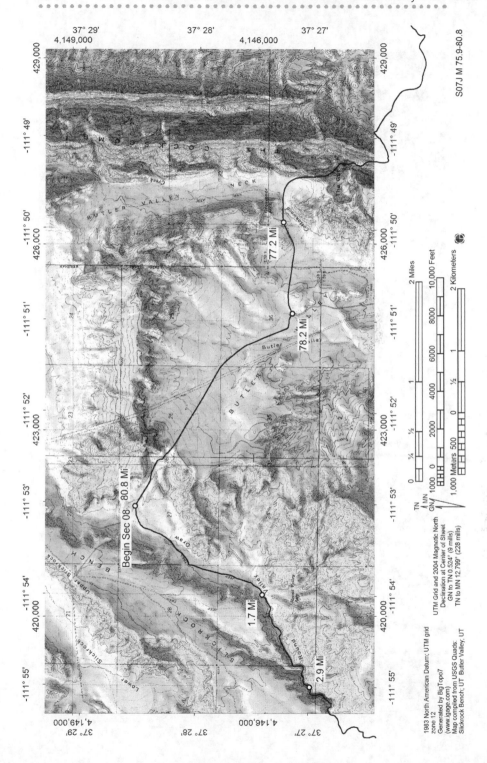

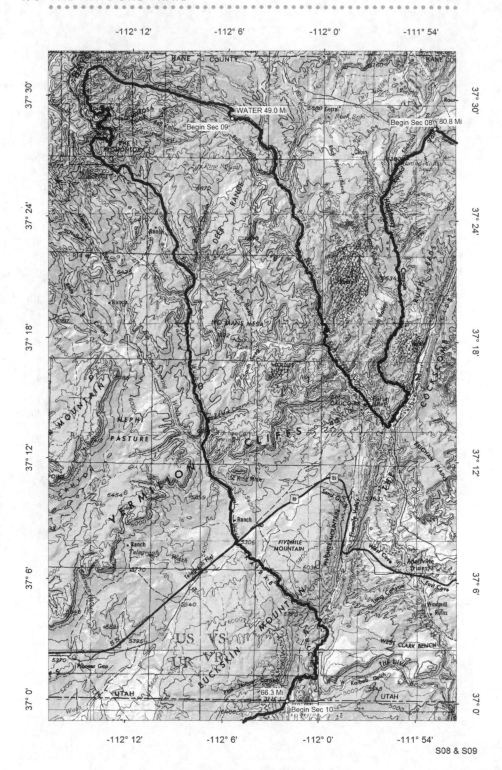

SECTION 8: OVERVIEW

■ SECTION 8
Round Valley Draw to Willis Creek

. . . .

APPROXIMATE TIME: 7 days

DISTANCE: 49.0 miles

EXERTION: moderate

NAVIGATION: easy

WATER: damp

DESOLATION FACTOR: backcountry

SPECIFIC HAZARDS: flash flood danger in Round Valley Draw, Hackberry Canyon, Paria River, Sheep Creek, and Willis Creek.

PERMITS: permits are required for overnight backcountry use in the Grand Staircase–Escalante National Monument.

"The day started ok, but quickly turned windy. Really windy. We were hiking along the Cottonwood Canyon Road between the Paria and Hackberry and at one point on the way the wind literally almost took me off my feet. The rest of the day was a giant wind and dust storm—probably the strongest winds we have walked through. In fact, we found all kinds of "damage" from the wind: downed trees and limbs, even a couple of rock falls. It was pretty nuts!

"Hackberry Canyon is another of those places on our route that is simply gorgeous. Big walls, trees, and water in most of the lower wash. Truly magnificent! There are also more wildflowers here than at any other place that we've seen on this trek.

"We hiked up a side canyon called Stone Donkey; very pretty, with a pour-off that has bored a hole right through the rock, forming a natural bridge. Always something new to contemplate, another formation that you have to see to believe."

MAY 11, 2000 [DAY 61 OF 104], NEAR HACKBERRY CANYON

". . . a peregrine falcon soared just over our heads while we ate our breakfast. This camp, at mile 400, is one of the good ones; the Paria joins the list of the best we've seen.

"The weather was looking decent, we needed a dry day, as Willis Creek has narrows which we intended to see. We got going fairly early and followed the Paria, with its clear-water feeds practically lining the river. Soon we came to Sheep Creek, which we headed up. Sheep Creek rocks! It could practically be mistaken for Zion: huge white walls, but a dry wash bottom. We found petroglyphs on three different panels. I was constantly stopping to take photos. By the time we got to Willis we were awestruck. It got better, too!

"Willis has about half a dozen sections with narrows, with a clear running creek flowing through the wash. After exiting one section, we found two large but young ravens on the wall. Neither seemed to be able to fly yet; they were so disturbed by our presence that one actually vomited."

MAY 31, 1998 [DAY 73 OF 94], WILLIS CREEK,
GRAND STAIRCASE–ESCALANTE NATIONAL MONUMENT

Meandering through a number of well-known drainages, this is another of the route's drop-dead gorgeous sections. It also has the only "slot" canyons of the Hayduke Trail. **Never enter a slot canyon when it is storming or storms are imminent.** Plan ahead and have either food enough to sit out the storm or maps to show you alternative routes.

You'll start this section by immediately dropping into one of the route's slot canyons, Round Valley Draw, which has tight-enough places that your packs will have to be dragged behind you to fit through. (To detour around Round Valley Draw head farther west on the road from Grosvenor Arch toward Kodachrome Basin, up the hill from Round Valley and to the old cattle gate. There you will find a faint double track that will take you south to a side drainage that accesses Round Valley Draw below the narrows.) Round Valley Draw empties into Hackberry Canyon, another beautiful deep canyon that leads down to the Paria River. Once you've come to the Paria River, you'll follow up the river drainage, past the old Paria Townsite movie set (many an old western was filmed there), until you reach Sheep Creek, which is followed up a short distance, past Bull Valley Gorge (a classic

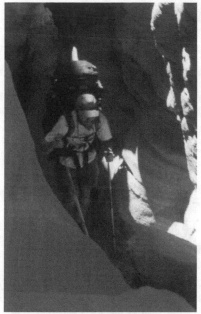

ROUND VALLEY DRAW

HACKBERRY CANYON

WILLIS CREEK NARROWS

Colorado Plateau "slot" that you can explore if you have time) to Willis Creek. All along the way you'll pass some pretty wild-looking geology; the rocks exhibit an amazing variety of colors as you hike from the Cockscomb formation through the Gap and up into the White Cliffs of the Grand Staircase. Just before entering Willis Creek, keep an eye out for a fairly large petroglyph panel above to the left. Willis Creek will lead through a couple of "narrows" sections before popping out by a dirt road, the Skutumpah Road, which is the end of this section.

■ **Resupply/Trailhead at Round Valley Draw:** See previous description.

■ **Resupply/Trailhead at Willis Creek:** From Highway 12 in Cannonville, Utah, turn south onto the Cottonwood Canyon Road. Follow this road for 3 miles until you come to the junction with the Skutumpah Road. Turn right onto this road and follow it generally south for 6 miles to the crossing of Willis Creek. The Skutumpah Road is a well-groomed dirt road that most vehicles will be able to handle, although it could become impassable after heavy rains.

■ **Topos:** Slickrock Bench, UT; Calico Peak, UT; Fivemile Valley, UT; Deer Range Point, UT; Bull Valley Gorge, UT.

ROUTE DESCRIPTION AND MILEAGE

1.7 ■ From the Cottonwood Canyon Road, take the jeep trail generally southwest down Round Valley Draw for 1.7 miles to a road junction.

2.9 ■ Leave the dirt road here and continue generally west-southwest down Round Valley Draw. In 1.2 miles you will enter the narrows via a short down-climb. You will need to lower your packs down here.

4.4 ■ Go generally southwest down Round Valley Draw for another 1.5 miles. You will exit the narrows and enter Hackberry Canyon.

6.0 ■ Now go down Hackberry Canyon, generally south-southwest, for 1.6 miles to the confluence with Death Valley Draw.

11.2 ■ Continue generally south-southeast down Hackberry Canyon for another 5.2 miles to a good spring. *You should have found plenty of water in the bottom of the canyon before you reach this spring.*

13.1 ■ Follow the canyon generally south for 1.9 miles to its confluence with a side canyon entering from the northwest. *A short distance up this canyon lies another spring.*

14.8 ■ Continue generally south down Hackberry Canyon. *In 1.7 miles you will reach a side canyon coming in from the west that contains yet another spring.*

20.8 ■ Keep following Hackberry Canyon generally southwest, south, and then southeast for 6.0 miles to its confluence with Cottonwood Creek.

23.7 ■ Now follow Cottonwood Creek generally southwest for 2.9 miles to the Paria River.

25.9 ■ Turn and follow the Paria River generally northwest for 2.2 miles, where you will intersect a dirt road at the Paria townsite. *You can expect to find varying amounts of water as you travel up the Paria River, anything from dank potholes to running water.*

30.1 ■ Continue generally northwest up the Paria River. In 4.2 miles you will come to the mouth of Kitchen Canyon.

36.7 ■ Keep going up the Paria River, now generally north, then northwest, for 6.6 miles to the mouth of Deer Creek Canyon.

41.4 ■ Continue generally north, then north-northwest, up the Paria River for 4.7 miles to the mouth of Sheep Creek.

42.9 ■ Now go up Sheep Creek, generally northwest, for 1.5 miles until you reach the mouth of Bull Valley Gorge. *If you have the time, Bull Valley Gorge has some of the best narrows in the region. It is well worth the hike up the gorge and back to see these narrows.*

46.7 ■ Continue generally north up Sheep Creek for another 3.8 miles to the mouth of Willis Creek.

49.0 ■ Now go up Willis Creek, generally northwest, for 2.3 miles to the Skutumpah Road. You will go through the eerie narrows of Willis Creek on the way. *You should also find good water running down the creek, especially in the narrows section.* This is the end of this section.

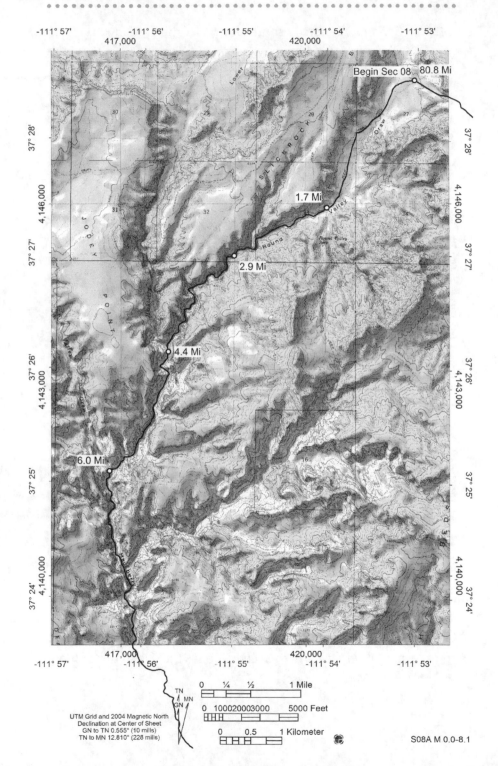

SECTION 8: 0.0–8.1 MILES

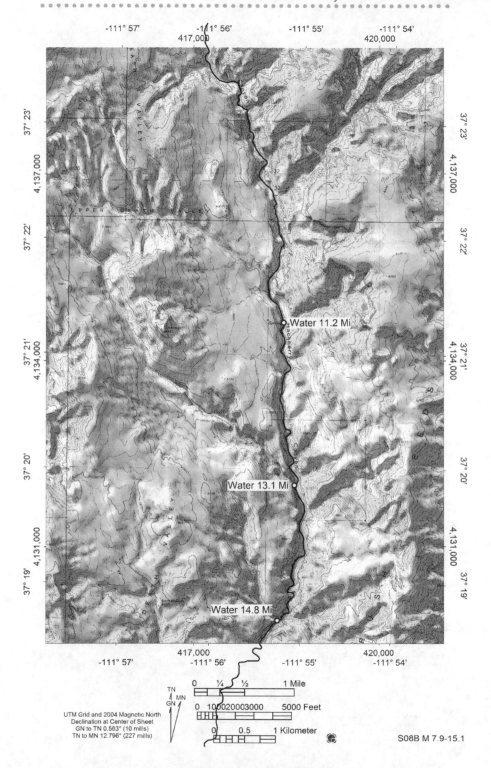

Water 11.2 Mi

Water 13.1 Mi

Water 14.8 Mi

0   ¼   ½   1 Mile

0   1000 2000 3000   5000 Feet

0   0.5   1 Kilometer

UTM Grid and 2004 Magnetic North
Declination at Center of Sheet
GN to TN 0.563° (10 mills)
TN to MN 12.796° (227 mills)

S08B M 7.9-15.1

SECTION 8: 7.9–15.1 MILES

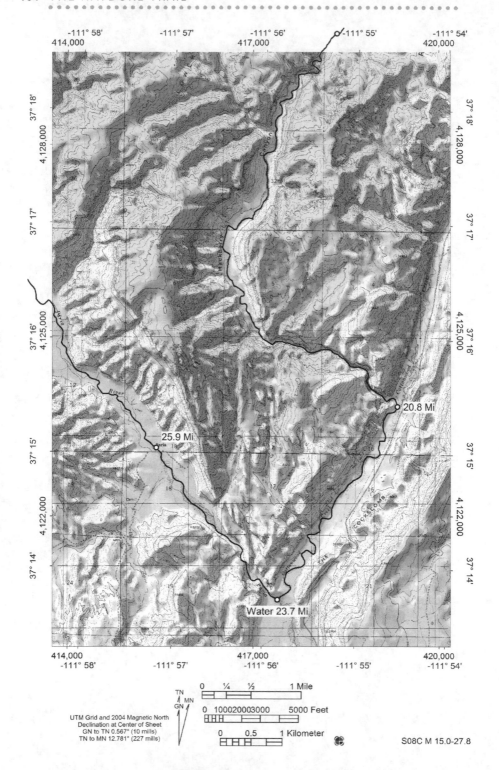

-111° 58'
414,000

-111° 57'

-111° 56'
417,000

-111° 55'

-111° 54'
420,000

37° 18'
4,128,000

37° 18'
4,128,000

37° 17'

37° 17'

4,125,000

37° 16'
4,125,000

37° 16'
4,125,000

37° 15'

20.8 Mi

25.9 Mi

4,122,000

37° 15'

37° 14'

4,122,000

37° 14'

Water 23.7 Mi

414,000

417,000

420,000

-111° 58'

-111° 57'

-111° 56'

-111° 55'

-111° 54'

TN

MN

GN

UTM Grid and 2004 Magnetic North
Declination at Center of Sheet
GN to TN 0.567° (10 mils)
TN to MN 12.781° (227 mils)

| 0 | ¼ | ½ | 1 Mile |

| 0 | 1000 | 2000 | 3000 | 5000 Feet |

| 0 | 0.5 | 1 Kilometer |

S08C M 15.0–27.8

SECTION 8: 15.0–27.8 MILES

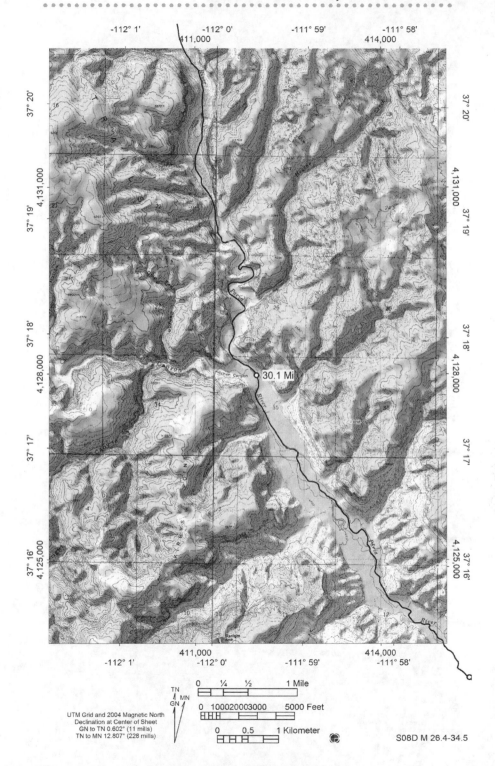

-112° 1'   -112° 0'   -111° 59'   -111° 58'

411,000   414,000

37° 20'

4,131,000   37° 19'

37° 19'

4,128,000   37° 18'

37° 18'

37° 17'   37° 17'

30.1 Mi

4,125,000   37° 16'

37° 16'   4,125,000

411,000   414,000

-112° 1'   -112° 0'   -111° 59'   -111° 58'

TN
MN
GN

UTM Grid and 2004 Magnetic North
Declination at Center of Sheet
GN to TN 0.602° (11 mils)
TN to MN 12.807° (228 mils)

0   ¼   ½   1 Mile

0   1000 2000 3000   5000 Feet

0   0.5   1 Kilometer

S08D M 26.4-34.5

SECTION 8: 26.4–34.5 MILES

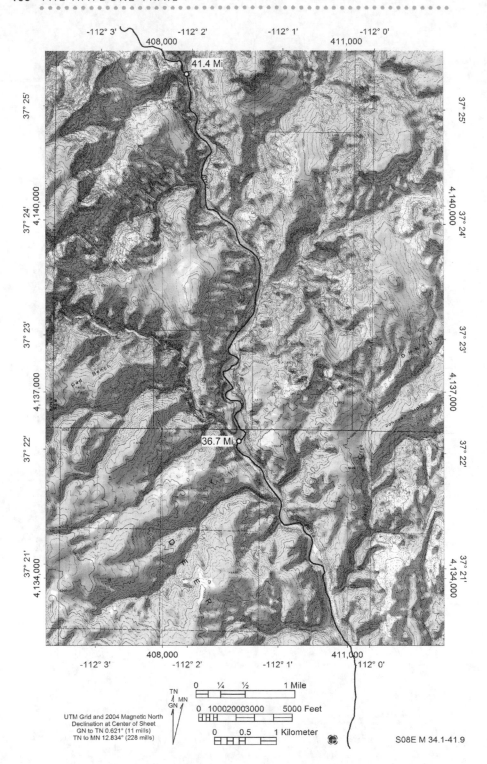

0 ¼ ½ 1 Mile

0 1000 2000 3000 5000 Feet

0 0.5 1 Kilometer

TN
GN MN

UTM Grid and 2004 Magnetic North
Declination at Center of Sheet
GN to TN 0.621° (11 mils)
TN to MN 12.834° (228 mils)

S08E M 34.1-41.9

SECTION 8: 34.1–41.9 MILES

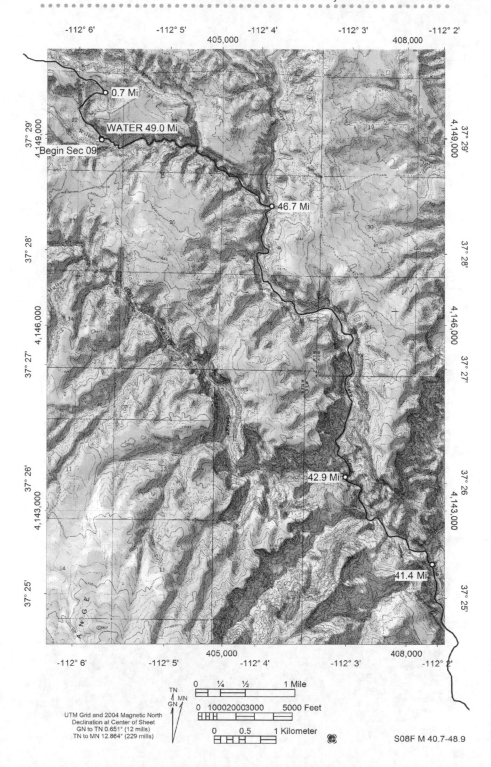

-112° 6'   -112° 5'   -112° 4'   -112° 3'   -112° 2'

405,000   408,000

37° 29'   37° 29'
4,149,000 4,149,000

0.7 Mi

WATER 49.0 Mi

Begin Sec 09

46.7 Mi

37° 28'   37° 28'

4,146,000 4,146,000

37° 27'   37° 27'

4,143,000

37° 26'   42.9 Mi   37° 26'
           4,143,000

37° 25'   41.4 Mi   37° 25'

405,000   408,000

-112° 6'   -112° 5'   -112° 4'   -112° 3'   -112° 2'

TN
MN
GN

0   ¼   ½   1 Mile

UTM Grid and 2004 Magnetic North
Declination at Center of Sheet
GN to TN 0.651° (12 mills)
TN to MN 12.864° (229 mills)

0   1000 2000 3000   5000 Feet

0   0.5   1 Kilometer

S08F M 40.7-48.9

SECTION 8: 40.7–48.9 MILES

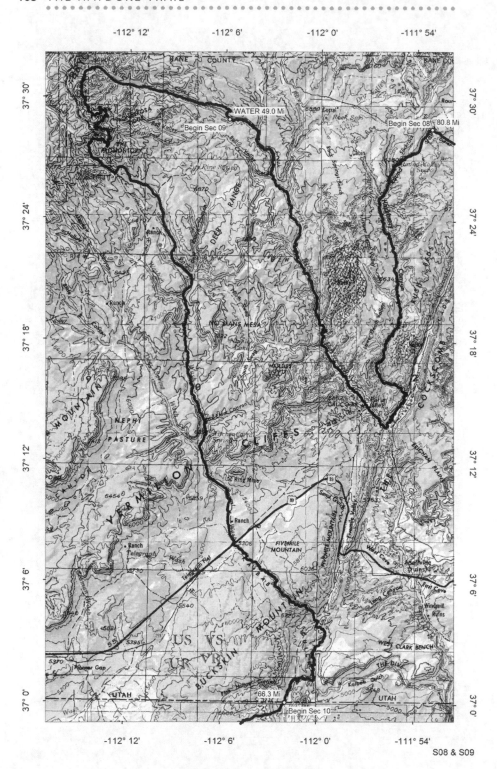

SECTION 9: OVERVIEW

■ SECTION 9
Willis Creek to Arizona Trail Stateline Trailhead

. . . .

APPROXIMATE TIME: 8 days

DISTANCE: 66.3 miles

EXERTION: moderate

NAVIGATION: easy

WATER: damp

DESOLATION FACTOR: backcountry

SPECIFIC HAZARDS: none

PERMITS: permits are needed in Grand Staircase–Escalante National Monument and Bryce Canyon National Park.

"What a killer day. It started early. We got up just before sunrise and walked about a mile north. We watched the first rays of the rising sun set the bright pinks of the cliff formations ablaze. These cliffs really can glow—the light reflecting off of seen and unseen faces. The formations are beyond my descriptive powers; they are simply amazing.

"We returned to camp separately, and I stumbled upon a deer skeleton, complete with four-point antlers. Mitch drew them when I showed him. I've never seen that before; it was all together, despite being dead for years. I'm feeling better today; Mitch is apparently getting ready for his turn. I think we must have picked up a virus or flu from someone earlier.

"By late morning we were finally ready to get going on our planned four-mile day. We left Willis, heading up Agua Canyon, where we quickly found Bryce's Under-the-Rim Trail. We also found the views we were looking for yesterday. The trail climbs quickly to a pass; our best view yet. We were back up at 8000 feet, the highest since the Henry Mountains.

"The pines are a pleasure to walk through, providing shade against what is becoming a scorching sun. Some places remind

me of hiking the mountains, it's so heavily vegetated with pines and aspens.

"Bryce has one thing though that we have not encountered before: helicopters. How is it that these loud, obnoxious, intrusive things are allowed in a national park? They disturb everything within earshot, and that's a lot."

JUNE 2, 1998 [DAY 75 OF 94], ENTERING BRYCE CANYON NATIONAL PARK

This section starts by following the dirt road that travels up along Willis Creek. There is a locked gate across the road, but you are allowed to continue on; the gate is in place because of damage done to a farmer's irrigation equipment by irresponsible four-wheelers (imagine that!), so please be aware that the land that this road passes through is private property. You will start to notice that the bottoms of the drainages in the area are turning to pink; they are stained by run-

NO MAN'S MESA AND MOLLIES NIPPLE, FROM
BRYCE CANYON NATIONAL PARK

BRYCE CANYON SCENE

off from the nearby Pink Cliffs of the Paunsaugunt Plateau, known since 1928 as Bryce Canyon National Park. After the farms, the road will take you into the Dixie National Forest, which offers a buffer zone around Bryce Canyon National Park. Agua Canyon will take you from the road into the national park and the Under-the-Rim Trail, which is then followed to Riggs Spring, where you head south out of the park. It is fairly simple to pop outside of the park border and camp without needing a park permit.

Upon exiting Bryce, you'll follow a dirt road a short way into Bull-rush Gorge (awesome!), which in turn leads you to No Man's Mesa (the only route to the top of the mesa will become quite apparent as you approach it) and Park Wash, which ultimately turns into Kitchen Corral Canyon, where a dirt road follows the drainage to U.S. Highway 89. You then follow the drainage farther south, where it becomes the Kaibab Gulch, an incredible, seldom-visited, deep canyon. This gulch becomes the start of the famed Buckskin Gulch (one of the Paria River drainages), which, if weather permits, you will travel about 6 miles through to Wire Pass. (If the weather is nasty, you will definitely want to be on the dirt road.) If you have time and can get the permits, Buck-skin Gulch should be explored farther down from Wire Pass; it is one of the most impressive (and narrowest) slots around. Take it through to the Paria, and even down that a couple of miles if you can, before heading back out to the Hayduke Trail. The Coyote Valley road leads south to the Arizona Trail Stateline Trailhead, where this section ends. There are four formal campsites, but no water, at this trailhead.

■ **Resupply/Trailhead at Willis Creek:** See previous description.

■ **Resupply/Trailhead at Arizona state line:** 40 miles east of Kanab, Utah, off U.S. Highway 89, on the southwest side of a hairpin turn, is the Coyote Valley road. Turn on to this good dirt road and follow it generally south-southwest for about 10.5 miles to the Arizona Stateline Trailhead. Most cars will make it down the dirt road if it's dry, but if it's wet it will require a 4WD with good clearance.

■ **Topos:** Bull Valley Gorge, UT; Rainbow Point, UT; Bryce Point, UT; Tropic Reservoir, UT; Deer Spring Point, UT; Nephi Point, UT; Eightmile Pass, UT; Pine Hollow Canyon, UT/AZ; West Clark Bench, UT/AZ.

ROUTE DESCRIPTION AND MILEAGE

0.7 ■ Get on the dirt Skutumpah Road and follow it northwest, then northeast, for 0.7 miles to the junction with the Willis Creek Road.

7.5 ■ Follow the dirt Willis Creek Road, generally west-northwest for 6.8 miles to the road junction at Black Birch Canyon. *Along the way you will pass through some private property. There is an easement through this property along the roadway, but make sure you don't camp there. Please treat this private land with respect.*

8.2 ■ Continue northwest up the Willis Creek Road for 0.7 miles to the road junction at Ponderosa Canyon.

8.9 ■ Stay on the dirt road and follow it another 0.7 miles, still northwest, to another road junction near the mouth of Bridge Canyon.

10.8 ■ Take the left fork. This dirt road is really just a faint double track that eventually turns into a pack trail. Follow it generally northwest, then west, into Bryce Canyon National Park, southwest, and then south for 1.9 miles to the junction with the Under-the-Rim Trail.

13.8 ■ Now follow the Under-the-Rim Trail generally south, then southeast, for 3 miles, around the heads of Ponderosa and Black Birch Canyons, to Birch Spring. *You should find water at Iron Spring or Birch Spring, but you will be within easy striking distance of Rainbow Point if you find them dry.*

16.8 ■ Continue on the Under-the-Rim Trail for 3 more miles as it swings you to the north, then around to the southwest, and up to a trail junction near Rainbow Point. *The right fork of this trail will take you a quarter mile up to the parking area at Rainbow Point if you feel the need to see some other people, get rid of some garbage, sit on a real toilet seat, or stage a resupply. Also, the views from there and at Yovimpa Point are something you probably shouldn't miss, and the trek doesn't take you very far out of your way. You will be able to see where you just came from as well as down the North Kaibab Plateau, where you will be going to in the coming weeks.*

20.9 ■ Follow the Under-the-Rim Trail for 4.1 miles to a trail junction in Mutton Hollow. You will be contouring around to the east, south, west, and then southwest below the Pink Cliffs and Yovimpa Point. *You will pass the somewhat questionable Bullberry Spring along the way.*

21.6 ■ Take the left, or south, fork and follow the trail south-southeast down Mutton Hollow for 0.7 miles to another trail junction at Riggs Spring. *This spring has been fenced off and is a reliable producer.*

22.5 ■ Go southeast for 0.9 miles on the trail down Lower Podunk Creek. The trail becomes a double track and leads you out of Bryce Canyon National Park to the parking area at Horse Hollow.

23.4 ■ Follow the dirt road southwest down Lower Podunk Creek for another 0.9 miles to the junction with a dirt road coming down from the north.

24.2 ■ Take the dirt road to the north and follow it generally northeast, then east, for 0.8 miles to Bullrush Hollow.

27.0 ■ Stay on the dirt track and follow it generally southeast down Bullrush Hollow for 2.8 miles to the Skutumpah Road.

27.9 ■ Cross this dirt road and follow the bed of Bullrush Hollow south-southeast for 0.9 miles to where the canyon starts to form up and a small trickle of water emerges from the sand. *Unless it has rained recently, take as much water from this source as you can carry.* For all practical purposes this is the transition point from Bullrush Hollow to Bullrush Gorge.

31.2 ■ Continue down the bed of Bullrush Gorge generally south-southeast, then south, for 3.3 miles to the junction with Park Wash.

32.8 ■ Pick up the dirt road in Park Wash and follow it southeast for 1.6 miles to a junction.

38.8 ■ Continue down Park Wash for 6 more miles generally southwest, then south, past No Man's Mesa, to another junction.

40.8 ■ Stay on the dirt road and follow it generally south-southeast for 2 miles down Park Wash to the junction with a dirt road that leads to Nipple Ranch.

47.3 ■ Continue on the dirt road for 6.5 miles, first southeast, then south, down Park Wash and then southeast down Kitchen Corral Wash to a road junction.

50.6 ■ Keep following the dirt road generally south for 3.3 miles to the junction with U.S. Highway 89.

50.9 ■ Cross the highway and follow a dirt track southwest for 0.3 miles to the bed of Buckskin Gulch, also called Kaibab Gulch on some maps.

58.5 ■ Go generally southeast down Buckskin Gulch for 7.6 miles to its junction with the dirt Coyote Valley Road. *We found some good pothole water in this stretch of Buckskin Gulch.*

63.2 ■ Continue generally southeast, then southwest, and then south down Buckskin Gulch for another 4.7 miles to the junction with Coyote Wash.

64.8 ■ Leave Buckskin Gulch and go west up Coyote Wash, also known as Wire Pass, for 1.6 miles to the Coyote Valley Road.

66.3 ■ Get on the Coyote Valley Road and follow it south-southwest for 1.5 miles to the Arizona Trail Stateline Trailhead. This is the end of this section.

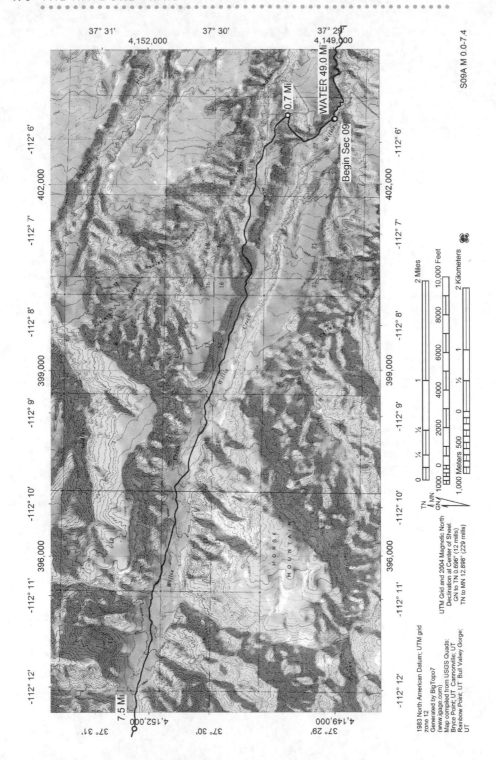

SECTION 9: 0.0–7.4 MILES

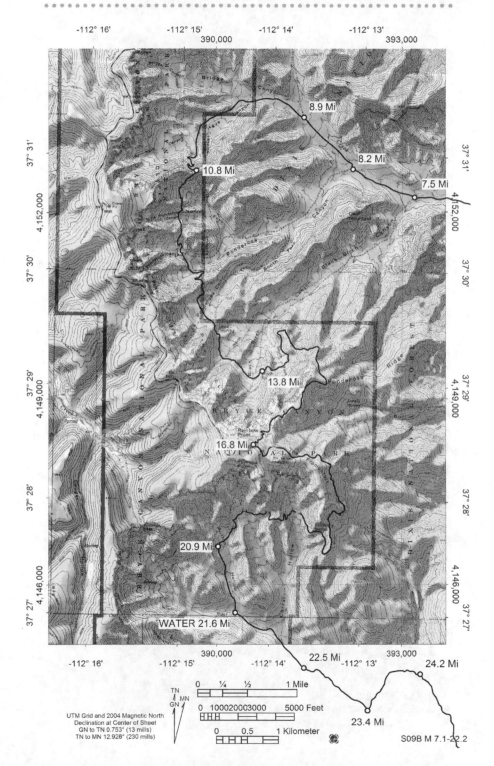

SECTION 9: 7.1–22.2 MILES

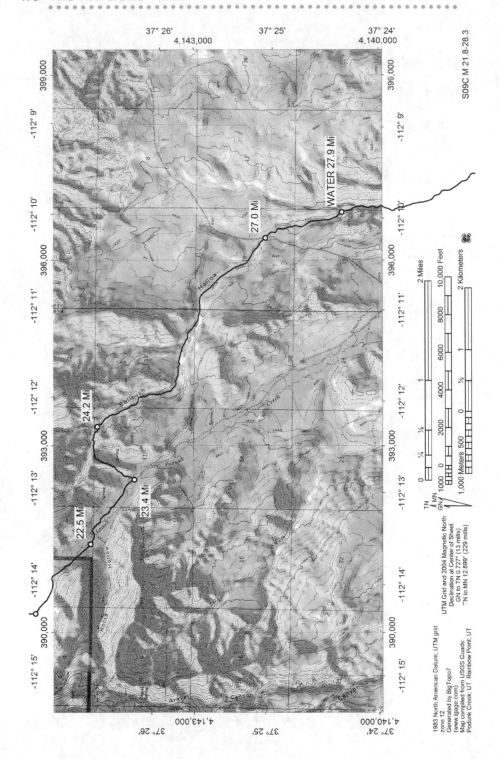

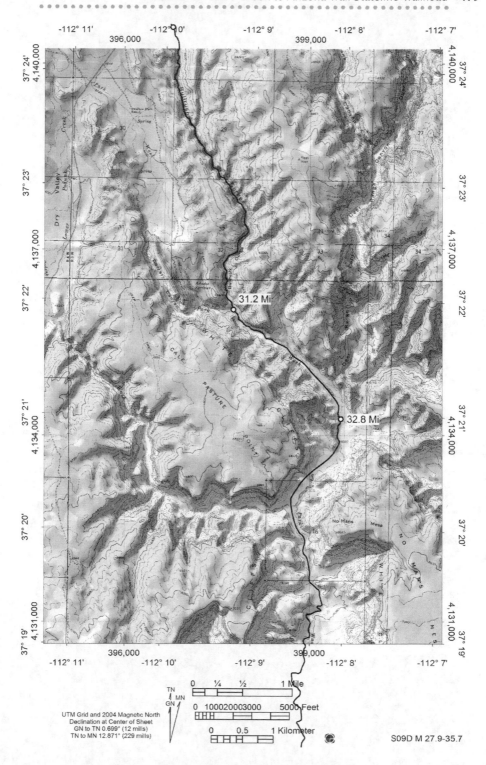

31.2 Mi

32.8 Mi

TN
MN
GN

UTM Grid and 2004 Magnetic North
Declination at Center of Sheet
GN to TN 0.699° (12 mils)
TN to MN 12.871° (229 mils)

0   ¼   ½   1 Mile

0   1000 2000 3000   5000 Feet

0   0.5   1 Kilometer

S09D M 27.9-35.7

SECTION 9: 27.9–35.7 MILES

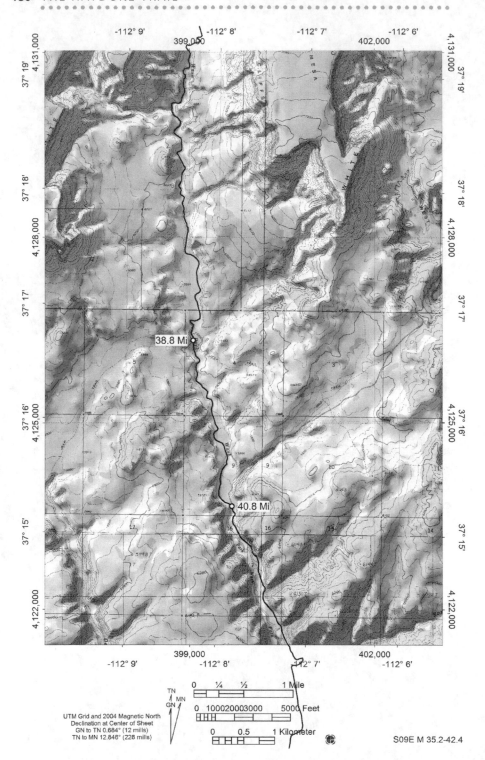

UTM Grid and 2004 Magnetic North
Declination at Center of Sheet
GN to TN 0.684° (12 mills)
TN to MN 12.846° (228 mills)

TN MN
GN

0   ¼   ½   1 Mile

0   1000 2000 3000   5000 Feet

0   0.5   1 Kilometer

S09E M 35.2-42.4

SECTION 9: 35.2–42.4 MILES

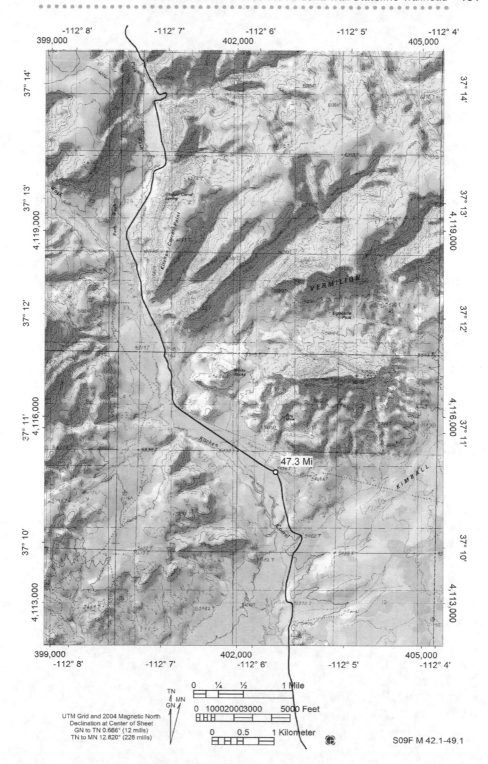

47.3 Mi

TN
MN
GN

UTM Grid and 2004 Magnetic North
Declination at Center of Sheet
GN to TN 0.666° (12 mils)
TN to MN 12.820° (228 mills)

0   ¼   ½   1 Mile

0   1000 2000 3000   5000 Feet

0   0.5   1 Kilometer

S09F M 42.1-49.1

SECTION 9: 42.1–49.1 MILES

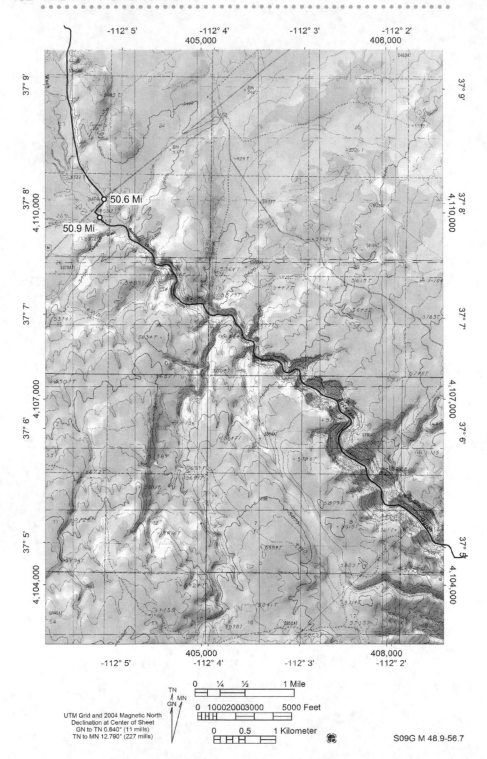

50.6 Mi

50.9 Mi

TN
MN
GN

UTM Grid and 2004 Magnetic North
Declination at Center of Sheet
GN to TN 0.640° (11 mils)
TN to MN 12.790° (227 mills)

0   ¼   ½   1 Mile

0 1000 2000 3000   5000 Feet

0   0.5   1 Kilometer

S09G M 48.9-56.7

SECTION 9: 48.9–56.7 MILES

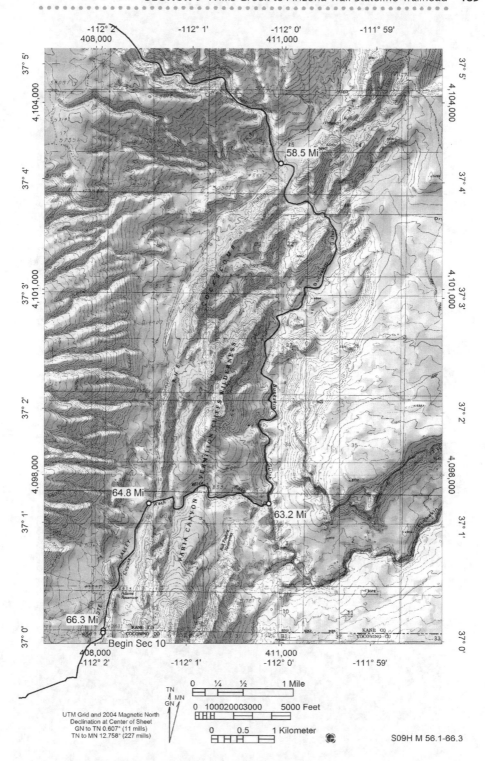

UTM Grid and 2004 Magnetic North
Declination at Center of Sheet
GN to TN 0.607° (11 mills)
TN to MN 12.758° (227 mills)

S09H M 56.1-66.3

SECTION 9: 56.1–66.3 MILES

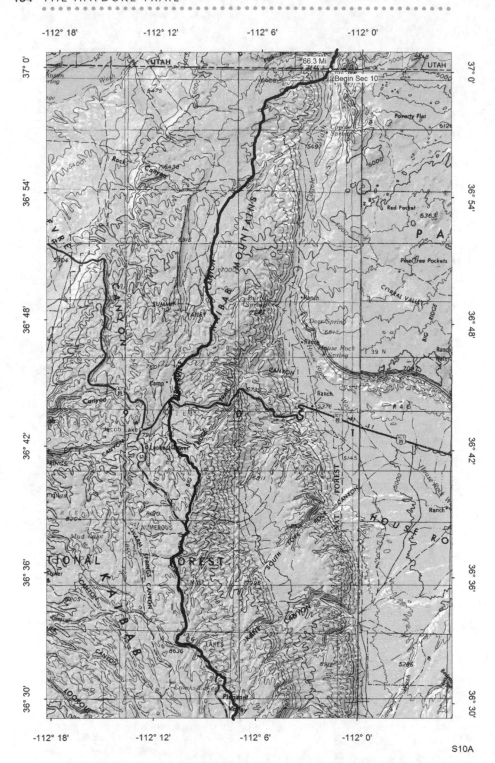

S10A

SECTION 10: OVERVIEW (continued on page 186)

■ SECTION 10
Arizona Trail Stateline Trailhead to Nankoweap Trailhead

APPROXIMATE TIME: 7 days

DISTANCE: 60.9 miles

EXERTION: easy

NAVIGATION: moderate (there is a confusing maze of trails)

WATER: dry

DESOLATION FACTOR: local

SPECIFIC HAZARDS: none

PERMITS: no permits are needed in this section

"We had been walking for a few days in the ponderosa forests of the Kaibab Plateau along the Arizona Trail when we came to the East Rim Overlook, a trailhead of the Arizona Trail. All of a sudden we had a view, and that view was stunning. We could see east all the way across the Arizona Strip, including into the gorge of Marble Canyon, whose entire course, snaking from Lees Ferry to Saddle Mountain, was visible from this vantage. Also visible were Navajo Mountain, the Kaiparowits Plateau, the Henry Mountains in the distance, the Vermilion Cliffs, the Echo Cliffs, and far beyond. What a wild, crazy, and colorful scene!

"The Arizona Trail has been tremendous, going from a sage desert up into the hills, gradually changing to a pinyon/juniper forest and then to a ponderosa forest. We have seen deer, turkeys, eagles, rabbits, the striking Kaibab squirrel, hawks, and even salamanders. The California condors remain elusive. We have heard surprising amounts of coyotes howling in the nights, which have been getting downright frigid lately. There have been a number of archaeological sites along the way; some even had quantities of broken arrowheads lying scattered on the ground."

OCTOBER 11, 2001 [DAY 6 OF 11], NORTH KAIBAB PLATEAU

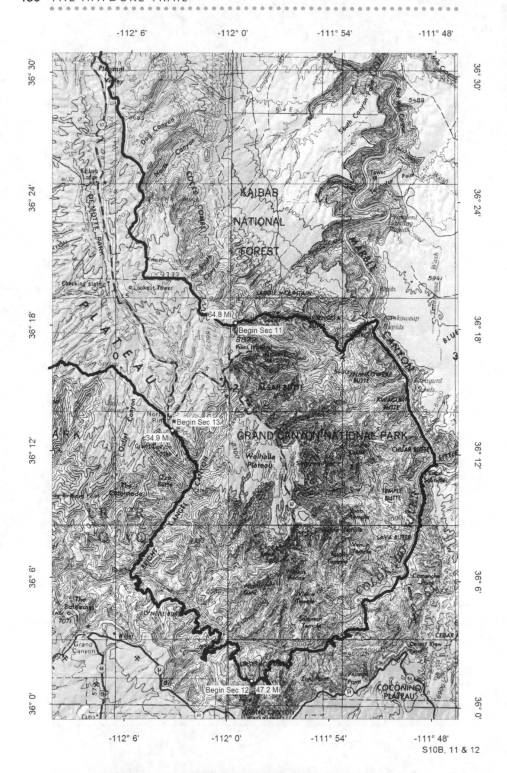

S10B, 11 & 12

SECTION 10: OVERVIEW (continued from page 184)

DEER ON KAIBAB

This section follows the Arizona Trail from the Utah border to the North Rim of the Grand Canyon. The Arizona Trail stretches from the state's southern border with Mexico to the Utah border on the north. Its creation began in the late 1980s, and it is still being "developed" today.

The stretch of the Arizona Trail that we have included here is fairly well marked and relatively easy to follow, but paying close attention will be necessary in a couple of places. The section starts with a 1,200-foot ascent into the trees and continues into the ponderosa forests, with moderate ups and downs along its length. The forest is quite beautiful, but keep in mind that the Kaibab Plateau reaches elevations of up to 9,000 feet, so it can get pretty cold, particularly during the evenings. The Kaibab is often snowed in from late fall through early spring, so check conditions before heading into this section. Most of the time views will be limited to the surrounding forest, but there are some notable exceptions where you approach the rim of the plateau and the views become huge.

The U.S. Forest Service recommends that water be cached at various points along the way, but we found adequate ponds and wildlife "guzzlers," though the quality of these sources is pretty low. There are, however, plenty of easy access places to cache water; many forest service roads intersect the Arizona Trail.

EAST RIM VIEW

Upon reaching the Grand Canyon National Park boundary, you will head along the dirt road east to the Saddle Mountain/Nankoweap Trailhead and the end of the section. The trailhead here will offer you your first view into the heart of the Grand Canyon, and we'll tell you now: it's impressive.

■ **Resupply/Trailhead at Arizona state line:** See previous description.

■ **Resupply/Trailhead at Nankoweap Trail:** From the Kaibab Lodge, go south on Arizona State Road 67 (the road to North Rim Village, Grand Canyon National Park) for 1 mile. Turn east off of the pavement onto a dirt road numbered 611. This is also about 4.5 miles north of the North Rim Entrance Station. Follow this dirt road generally south-southeast, then north, for 1.4 miles to a road junction. Turn right onto the 610 dirt road and follow it generally south, then east, and then southeast for 12.7 miles until you reach the parking area.

■ **Topos:** Pine Hollow Canyon, UT/AZ; Dog Point, AZ; Little Park Lake, AZ; Point Imperial, AZ.

VIEW BY SECTION END

■ **Special Note About the Arizona Trail**: Currently, the Arizona Trail Association is precisely plotting the entire Arizona Trail; but they have started at the Arizona/Mexico border and are working their way north. At the time of this writing, the latest maps show the area we are concerned with as the provisional Kaibab Plateau Arizona Trail, and its placement is approximate. The good news is that the Arizona Trail is very well marked and signed, and we found it very easy to follow on the ground. If our description and maps do vary from the actual course of the Arizona Trail, don't worry. **Just be sure to follow the trail signs and you won't get lost!** Check the Arizona Trail Association website at www.aztrail.org for current information.

ROUTE DESCRIPTION AND MILEAGE

4.3 ■ Take the Arizona Trail generally southwest, then west-southwest, for 4.3 miles as you switch back and forth up the flank of Buckskin Mountain to a road junction near the head of Larkum Canyon. *Along this entire section, keep your eyes peeled for the condors* *released in this area. They are said to travel great distances along the Kaibab Plateau and some of them return in the evening to roost here in the Vermilion Cliffs.*

8.5 ▣ Now go generally south-southwest on the trail for 4.2 miles, across the heads of Basin, Red, and Dead Man Canyons, to another junction.

9.9 ▣ Follow the trail southwest for 1.4 miles, paralleling the upper reaches of Long Canyon, to another junction.

14.1 ▣ Continue on the trail generally south-southwest for 4.2 miles, following Summit Valley to the Navajo Trail junction.

19.0 ▣ Go 4.9 miles generally south on the Arizona Trail to the head of Summit Valley, up the draw that's just east of Orderville Canyon, and then to dirt road #249 on the plateau.

23.9 ▣ Cross the dirt road and follow the trail generally southwest, then south, and then west-southwest for 4.9 miles to where the trail crosses U.S. Highway Alt. 89.

29.6 ▣ Follow the trail for another 5.7 miles. You will be going generally south past Big Ridge Tank, then southeast, and then south-southwest past the Buffalo Trick Tank to dirt road #205B. *Keep your eyes and ears open for the many wild turkeys that call the Kaibab Plateau their home. We saw their tracks everywhere, especially near the guzzlers, and we startled a group of about twenty that were drinking from a dank pond.*

33.4 ▣ After crossing the dirt road, the trail turns south. Continue on the trail, generally south, then southwest, for 3.8 miles to a dirt road at Sixty-Seven Apron.

39.0 ▣ Take the trail southwest, then generally south-southeast, and then southwest again for 5.6 miles. You will be paralleling the North Rim Parkway here. On the western end of Telephone Hill the trail turns to the southeast. *The Kaibab is also home to an incredible number of mule deer. In the summer months you could expect to see deer throughout the region. A large number of these deer will spend the winter at the lower elevations on Buckskin Mountain.*

43.6 ■ Follow the trail generally east, then southeast, for 4.6 miles, in and out of Little Round Valley and then into Little Pleasant Valley and a dirt road.

46.1 ■ Stay on the trail and go generally south-southeast for 2.5 miles to the junction with the road that leads to Tater Ridge. You will cross Cane Ridge and Pleasant Valley Outlet along the way.

47.7 ■ Continue on the trail generally south-southeast for another 1.6 miles until you reach Upper Tater Canyon. *Another animal to keep an eye out for is the unique Kaibab squirrel. Easy to recognize due to its large ear tufts, it is found nowhere else on earth.*

49.2 ■ Go south on the trail through Upper Tater Canyon for 1.5 miles. Here the trail turns to the southeast.

51.0 ■ Follow the trail southeast for 1.8 miles. After climbing out of Upper Tater Canyon, the trail crosses Dog Canyon and takes you to the edge of North Canyon at a developed trailhead. Definitely take the time to hike southeast down the short trail to the East Rim Viewpoint. You won't be disappointed by the view.

53.4 ■ The trail skirts along the rim generally south-southwest for 2.4 miles to Crystal Spring.

55.9 ■ Now go 2.5 miles, heading south, then southwest, up the draw and then generally southeast into Upper North Canyon.

57.9 ■ Follow Upper North Canyon generally south for 2 miles until you intersect dirt road #610. You will be leaving the Arizona Trail here.

60.1 ■ Follow the dirt road due east for 2.2 miles. Here the road turns to the southeast. You will be following the Grand Canyon National Park boundary.

64.8 ■ Continue on the dirt road generally southeast, then east, for 4.7 miles to the trailhead parking area and the end of this section.

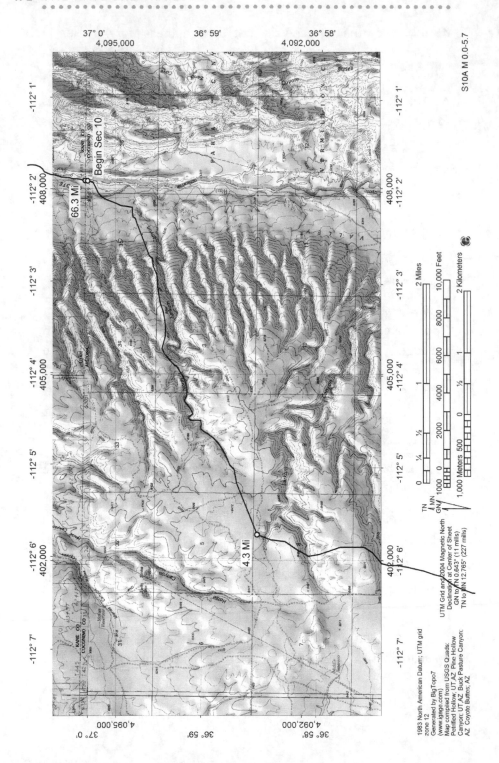

SECTION 10: 0.0–5.7 MILES

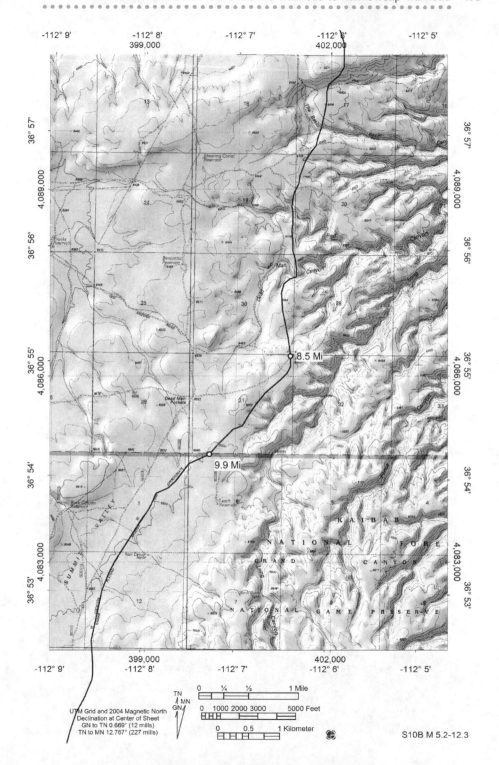

UTM Grid and 2004 Magnetic North
Declination at Center of Sheet
GN to TN 0.669° (12 mils)
TN to MN 12.767° (227 mils)

S10B M 5.2-12.3

SECTION 10: 5.2–12.3 MILES

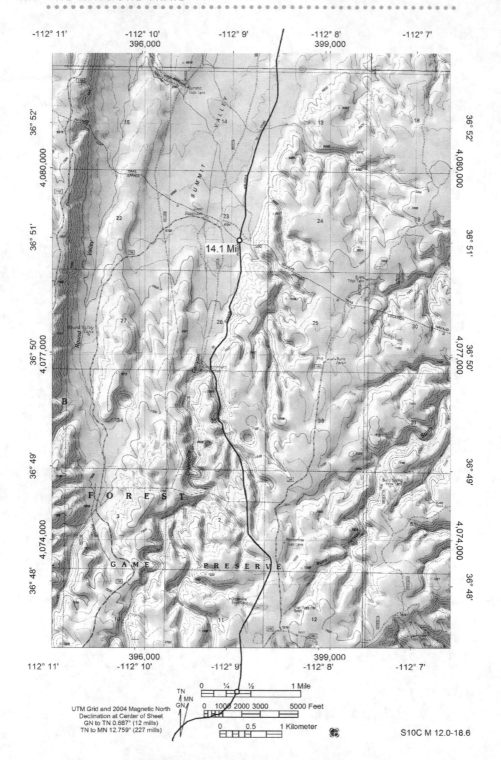

SECTION 10: 12.0–18.6 MILES

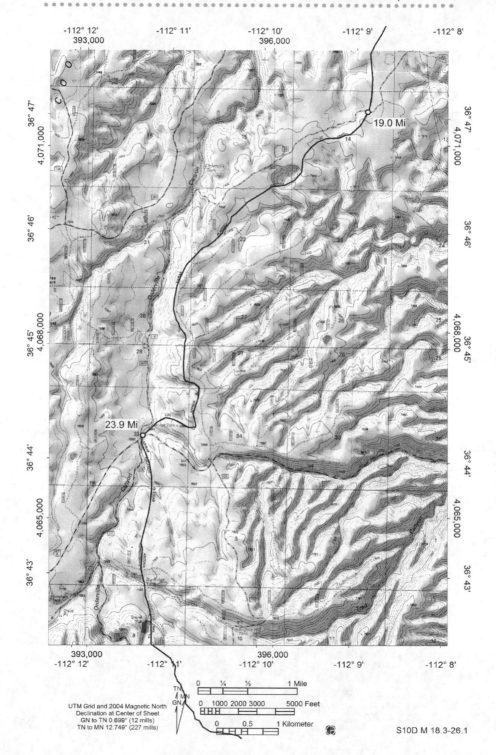

UTM Grid and 2004 Magnetic North
Declination at Center of Sheet
GN to TN 0.699° (12 mills)
TN to MN 12.749° (227 mills)

0   ¼   ½   1 Mile

0   1000 2000 3000   5000 Feet

0   0.5   1 Kilometer

S10D M 18.3-26.1

SECTION 10: 18.3–26.1 MILES

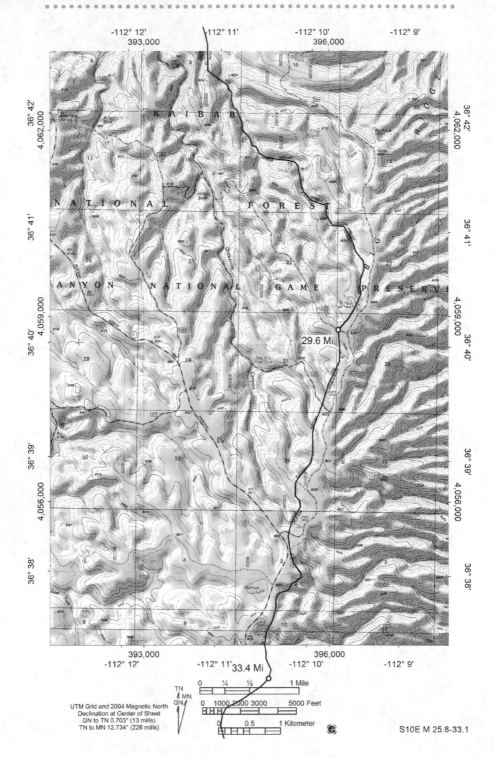

29.6 Mi

33.4 Mi

TN
MN
GN

UTM Grid and 2004 Magnetic North
Declination at Center of Sheet
GN to TN 0.703° (13 mils)
TN to MN 12.734° (226 mils)

| 0 | ¼ | ½ | 1 Mile |

| 0 | 1000 | 2000 | 3000 | 5000 Feet |

| 0 | 0.5 | 1 Kilometer |

S10E M 25.8-33.1

SECTION 10: 25.8–33.1 MILES

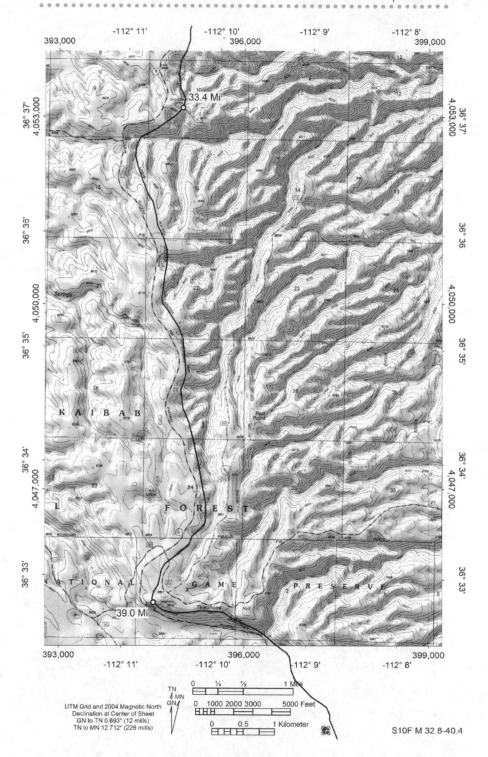

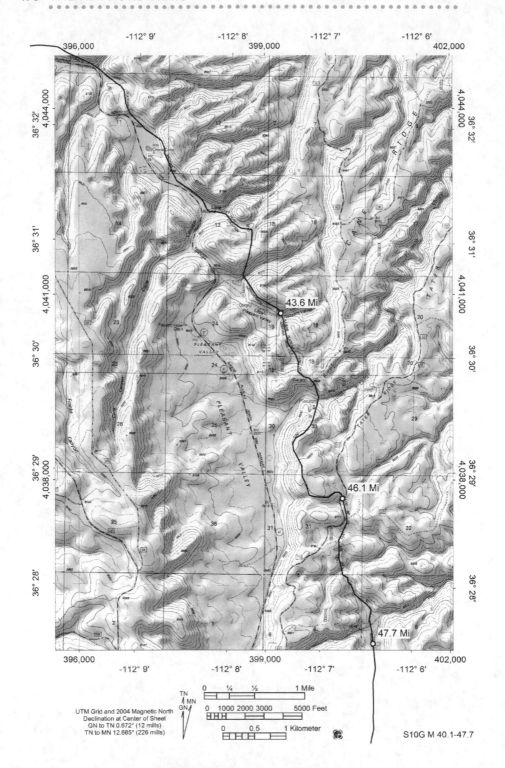

43.6 Mi

46.1 Mi

47.7 Mi

TN
MN
GN

UTM Grid and 2004 Magnetic North
Declination at Center of Sheet
GN to TN 0.672° (12 mills)
TN to MN 12.685° (226 mills)

| 0 | ¼ | ½ | 1 Mile |

| 0 | 1000 | 2000 | 3000 | 5000 Feet |

| 0 | 0.5 | 1 Kilometer |

S10G M 40.1-47.7

SECTION 10: 40.01–47.7 MILES

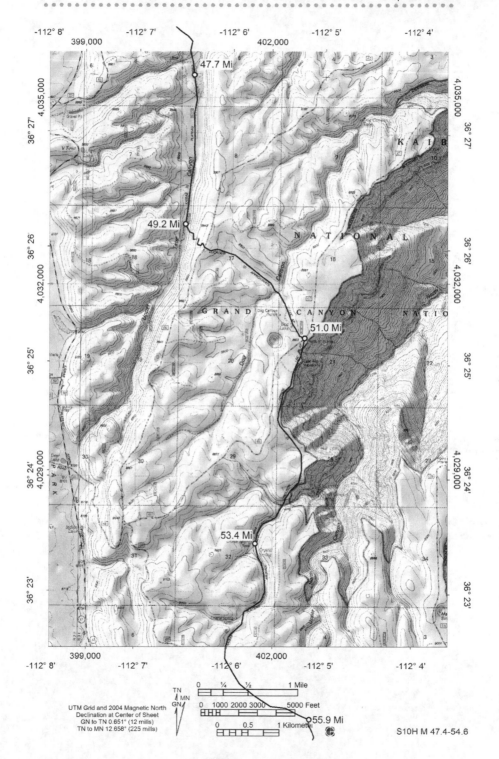

47.7 Mi

49.2 Mi

51.0 Mi

53.4 Mi

55.9 Mi

TN
MN
GN

UTM Grid and 2004 Magnetic North
Declination at Center of Sheet
GN to TN 0.651° (12 mils)
TN to MN 12.658° (225 mils)

0   ¼   ½   1 Mile

0   1000 2000 3000   5000 Feet

0   0.5   1 Kilometer

S10H M 47.4-54.6

SECTION 10: 47.4–54.6 MILES

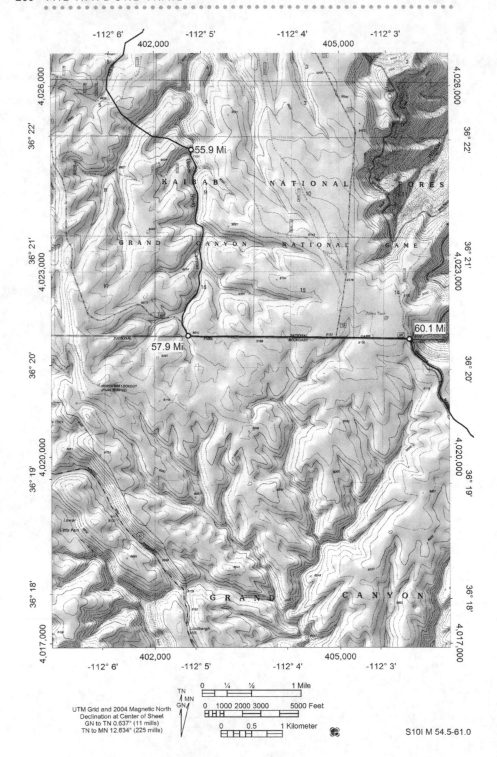

55.9 Mi

KAIBAB NATIONAL FORES

GRAND CANYON NATIONAL GAME

57.9 Mi

60.1 Mi

NORTH RIM LOOKOUT
(PARK SERVICE)

GRAND CANYON

TN MN GN

UTM Grid and 2004 Magnetic North
Declination at Center of Sheet
GN to TN 0.637° (11 mills)
TN to MN 12.634° (225 mills)

0   ¼   ½   1 Mile

0   1000 2000 3000   5000 Feet

0   0.5   1 Kilometer

S10I M 54.5-61.0

SECTION 10: 54.5–61.0 MILES

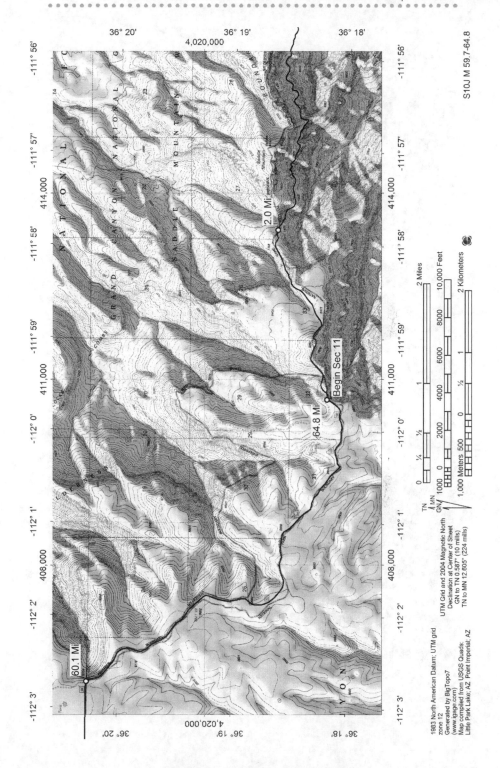

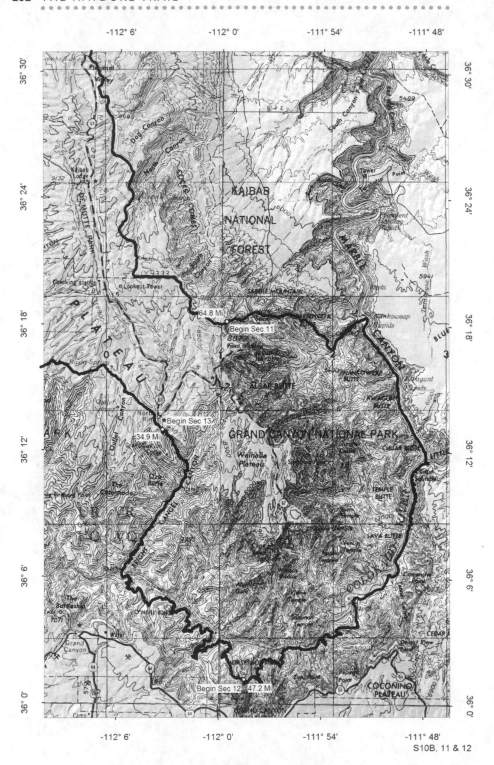

S10B, 11 & 12

SECTION 11: OVERVIEW

■ SECTION 11
Nankoweap Trailhead to Horseshoe Mesa, Grand Canyon National Park

• •

APPROXIMATE TIME: 9 days

DISTANCE: 47.1 miles

EXERTION: moderate to difficult

NAVIGATION: moderate

WATER: wet

DESOLATION FACTOR: backcountry

SPECIFIC HAZARDS: exposure, difficult water crossing (Little Colorado River, Colorado River), rattlesnakes, heat

PERMITS: Grand Canyon National Park requires permits for overnight backcountry camping.

"We didn't get to sleep under the stars last night, and we were lucky too! That plan changed when I went down to the river for one last pee break before turning in for the night and narrowly missed stepping on a quietly coiled pink Grand Canyon rattlesnake. The damn thing just about gave me a heart attack, but at least it didn't bite me. Anyway, it was way too close to where we were going to be sleeping, so the screen sections of the tents went up, particularly in light of the fact we lost track of the critter. Just as dawn was breaking, it started to rain. On went the flys. Now we're waiting for it to quit. A break in the rain allowed us to access our packs real quick, and that allowed us to see the big picture: snow on both rims! We're more than a bit curious as to the storm's effect on the Little Colorado River, as we need to cross it later today."

APRIL 18, 2000 [DAY 38 OF 101], ON THE COLORADO RIVER,
GRAND CANYON NATIONAL PARK

"We're on the other side of the river again. We just had to wait a bit for a boat to come by. A Colorado River and Trails Expedition raft finally came along and ferried us across the river (thanks, Bill!). It was quick; we saw them coming, they saw us, we shouted

that we needed a ride, they beached, and we hopped on and went across. The whole process took about a minute.

"We are just barely upriver of Awatubi Creek, in Marble Canyon. The scene is sublime. Truly. Massive rock walls line both sides of the canyon. The river is visible up and down the canyon, the water turning the color of gold with the reflection of the setting sun on the walls. Small rapids are everywhere. There is actually a trail (sort of) along our way, probably a game trail, but it sure makes the way easier."

APRIL 19, 2000 [DAY 39 OF 101], ON THE COLORADO RIVER,
GRAND CANYON NATIONAL PARK

This is an incredible section, wholly within Grand Canyon National Park and offering a big taste of the inner gorge of the Grand Canyon. This section also has a unique challenge built into it: you need to get across the mighty Colorado River. Starting at the Saddle Mountain/ Nankoweap Trailhead, you descend about a vertical mile into Nankoweap Canyon. The route down is steep and exposed; the national park considers this to be the most difficult named trail in the entire park (though we think the North Bass Trail rightly deserves that title). A short walk down Nankoweap Canyon will take you to the river

NANKOWEAP GRANARIES

MARBLE CANYON SCENE, GRAND CANYON NATIONAL PARK

as well as to a beautiful set of granaries. A faint trail is the easiest way to head down river, and we suggest that you stay on the right side of the river until you are at least within a mile of the Little Colorado River before attempting to find a ferry across the water. **We strongly advise not trying to swim the Colorado River; the water is much too cold and the current too strong to safely pull that off!** Wait for a passing raft or boat, or bring inner tubes or a small raft instead (you can float yourself *across* the river without a boating permit; but pack it out if you pack it in).

Once across the river, you will need to ford the Little Colorado River, which should be fairly simple, as the water isn't that fast, though it could be waist deep. Waiting out high water, in the event you can't

CROSSING THE LITTLE COLORADO RIVER, GRAND CANYON NATIONAL PARK

CAMP AT CARDENAS, GRAND CANYON NATIONAL PARK

safely cross, generally shouldn't take more than a day (except in the case of a melting snowpack, at which time early mornings should have the day's lowest flows). From the Little Colorado River there are trails (Beamer, Escalante, and Tonto) you can follow all the way to Horseshoe Mesa, where this section ends. The trails often skirt along the river; at other times you'll climb to ridges high above the water. There are frequent stretches with pretty serious exposure, but, for the most part, these are fairly simple, easy-to-follow trails. We had a food cache at Horseshoe Mesa on our journey through the canyon, but there is also a trail to the rim (the Grand View Point Trail) from here for a resupply meeting.

■ **Resupply/Trailhead at Nankoweap Trail:** See previous description.

■ **Resupply/Trailhead at Horseshoe Mesa:** The actual terminus of this section is on Horseshoe Mesa, below the South Rim of the Grand Canyon, but, depending on your itinerary, you may wish to end this section at Grand View Point Trailhead on the rim. If your plan is to continue on to the next section (as we did), you will need either to hike a resupply down to Horseshoe Mesa and cache it somewhere, or arrange to be resupplied on the mesa or on the rim. **You must check in with and gain permission from Grand Canyon National Park**

before caching anything in the
backcountry! It is your responsibility to remove your empty
cache buckets/water jugs in a
reasonable amount of time after
your trek. Please don't litter the
canyon or force other hikers or
park service personnel to carry
out your spent cache items. If
we abuse this privilege, we may
not be able to leave caches in
the park in the future. Leave No
Trace! If you are beginning or
ending your trek here, you will
need to do so up on the South
Rim at the Grand View parking
area. There is a 2.3-mile, well-
worn trail that connects Horseshoe

UNCONFORMITY BY HANCE RAPID, GRAND
CANYON NATIONAL PARK

Mesa and the Grand View parking area. **Please note that there is a
2,540-foot difference in elevation between the mesa and the rim!**

■ **Topos:** Point Imperial, AZ; Nankoweap Mesa, AZ; Cape Solitude,
AZ; Desert View, AZ; Cape Royal, AZ.

ROUTE DESCRIPTION AND MILEAGE

2.0 ■ From the parking area, follow National Forest Service Trail 57
generally east-northeast for 2 miles to the Nankoweap Trailhead. **You
will be entering Grand Canyon National Park here, so make sure you
have the appropriate permits!**

7.8 ■ Go down the Nankoweap Trail generally east, then southeast,
for 5.8 miles to the floor of Nankoweap Creek. The trail is easy to follow, but you will be descending a whopping 4,160 feet of elevation
between the rim and the creek! You will pass a very small seep on the
way down that may or may not be flowing. *People often leave water
jugs under this dripping seep to slowly fill up (while they are in the
canyon) so they will have water for the trip back up to the rim.*

Although in our opinion this is a questionable practice (expressing too much faith in the goodwill of others), **someone may have their life staked on that water being there when they need it. Please leave it alone!** *There will be plenty of cold, clear water in the creek and more than you could ever need in the river a few miles down the canyon.*

10.6 ◼ Now follow Nankoweap Creek downstream, generally northeast, for 2.8 miles to the Colorado River. To the southwest are the famous Anasazi granaries perched high on the cliffs above you. They are marked on the quad map of this area, and a well-worn trail will lead you up through the talus to these ruins.

14.4 ◼ You will turn south here and then bushwhack and boulder hop alongside the river, generally southeast, for 3.8 miles to the mouth of Kwagunt Creek. There is no formal trail to follow but you will find a maze of game trails leading you downstream through the brush and talus. *As you follow these game trails, an important thing to know is the difference between deer tracks and those of bighorn sheep. You'll figure it out soon enough. Typically, the deer are going to stick to the more sane terrain, following the path of least resistance. The sheep, being unparalleled climbers, do not need to conform to these conventions and you could find yourself following them into serious trouble.*

15.9 ◼ Continue boulder hopping south alongside the river for another 1.5 miles to the mouth of Malgosa Canyon.

16.6 ◼ After traveling generally south for another 0.7 miles downriver you will reach the mouth of Awatubi Canyon.

18.1 ◼ Now go south-southeast alongside the river for 1.5 miles to the mouth of Sixtymile Canyon.

19.2 ◼ Continue south-southeast alongside the river for another 1.1 miles. This is where you put all your eggs in one basket and start waiting for a ride across the river. Start by looking for a safe and easy place for a raft to pull over to pick you up. *While most river runners we know would be glad to help out a fellow adventurer, they are not obligated to do you any favors and would never jeopardize their party's safety just to give you a ride. We found this small area to be the most logical* *place to catch a ride, as the currents are not too swift and, once on the other side, you will find the boulder hop down to the Little Colorado a piece of cake. Make it very clear to any rafters you hail that you are not in trouble and merely wish to be ferried to the other side of the river. You must convey your message quickly. By the time you spot a raft coming downstream, or, more importantly, they spot you, the captain will only have a moment to make and then act on a decision to pick you up or not. It is illegal for a rafter to transport you downstream unless you are specifically named on their trip permit, so don't even ask. They are, fortunately, allowed to ferry hikers from one shore to the other.* **But they are not obligated!** *Hopefully, you planned your trip during the commercial rafting season, when there are lots of boats in the canyon, or you may find yourself waiting for a very long time. Better yet, set up a ferry in advance with one of the many commercial rafting outfits running the canyon. Even so, be prepared to wait at least one full day for a ride, and always have all your gear packed and be ready to jump on board at a moment's notice.* **Whatever you do, do not attempt to swim across the Colorado River anywhere in the Grand Canyon! The water issuing out of Lake Powell is so cold that you would surely die before you made it to the other side!** *If catching a ride becomes a hopeless prospect, it's only 19.2 miles back to the trailhead on the North Rim.*

20.0 ▪ Once you are safely on the east (or left) side of the river, continue boulder hopping south for 0.8 miles, turning east into the mouth of the Little Colorado River Canyon. Under normal flows, the Little Colorado can be safely waded here. If it happens to be flooding or running high, you must sit and wait again. **You have to be prepared for this!** *Either wait for the Little Colorado to recede or wait for another passing raft to ferry you over. Fortunately, most rafting parties stop here to check out the normally turquoise waters of the Little Colorado.* However you actually have to do it, cross the Little Colorado here and then find the Beamer Trail on the other side. Before you do, grab enough water from the Colorado River (upstream of the Little Colorado River) to see you the 6.4 miles to Lava Canyon Rapid.

26.4 ■ You are now standing on one end of the national park's large network of linked trails through the inner Grand Canyon. The Beamer is definitely one of the most exciting trails in the system. Follow it southwest, then generally south, for 6.4 miles. It will lead you up onto a narrow, sloping bench, high above the Colorado River. The trail traverses along this sketchy bench almost all the way to Palisades Creek. You will pass in and out of countless little hanging side canyons, and sometimes be looking straight down on the river. **There are several places where this trail is seriously sloping off toward disaster, so make every step count!** Just before you reach Palisades, the trail leads you back down to river level and then to the beach beside Lava Canyon Rapid.

29.5 ■ Continue following the Beamer Trail, now at river level, generally south-southwest for 3.1 miles. You will pass Espejo Creek, then Commanche Creek, and come to the junction with the Tanner Trail and Escalante Route at Tanner Creek. (Notice that the Beamer Trail is mistakenly named the "Beaver Trail" on the quad map.)

32.0 ■ *If you are hating it at this point, the Tanner Trail will lead you up to the South Rim and the relative safety of motoring tourists.* If everything is going fine, then head downstream on the Escalante Route. Follow this sometimes faint trail, just above river level for 2.5 miles generally southwest, to the mouth of Cardenas Creek. Take enough water from the river here to see you the next 6.3 miles to Nevills Rapid.

35.2 ■ Now follow the Escalante Route west and then generally south for 1.3 miles, climbing up onto the ridge separating Cardenas Creek from the Colorado River. The trail veers off of the crest and onto the west side of the ridge. Continue on the Escalante Route for another 1.9 miles, first contouring south into the head of a drainage and then west back out of it and onto the ridge separating this drainage from Escalante Creek. *The river is now 1,360 feet below you, and the view of the Unkar Delta and the cliffs of the Palisades of the Desert is hard to beat.*

35.7 ■ Follow the trail southwest, then east-southeast, for 0.5 miles to the bed of Escalante Creek.

36.3 ■ The trail crosses the creek bed and contours west-southwest for 0.6 miles to the bottom of the South Fork of Escalante Creek.

37.7 ■ Now the trail contours up and generally west-northwest, then southwest parallel to (but 200 feet above) the Colorado, then southeast into Seventyfive Mile Creek. It is 1.4 miles from the South Fork of Escalante Creek to the bed of Seventyfive Mile Creek.

38.3 ■ After crossing the creek bed, follow the Escalante Route northwest for 0.6 miles as it leads you out of Seventyfive Mile Creek and back down to the river.

39.7 ■ Follow the trail generally southwest, then west, for 1.4 miles alongside the river to the junction with the Hance Trail and Tonto Trail at the mouth of Red Canyon. *The Hance Trail is the next escape route to the rim.*

41.9 ■ The next water you find will be 6.8 miles away at Miners Spring. Get on the Tonto Trail and follow it generally west, then south, for 2.2 miles as you first parallel the river and then head back into Mineral Canyon. The Tonto Trail is the beginning of your gradual ascent from 2,600 feet at the river to 5,160 feet at Horseshoe Mesa.

45.4 ■ Continue on the Tonto Trail for 3.5 miles, generally west-northwest, then around to the south, to the bed of Hance Creek.

45.8 ■ Now the trail contours out of Hance Creek to the northwest for 0.4 miles to a trail junction. The Tonto Trail continues on the right.

46.5 ■ Take the trail on the left and follow it first northwest, then southwest, for 0.7 miles to another trail junction. *The trail on the left will take you a short distance to Miners Spring.*

47.1 ■ Stay to the right-hand trail and follow it another 0.6 miles as it zigzags up onto Horseshoe Mesa and the junction with the Grandview Trail.

If you are continuing on from here, this ends this section. Time to dig out your cache and take a day off, taking it easy or exploring the mesa, the Cave of the Domes, and Grandview Point. If not, the Grandview Trail will take you south for another 2.3 miles up to the rim.

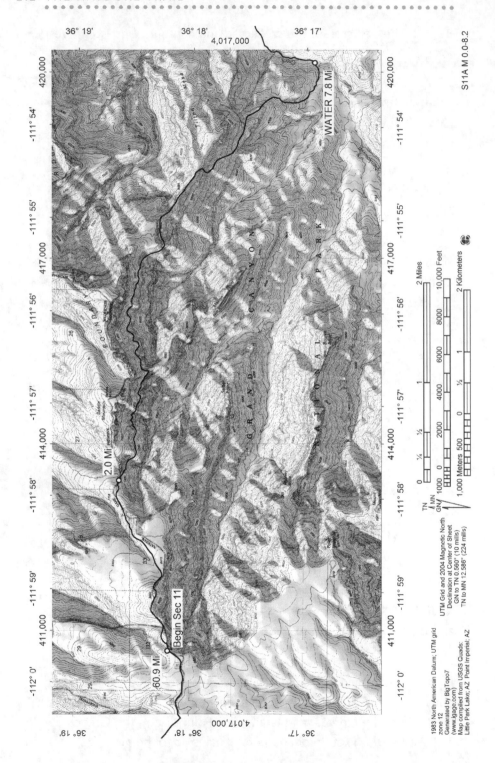

S11A M 0.0-8.2

WATER 7.8 Mi

2.0 Mi

Begin Sec 11

60.9 Mi

1983 North American Datum; UTM grid
zone 12
Generated by BigTopo7
(www.igage.com)
Map compiled from USGS Quads:
Little Park Lake; AZ Point Imperial; AZ

UTM Grid and 2004 Magnetic North
Declination at Center of Sheet
GN to TN 0.560° (10 mils)
TN to MN 12.586° (224 mils)

SECTION 11: 0.0–8.2 MILES

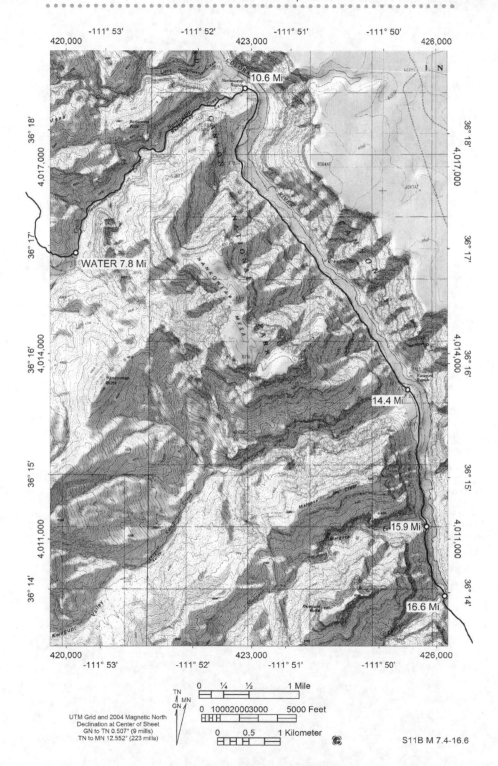

10.6 Mi

WATER 7.8 Mi

14.4 Mi

15.9 Mi

16.6 Mi

0   ¼   ½   1 Mile

0 1000 2000 3000   5000 Feet

0   0.5   1 Kilometer

TN
MN
GN

UTM Grid and 2004 Magnetic North
Declination at Center of Sheet
GN to TN 0.507° (9 mills)
TN to MN 12.552° (223 mills)

S11B M 7.4-16.6

SECTION 11: 7.4–16.6 MILES

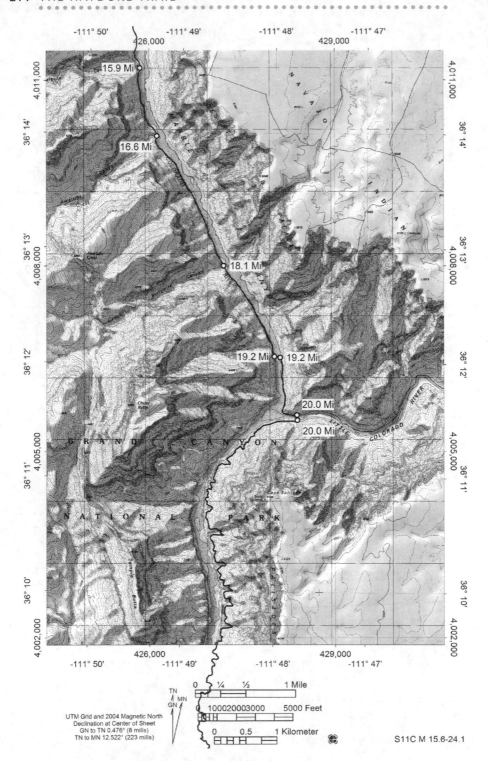

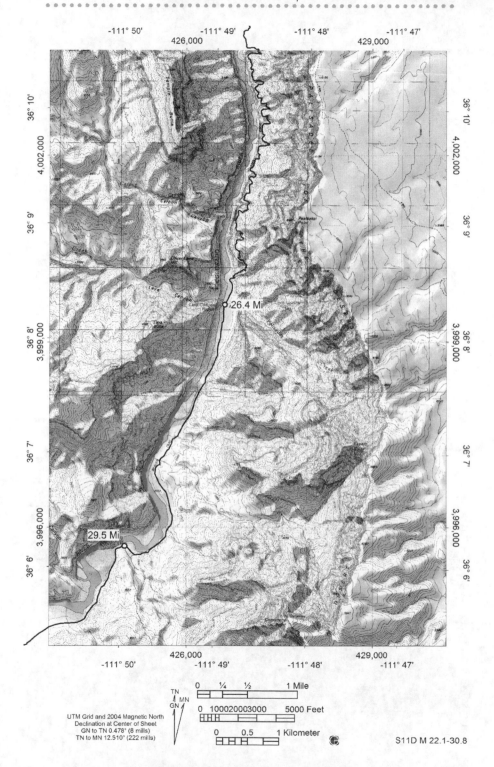

26.4 Mi

29.5 Mi

TN
MN
GN

UTM Grid and 2004 Magnetic North
Declination at Center of Sheet
GN to TN 0.478° (8 mills)
TN to MN 12.510° (222 mills)

0   ¼   ½   1 Mile

0   1000 2000 3000   5000 Feet

0   0.5   1 Kilometer

SECTION 11: 22.1–30.8 MILES

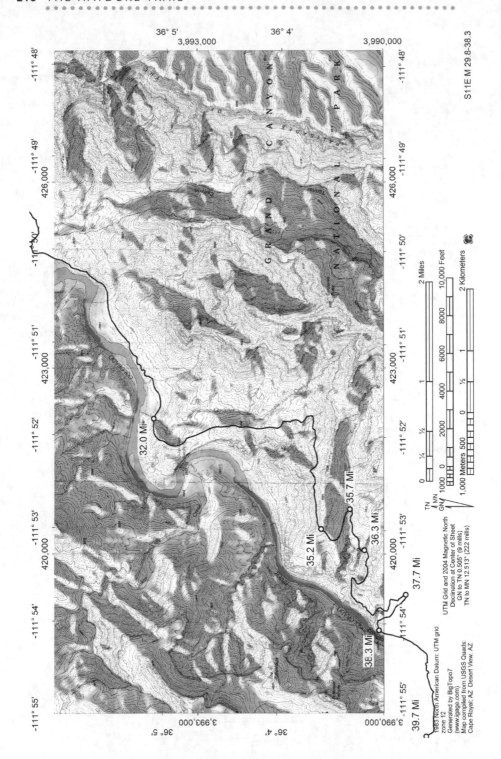

SECTION 11: 29.8–38.3 MILES

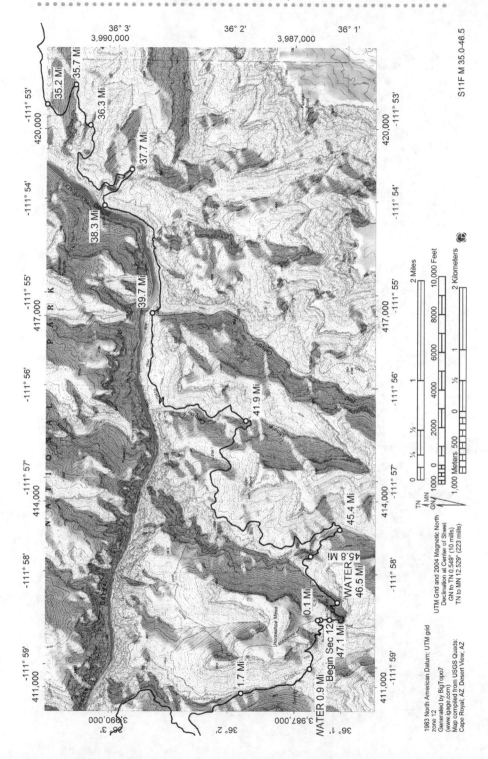

S11F M 35.0-46.5

2 Miles

10,000 Feet

2 Kilometers

1983 North American Datum: UTM grid
zone 12
Generated by BigTopo7
(www.igage.com)
Map compiled from USGS Quads:
Cape Royal, AZ Desert View, AZ

UTM Grid and 2004 Magnetic North
Declination at Center of Sheet
GN to TN 0.549° (10 mils)
TN to MN 12.529° (223 mils)

SECTION 11: 35.0–46.5 MILES

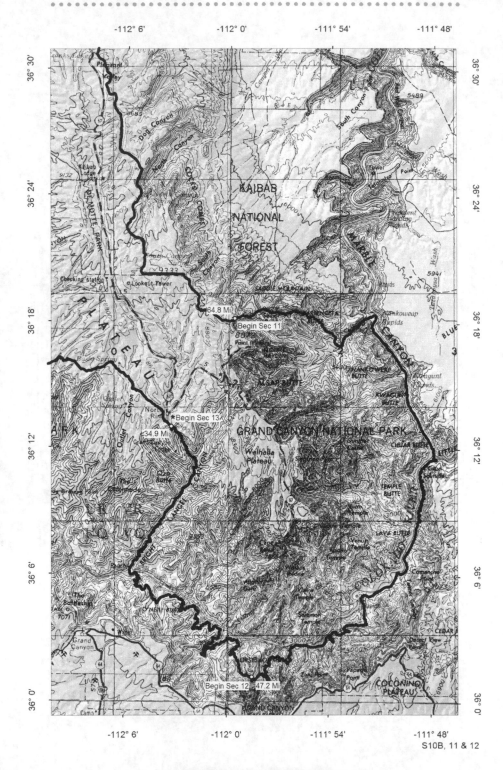

S10B, 11 & 12

SECTION 12: OVERVIEW

■ SECTION 12
Horseshoe Mesa to the North Rim, Grand Canyon National Park

● ●

APPROXIMATE TIME: 6 days

DISTANCE: 34.9 miles

EXERTION: moderate to difficult

NAVIGATION: easy

WATER: damp

DESOLATION FACTOR: backcountry

SPECIFIC HAZARDS: exposure, heat, rattlesnakes

PERMITS: Grand Canyon National Park requires permits for overnight backcountry use.

"The canyon experience has been one of the most intense and rewarding of my life. Never before have I felt so isolated, so totally on my own. Never before have I undertaken such a difficult task, with quite so many life-threatening hazards. There were times when the going was so tough, so slow, that we wondered if we were getting anywhere, if we'd make it through. Other times were flat-out dangerous. Climbing on slick or broken rock, falling was not an option. Fear became irrelevant. The bottom line: we had to go on.

"I found that fear is something your mind must create to try to prevent you from doing something foolish. But it's all in your head. For the first time in my life, I've learned how to use that fear, to channel it into intense concentration to deal with the task at hand. There were times when it all seemed almost overwhelming: the size of the canyon systems, the severity of the terrain and vegetation. But you make yourself continue on (as if there's a choice!). And all of a sudden, Bam! You're at the last pass, or you've finished that final ascent. Not only another day done, but another goal achieved."

APRIL 13, 2000 [DAY 33 OF 101], DEEP IN THE GRAND CANYON

**LOOKING INTO GRANITE GORGE,
GRAND CANYON NATIONAL PARK**

This is another killer section, with amazing scenery and the impact of the inner gorge of the Grand Canyon. The section starts by descending Horseshoe Mesa to the East Tonto Trail, which skirts around south-side drainages such as Grapevine and Cremation Creeks. There are places with exposure, but the route is always obvious and easy to follow. We found the worst part of this section to be the flies, particularly when we stopped moving. We had little difficulty locating water; but these are not perennial streams and will dry out as the heat of the summer wears on.

Don't count on being able to reach the river for water on the south side—it would require a highly technical descent and ascent. The East Tonto Trail will lead you to the South Kaibab Trail, which you will take to Bright Angel Creek and campground on the north side (there are a pair of footbridges crossing the river here). Cold beer is available at Phantom Ranch, and the hiker's stew dinner is highly recommended if you crave a hot cooked meal.

The North Kaibab Trail will lead you 14 miles and 6,000 feet up, out of the gorge (Cottonwood Campground is halfway up), and to the end of the section at the North Rim. There is plenty of water on the North Kaibab; enough to keep you and your clothes soaked (evaporative cooling!) for the sun-exposed ascent out of the gorge.

■ **Resupply/Trailhead at Horseshoe Mesa:** See previous description.

■ **Resupply/Trailhead at North Rim Village:** From Jacob Lake on Arizona Highway Alt. 89, drive south on Highway 67, also known as the Kaibab Plateau North Rim Parkway. In about 31 miles you will come to the Grand Canyon National Park boundary and entry station. Continue

AT THE TIPOFF, GRAND CANYON NATIONAL PARK

generally southeast down the road another 10 miles to a junction. Go straight through the junction and continue another mile to the North Kaibab Trailhead.

■ **Topos:** Cape Royal, AZ; Phantom Ranch, AZ; Bright Angel Point, AZ.

If you are continuing on from the last section, you will already be at the start of this one. If you are beginning your trip with this section, the mileage actually starts 2.3 miles down the Grandview Trail at the first trail junction on Horseshoe Mesa.

0.1 ■ Follow the Grandview Trail north for 0.1 miles to a trail junction.

0.9 ■ Take the trail on the left and follow it generally west-northwest for 0.8 miles off of Horseshoe Mesa and down to Cottonwood Creek on the Tonto Platform. *There should be a small flow of water in the creek.*

1.7 ■ Travel northwest, then north, for another 0.8 miles along this trail. This will bring you to the Tonto Trail.

6.6 ■ At the junction, go left and follow the Tonto Trail for 4.9 miles generally north out of Cottonwood Creek, west-northwest parallel to the Colorado River, and then southwest way back into the bed of Grapevine Creek.

12.0 ■ Follow the trail across Grapevine Creek and for 5.4 miles, generally northeast out of Grapevine, northwest parallel to (but 1,200 feet above) the Colorado River again, and then west-southwest to cross Boulder Creek.

14.9 ■ The trail continues on the Tonto Platform generally north, then west-southwest, for 2.9 miles to the bed of Lonetree Canyon.

17.7 ■ Now the trail leads you 2.8 miles around to the west side of Pattie Butte and the bed of Cremation Creek.

20.0 ■ Continue on the Tonto Trail for another 2.3 miles generally north-northwest out of Cremation Creek and then around to the west to the junction with the Kaibab Trail.

21.6 ■ Take the Kaibab Trail generally north for 1.6 miles, over the Tipoff and down the switchbacks to a trail junction about 200 feet above the river.

21.8 ■ Go right at the junction and you will reach a tunnel. Another 0.2 miles through the tunnel and northwest across the bridge brings you to the north (or right) side of the Colorado River.

22.1 ■ Follow the North Kaibab Trail generally southwest for 0.3 miles to the mouth of Bright Angel Creek. It's all uphill from here, 5,750 feet to the rim!

22.5 ■ Go north on the trail up Bright Angel Creek. In 0.4 miles you will be at the center of Phantom Ranch.

23.0 ■ Continue generally north-northeast for 0.5 miles on the trail up Bright Angel to a trail junction. Bright Angel Creek is a perennial stream and always has a little water in it. The problem is when it has a lot of water in it. *Don't think that just because there is a well-used park service trail running alongside the creek that it is not subject to the same dangers as every other deeply entrenched desert canyon!* **Bright Angel Creek floods regularly and has even taken out Phantom**

Ranch! *Make sure you get a weather forecast from the ranger outpost at the ranch before venturing on.*

23.6 ■ Go left at the junction and generally northeast, then north, up the North Kaibab Trail for 0.6 miles until you reach the mouth of Phantom Canyon.

28.1 ■ Stay on the North Kaibab Trail and follow it generally northeast up Bright Angel Creek. After 4.5 miles you will reach a trail junction. The trail on the left leads you west a short distance to Ribbon Falls.

29.2 ■ Continue up the trail, generally northeast, for 1.1 miles to Cottonwood Camp.

30.5 ■ Another 1.3 miles generally northeast up the trail will bring you to a junction at a footbridge just to the south of a heliport.

31.2 ■ Go left at the junction and head north for 0.7 miles to another trail junction. You will be leaving Bright Angel Creek here.

32.9 ■ Turn left at this junction and follow the North Kaibab Trail generally northwest for 1.7 miles up Roaring Springs Canyon to a footbridge.

33.6 ■ Go north across the bridge and continue generally north-northwest up the trail for 0.7 miles to the top of the switchbacks and a tunnel.

34.9 ■ Continue on through the tunnel and then another 1.3 miles generally northwest on the trail, up another series of switchbacks, and on to the North Kaibab Trailhead. This is the end of this section.

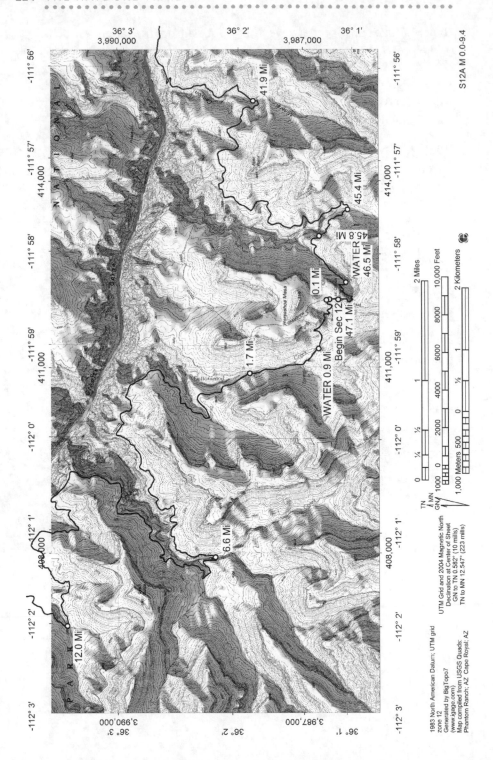

41.9 Mi

45.4 Mi

45.8 Mi

WATER 46.5 Mi

0.1 Mi

Begin Sec 12

47.1 Mi

1.7 Mi

WATER 0.9 Mi

6.6 Mi

12.0 Mi

1983 North American Datum; UTM grid
zone 12
Generated by BigTopo7
(www.igage.com)
Map compiled from USGS Quads:
Phantom Ranch, AZ; Cape Royal, AZ

UTM Grid and 2004 Magnetic North
Declination at Center of Sheet
GN to TN 0.582° (10 mils)
TN to MN 12.547° (223 mils)

TN
MN
GN

2 Miles

10,000 Feet

2 Kilometers

SECTION 12: 0.0–9.4 MILES

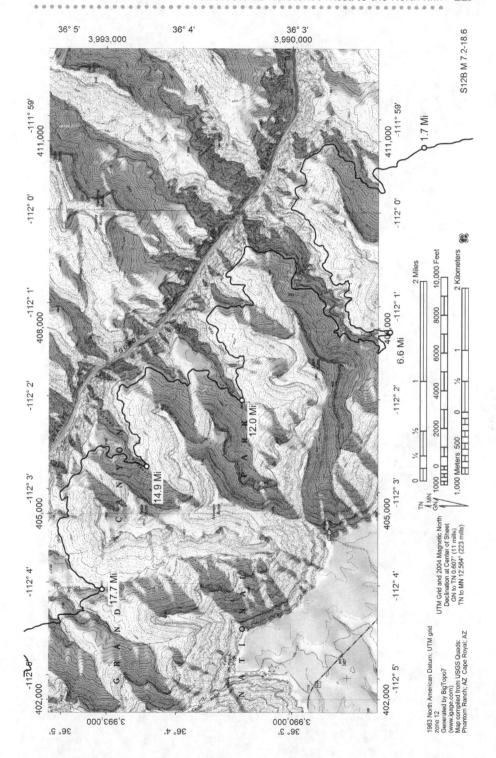

S12B M 7.2-18.6

1.7 Mi

6.6 Mi

12.0 Mi

14.9 Mi

17.7 Mi

2 Miles

10,000 Feet

2 Kilometers

1983 North American Datum; UTM grid
zone 12
Generated by BigTopo7
(www.igage.com)
Map compiled from USGS Quads:
Phantom Ranch, AZ Cape Royal, AZ

UTM Grid and 2004 Magnetic North
Declination at Center of Sheet
GN to TN 0.607° (11 mills)
TN to MN 12.564° (223 mills)

SECTION 12: 7.2–18.6 MILES

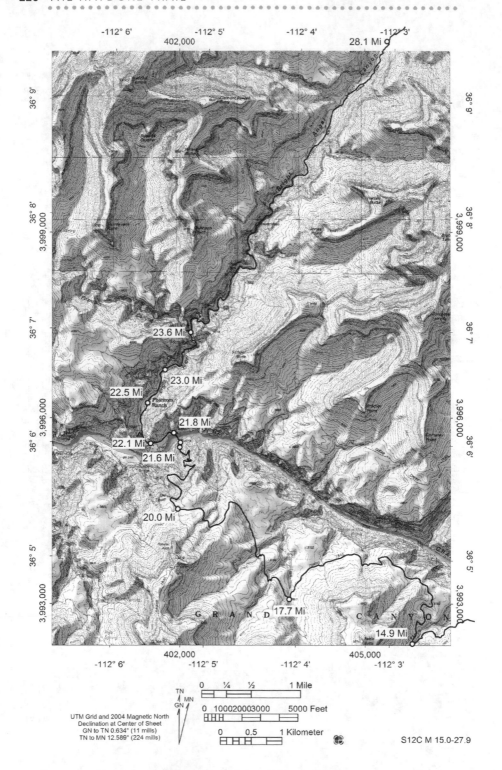

UTM Grid and 2004 Magnetic North
Declination at Center of Sheet
GN to TN 0.634° (11 mills)
TN to MN 12.589° (224 mills)

0   ¼   ½   1 Mile

0 1000 2000 3000   5000 Feet

0   0.5   1 Kilometer

S12C M 15.0-27.9

SECTION 12: 15.0–27.9 MILES

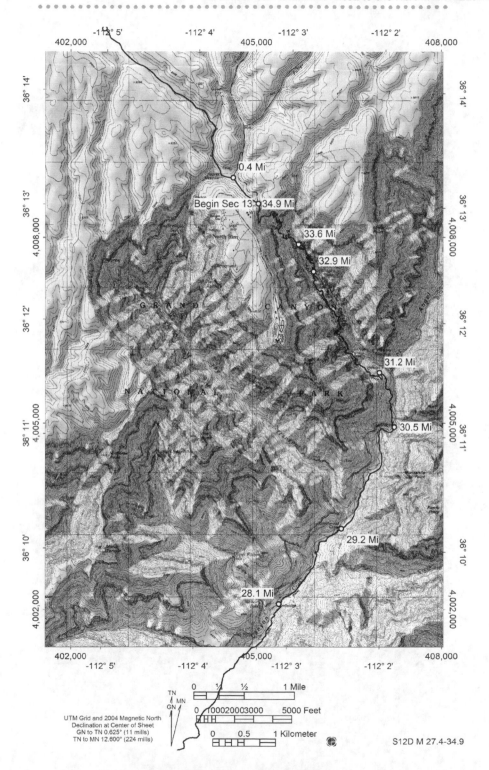

SECTION 12: 27.4–34.9 MILES

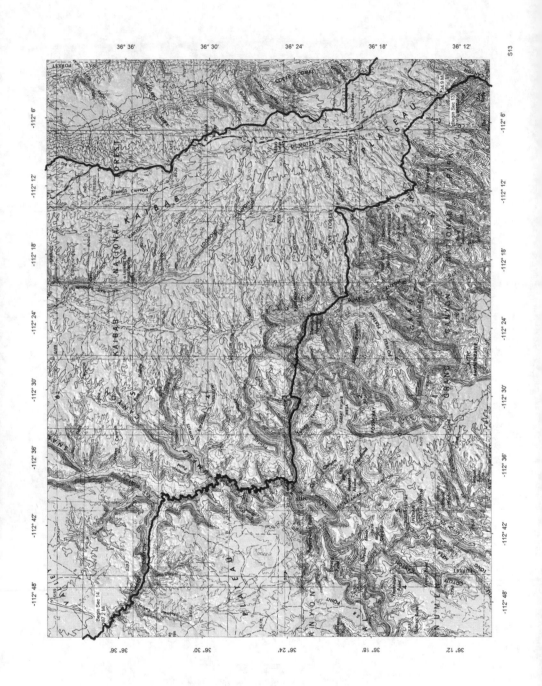

SECTION 13: OVERVIEW

North Rim, Grand Canyon National Park to Hack Canyon

• •

APPROXIMATE TIME: 12 days

DISTANCE: 87.2 miles

EXERTION: extreme

NAVIGATION: difficult

WATER: wet

DESOLATION FACTOR: out there!

SPECIFIC HAZARDS: exposure, swift-water crossing, flash floods

PERMITS: Grand Canyon National Park requires permits for overnight backcountry use.

"We camped at Surprise Valley. Our tents held up to the windy night pretty well. A group of people we saw said that it was full blizzard conditions up top. Glad to miss it!

"We're now in Saddle Canyon, coming about 6 miles to the confluence of Stina Canyon, which gives us a jump on tomorrow's climb to the Muav Saddle. Tapeats was killer, Thunder River bizarre. Thunder River, the world's shortest river, plunges from a leak in the huge Redwall cliff face, cascades through a talus field, now lined with trees until it meets with Tapeats. We had to cross and walk in Tapeats numerous times. I sure can understand why you don't want to try in high water; it's way too steep. The walk involved a lot of bouldering, climbing, and scratching through trees and shrubs. Why is everything here so sharp? The plants are all sharp, even the rocks are sharp.

"We only caught glimpses of the sun today; it figures, we had wet feet all day! I guess it was another rough one up top. . . ."

MARCH 31, 2000 [DAY 20 OF 101], AT THE BASE OF SADDLE CANYON

"We're in Teddy's Cabin, at the Muav Saddle. Our cache is intact. That's the good part. Getting here yesterday was tough. Probably the toughest 4 miles I've ever done. Call it Mitch and Mike's

Misery Part II: Saddle Canyon. [Part I was forcing our way out of the Barracks, a deep, narrow section of the East Fork of the Virgin River.] *Yesterday started off nice, but traveling got nasty fast: George Steck's slip and slide chutes. First we had to wade through a waist-deep pool, just to climb up a nasty pour-off, and then we got to another pool. It not only was neck deep but ice cold as well. Near hypothermic. We found a sliver of sun in the depths to warm us after our chilly swim. Then came the navigation hell; bushwhacking through the thorniest shit you could imagine, skin and clothes getting torn. Up a ridge, then down the other side. And again. And again. Every now and then we'd see a cairn to let us know that somebody else had once been there too. The 4 miles took us 9 hours to complete. We were starting to think that we'd be finishing in the dark. Oh, what a sight it was to finally see the cabin!"*

APRIL 2, 2000 [DAY 22 OF 101], MUAV SADDLE

TAPEATS CANYON, GRAND CANYON NATIONAL PARK

This section is both extremely difficult and extremely scenic. It is also the only section of the Hayduke Trail that should *only* be traveled in the direction described—climbing up Saddle Canyon instead of down is infinitely harder.

Leaving the North Rim Village, you'll head towards the Widfors Trailhead. The dirt fire road that leads to the trailhead from the main paved park road will bring you along the rim towards Point Sublime and then out to Swamp Point. Basin Spring, listed on most maps near the head of the Tiyo Point Trail, is dry (a check in early 2002 showed that it has been dry for at least a few years). From Swamp Point, you venture down the beginning of the North Bass Trail to the saddle 800 feet below, which is Muav Saddle. From the saddle, you descend Saddle Canyon, whose 4 miles are among the hardest of the Hayduke Trail. The way quickly leaves the ponderosa forest and becomes choked with thorn-covered vegetation, and at times is very steep. Repeated pour-offs force constant detours up and down the canyon's west wall. A pair of water-worn chutes towards the bottom will require you to slide down into chilly pools where you can expect that you and your pack will get wet. Once you pass these slip-and-slide chutes, reaching Tapeats Creek is pretty simple.

Following Tapeats Creek down to the Thunder River Trail is a constant boulder-hopping, in-and-out-of-the-water experience. **Do not attempt to travel down Tapeats Creek if the creek is in the midst of its springtime run-off!** The water level may be barely knee deep, but, with its steep descent, it can easily sweep you off your feet, possibly to your death. Thunder River is another of those places that defies adequate description: a huge hole in a cliff face simply erupts with an amazing amount of water, forming a massive waterfall. As you look at it, it's hard to believe all that water is seemingly just squeezing out of rock.

The Thunder River Trail is fairly steep as it leads up to Surprise Valley (the view back into Tapeats is pretty impressive from the top of the Thunder River Trail; it's also the last time on the Hayduke Trail that

THUNDER RIVER WITH TAPEATS CREEK ON RIGHT SIDE, GRAND CANYON NATIONAL PARK

MOUTH OF KANAB CREEK, GRAND
CANYON NATIONAL PARK

UPPER KANAB CREEK

you'll see the Grand Canyon from anywhere but deep in the gorge). You'll cross Surprise Valley until you join with the Deer Creek Falls Trail, which follows a tight, exposed ledge above the creek, which is now hidden in the bottom of a very narrow and very deep gorge. The Deer Creek Falls Trail brings you all the way down to the level of the Colorado River, where you'll begin a grueling seven-mile boulder-hopping ordeal to Kanab Creek.

Going up quite pretty Kanab Creek is moderately strenuous. Make sure you seek out Whispering Springs, located up the first major drainage on the right side, as you ascend Kanab Creek Canyon; it is amazing! There are a number of decent springs in the gorge. However, Hack Canyon, which leads off Kanab Creek, most likely will not have much water. Look for the faint petroglyph panel at the confluence. Hack Canyon takes you out of the Kanab Creek Wilderness, where you will pick up a dirt road that leads out of the canyon system, passing through a thick band of fossils on the way, and onto the Arizona Strip. This section ends when there ceases to be canyon walls and you are out on the Strip.

HACK CANYON CAMPSITE

■ **Resupply/Trailhead at North Rim Village:** See previous description.

■ **Resupply/Trailhead at Hack Canyon:** About 8.5 miles southwest of Fredonia on Arizona Highway 389, is the dirt road to Toroweap, marked #109. Turn onto this sometimes rough dirt road and follow it 23 miles to the junction with the Hack Canyon Road, #1123.

■ **Topos:** Bright Angel Point, AZ; Little Park Lake, AZ; Kanabownits Spring, AZ; King Arthur Castle, AZ; Powell Plateau, AZ; Tapeats Amphitheater, AZ; Fishtail Mesa, AZ; Kanab Point, AZ; Grama Spring, AZ; Robinson Canyon, AZ.

ROUTE DESCRIPTION AND MILEAGE

You would be wise to cache some water somewhere between the car park and Swamp Point. It is about 28 waterless miles across the plateau until you reach a questionable seep on the Muav Saddle. Although there are several springs shown on the maps, don't count on them always (or ever) flowing. All springs on the plateau should be considered questionable.

0.4 ■ Much of this area of the Kaibab Plateau was recently burned. Check with the Park Service and Forest Service offices to find out the current conditions. Large areas of this forest are periodically control burned and the roads through those areas are frequently closed. *Make sure you check ahead and have the appropriate permits!* From the car park at the North Kaibab Trailhead follow your compass north-west across the road and into a small drainage. Follow this drainage 0.4 miles to the Point Sublime Road in the meadow.

2.5 ▥ Follow this road west-northwest, then north-northwest, and then northwest for 2.1 miles to a road junction. You will be strolling through forest and meadow, gradually climbing up a shallow drainage.

3.2 ▥ Go straight, or northwest, through the junction and continue down the road for 0.7 miles into the bottom of a south-coursing drain-age. Keep your eyes open for deer, turkeys, and Kaibab squirrels as you cross the plateau.

4.3 ▥ Follow the road 1.1 miles, first north out of this drainage and then northwest to the road junction in Outlet Canyon.

7.8 ▥ Take the right fork and follow the road for 3.5 miles, first north-west, then west-southwest, and then northwest again until you cross Milk Creek.

8.9 ▥ The road turns west here. Follow it generally west-northwest for 1.1 miles across Crystal Ridge and down into Crystal Creek.

11.1 ▥ Follow the road generally southwest for 2.2 miles out of Crys-tal Creek to the brink of Crystal Creek Gorge.

11.7 ▥ Now the road swings north, then west, and in 0.6 miles you will reach a road junction in Walhalla Valley. The road to the left, or south, leads out to Point Sublime, one of the best views in the entire canyon system.

14.3 ▥ Go right, or north, on the dirt road and follow it generally north, then north-northwest, for 2.6 miles to a road junction in Kanabownits Canyon.

14.6 ▥ Take the left fork, generally southwest, for 0.3 miles to another road junction.

14.7 ▥ Take the right fork and follow the dirt road north for 0.1 miles to a junction. The right fork leads you to a lookout tower.

17.3 ▥ Follow the dirt road on the left generally north-northwest for 2.6 miles to the divide between Kanab Canyon and a drainage leading north into Big Spring Canyon.

18.4 ▥ Continue north on this dirt road for 1.1 miles to the bottom of Big Spring Canyon.

19.8 ▥ Stay on the dirt road and follow it generally north-northeast for 1.4 miles up Tipover Canyon.

20.3 ▥ The road switches back and climbs out of the canyon here. Follow it another 0.5 miles, generally northwest, to a junction on Swamp Ridge.

27.9 ▥ Take the left fork and follow this dirt road generally southwest, then west, for 7.6 miles down Swamp Ridge to its end at Swamp Point. Here you will find the trailhead for the North Bass Trail.

28.5 ▥ Take this winding trail generally west-southwest for 0.6 miles down to a trail junction on the Muav Saddle.

28.6 ▥ The North Bass Trail continues to the left while the trail to the southwest will take you up onto the Powell Plateau. *A short distance farther down the North Bass Trail is a small, hit-or-miss seep. If this seep is dry, your next chance for water is not too far away in Saddle Canyon.* Hidden in the trees, 0.1 miles to the northwest, is Teddy's Cabin, a backcountry ranger cabin named in honor of Theodore Roosevelt. A trail will lead you right to it.

30.2 ▥ From the cabin, go northwest down into Saddle Canyon. Then head north-northwest, then northwest, down the canyon. After 1.6 miles of serious bushwhacking (don't forget your long pants), you will come to a point where you will need to climb out of the bottom of the canyon in order to bypass a pour-off. *You may miss the faint trail leading up the side of the canyon, but if you miss it, don't worry too much. When you get to the top of a pretty large pour-off just turn around and go back up the canyon until you find the route up.*

31.0 ▧ You will want to go generally west-northwest as you climb up to the long finger of land 200 feet above. Once you gain the crest, follow the northwest spit of land for 0.8 miles back down to the bottom of Saddle Canyon.

32.6 ▧ Now continue generally north-northwest down Saddle Canyon. In 1.6 miles you will come to the junction with Stina Canyon, but not before you must negotiate a couple of slippery sandstone chutes that pour off into plunge pools. *Make sure you have waterproofed your gear before you jump in, as you're going to want something dry to change into when you get out. The sun doesn't spend too much time down in the bottom of this part of the canyon, so the water is probably going to be ice cold.*

33.1 ▧ Another 0.5 miles north-northwest down Saddle Canyon will bring you to the junction with Crazy Jug Canyon and the beginning of Tapeats Creek.

37.4 ▧ Now go generally west, northwest, then west again for 4.3 miles down Tapeats Creek to the junction with Thunder River. It may be best to hike right down the creek itself, but only if the water isn't too high. Judge it for yourself. If the water is up, you will have to cross the stream repeatedly or use the faint high-water routes on either side of the creek in the talus. *If the water is too high, you will be unable to safely cross to the north side of Tapeats Creek in order to access the trail on the west side of Thunder River. Make sure you time this right or you may find yourself turning around and climbing back up the slimy chutes.*

38.3 ▧ Follow the trail generally west-northwest for 0.9 miles, 1,400 feet up through the talus, past Thunder Spring and onto the saddle at the eastern end of Surprise Valley.

39.5 ▧ Continue west-northwest on the trail for 1.2 miles across Surprise Valley to the second trail junction. Either of these trails coming in from the north will take you to the trail leading up to the North Rim at Indian Hollow.

40.9 ▧ Stay on the trail and follow it another 1.4 miles west-northwest, over the saddle on the western end of Surprise Valley, into the Deer

Creek drainage and down to Deer Spring. *This is a great little spring. Besides being reliable, it is also lush and shady—a perfect spot for a siesta!*

41.1 ▦ From the spring, follow the trail generally west-southwest for 0.2 miles to the bottom of Deer Creek Canyon. Deer Creek is normally flowing at this point.

41.5 ▦ Now follow this trail generally south for 0.4 miles, alongside the creek, to the Deer Creek Campground.

42.1 ▦ Stay on the west side of the creek and follow the trail 0.6 miles south-southwest to the Colorado River. You will be following a skinny ledge halfway up the wall of an amazing little narrows and then down a series of switchbacks to the river. You will land at the base of Deer Creek Falls, one of the prettiest waterfalls in the Grand Canyon.

42.8 ▦ Now start heading downriver. Pick your way through the boulders for 0.7 miles, west-northwest along the river, until you come to the place where the Tapeats Sandstone cliffs pop up through the talus and start to get closer to the river.

44.3 ▦ Start looking for a game trail that leads you generally northwest up through the talus to the top of the cliffs. Follow the trail generally west-northwest, traversing the talus field atop the cliffs. In 1.5 miles you will come to the edge of the side canyon east of Fishtail Canyon.

44.4 ▦ The trail turns southwest here and takes you another 0.1 miles back down to the river.

45.0 ▦ Resume boulder hopping downriver, or west. *This is one of the most tedious boulder fields you may ever encounter. Take your time and make sure of every step. There are plenty of opportunities to twist an ankle, break a leg, never be heard from again, etc.* After 0.6 miles you will reach the mouth of Fishtail Canyon.

49.4 ▦ Continue the boulder hop downriver for 4.4 miles to the mouth of Kanab Creek. *There is an exceptional established campsite on the east side of the creek.* You will be going generally west-southwest as the canyon winds along through this stretch.

57.9 ▒ Now leave the river and start heading up Kanab Creek. You will be going generally north and will have to cross the creek many times. Plan on getting your feet wet. Kanab Creek Canyon is an exceptionally beautiful place, but don't linger here too long. **The flash-flood potential on Kanab Creek is outstanding!** Unlike most tributary canyons in the Grand Canyon that originate not far beyond the rim, Kanab Creek originates a long way off, in the high country of southern Utah, and has many large tributaries itself. *Be aware that a storm as far away as Bryce Canyon National Park could send an unchecked flood racing around the next corner.* In 8.5 miles you will come to Showerbath Spring.

62.6 ▒ Continue winding your way generally north-northeast up Kanab Creek. In 4.7 miles you will come to the national park boundary at the mouth of Jumpup Canyon.

71.5 ▒ Another 8.9 miles generally north up Kanab Creek will bring you to the mouth of Hack Canyon. *Depending on the flow, Kanab Creek will probably come and go as you work your way upstream. Take enough water from the creek to see you to the end of this section (and hopefully your resupply, cache, jug of water you remembered to leave in the car), as Willow Spring may not be too reliable.*

77.1 ▒ There is a pretty decent trail coming down Hack Canyon. Get on the trail and follow it generally west-northwest, then west, up Hack Canyon for 5.6 miles to Willow Spring.

81.4 ▒ The trail becomes dirt road #1123 here. Follow the road generally west, then northwest, up Hack Canyon. In 4.3 miles you will reach the Hack Canyon Mine.

87.2 ▒ Another 5.8 miles generally northwest up the road will bring you to the head of Hack Canyon and the junction with #109 road. This is the end of this section.

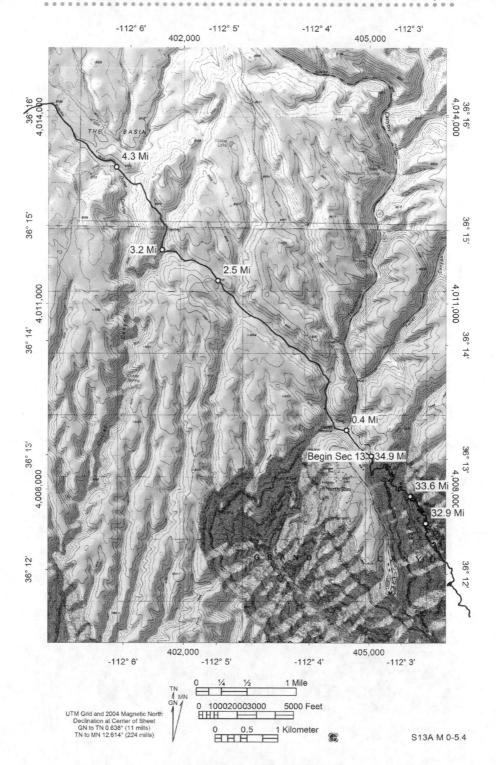

TN
MN
GN

UTM Grid and 2004 Magnetic North
Declination at Center of Sheet
GN to TN 0.638° (11 mils)
TN to MN 12.614° (224 mils)

0   ¼   ½   1 Mile

0   1000 2000 3000   5000 Feet

0   0.5   1 Kilometer

S13A M 0–5.4

SECTION 13: 0.0–5.4 MILES

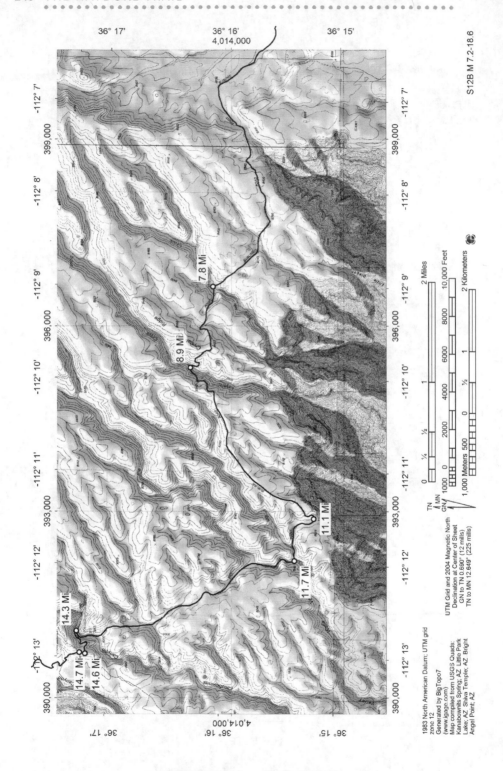

36° 17'

36° 16'
4,014,000

36° 15'

S12B M 7.2-18.6

-112° 7'

-112° 7'

399,000

399,000

-112° 8'

-112° 8'

7.8 Mi

-112° 9'

-112° 9'

396,000

Ridge

8.9 Mi

396,000

-112° 10'

-112° 10'

-112° 11'

-112° 11'

393,000

393,000

11.1 Mi

-112° 12'

-112° 12'

11.7 Mi

14.3 Mi

-112° 13'

-112° 13'

390,000

14.7 Mi
14.6 Mi

390,000

36° 17'

36° 16'
4,014,000

36° 15'

1983 North American Datum; UTM grid
zone 12
Generated by BigTopo7
(www.igage.com)
Map compiled from USGS Quads:
Kanabownits Spring, AZ, Little Park
Lake, AZ, Shiva Temple, AZ, Bright
Angel Point, AZ

UTM Grid and 2004 Magnetic North
Declination at Center of Sheet
GN to TN 0.690° (12 mils)
TN to MN 12.649° (225 mils)

TN
MN
GN

2 Miles
10,000 Feet
1000   0   2000   4000   6000   8000
1,000 Meters   500   0   1   2
2 Kilometers
¼   ½   ¾   1
0   ½   1

SECTION 13: 4.6–15 MILES

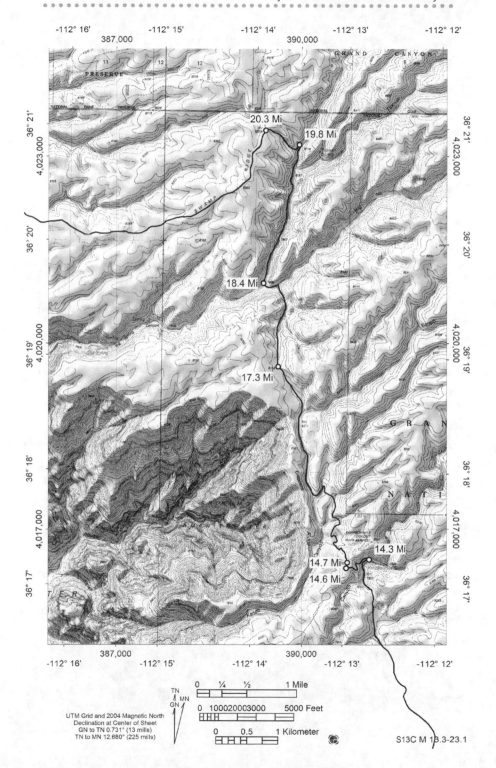

SECTION 13: 13.3–23.1 MILES

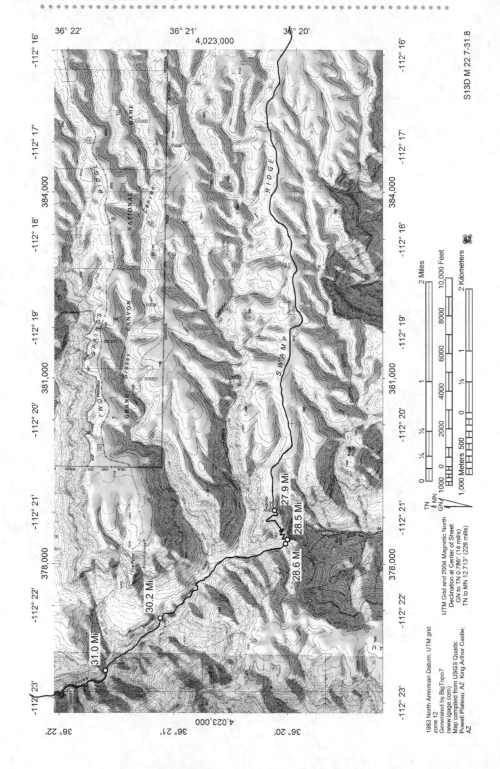

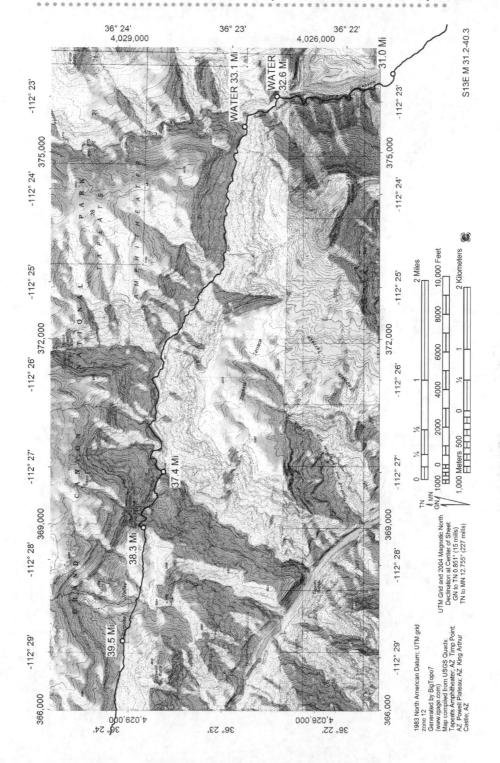

36° 24'
4,029,000

36° 23'

36° 22'
4,026,000

31.0 Mi

S13E M 31.2-40.3

WATER 33.1 Mi

WATER 32.6 Mi

-112° 23'

375,000

-112° 24'

-112° 25'

372,000

-112° 26'

-112° 27'

369,000

37.4 Mi

-112° 28'

38.3 Mi

-112° 29'

39.5 Mi

366,000

4,029,000

4,026,000

36° 24'

36° 23'

36° 22'

TN
MN
GN

UTM Grid and 2004 Magnetic North
Declination at Center of Sheet
GN to TN 0.851° (15 mills)
TN to MN 12.755° (227 mills)

2 Miles

10,000 Feet

2 Kilometers

1,000 Meters 500

1983 North American Datum; UTM grid
zone 12
Generated by BigTopo7
(www.sjgage.com)
Map compiled from USGS Quads:
Tapeats Amphitheater, AZ Timp Point;
AZ Powell Plateau, AZ King Arthur
Castle, AZ

SECTION 13: 31.2–40.3 MILES

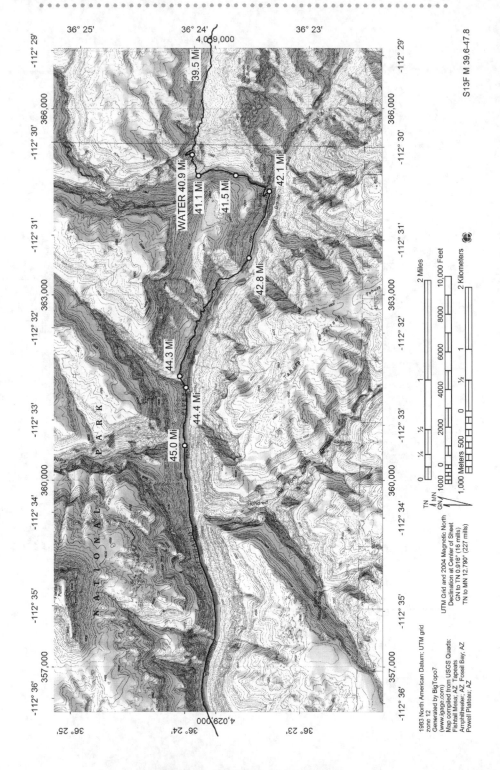

WATER 40.9 Mi

39.5 Mi

40.9 Mi

41.1 Mi

41.5 Mi

42.1 Mi

42.8 Mi

44.3 Mi

44.4 Mi

45.0 Mi

PARK

NATIONAL

1983 North American Datum; UTM grid
zone 12
Generated by BigTopo7
(www.igage.com)
Map compiled from USGS Quads:
Fishtail Mesa, AZ Tapeats
Amphitheater, AZ Fossil Bay, AZ
Powell Plateau, AZ

UTM Grid and 2004 Magnetic North
Declination at Center of Sheet
GN to TN 0.916° (16 mills)
TN to MN 12.790° (227 mills)

S13F M 39.6-47.8

SECTION 13: 39.6–47.8 MILES

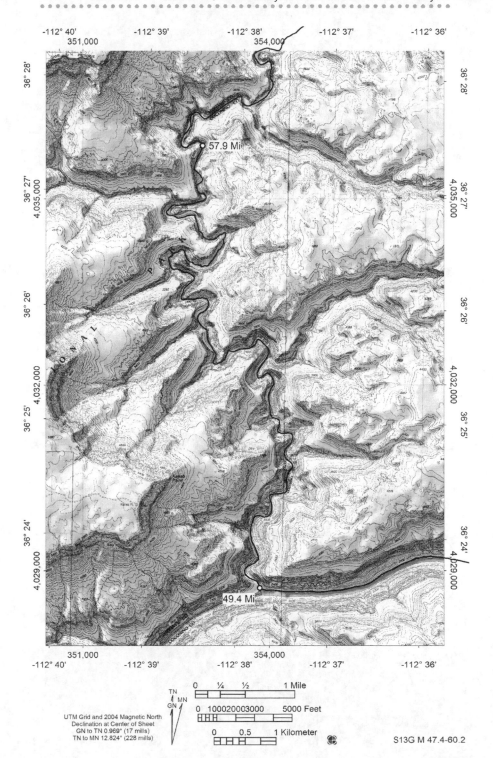

-112° 40'
351,000

-112° 39'

-112° 38'
354,000

-112° 37'

-112° 36'

36° 28'

36° 27'
4,035,000

36° 26'

4,032,000
36° 25'

36° 24'
4,029,000

57.9 Mi

49.4 Mi

TN
MN
GN

UTM Grid and 2004 Magnetic North
Declination at Center of Sheet
GN to TN 0.969° (17 mils)
TN to MN 12.824° (228 mils)

0   ¼   ½   1 Mile

0 1000 2000 3000   5000 Feet

0   0.5   1 Kilometer

S13G M 47.4-60.2

SECTION 13: 47.4–60.2 MILES

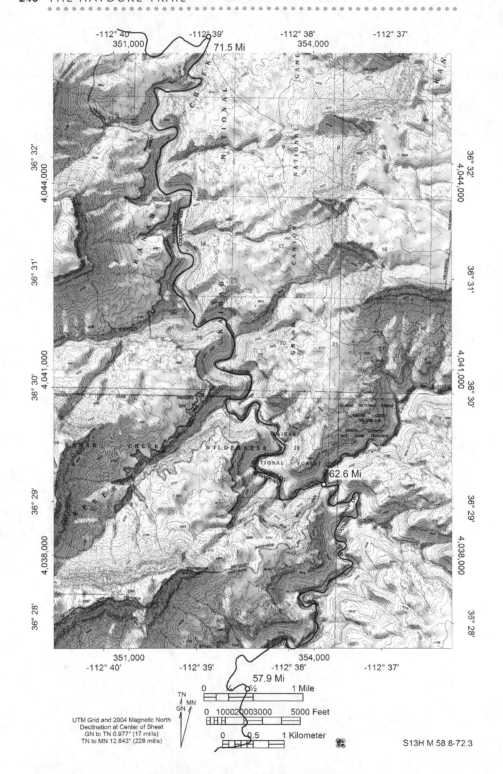

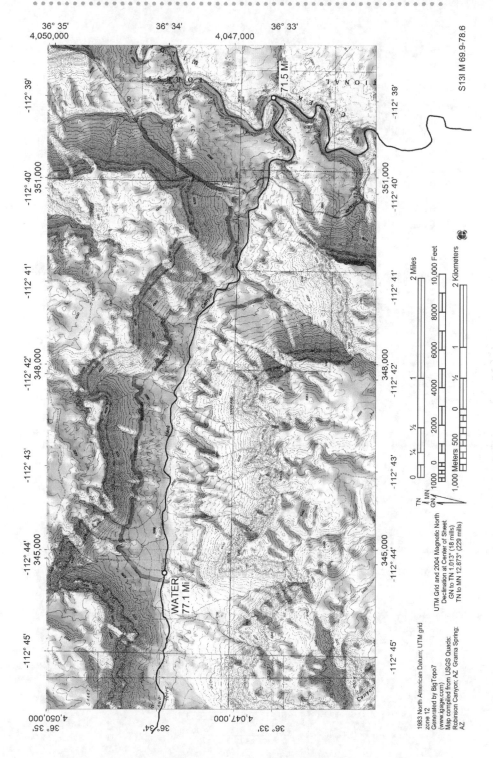

36° 35'
4,050,000

36° 34'

36° 33'

4,047,000

S13I M 69.9-78.6

-112° 39'

-112° 40'
351,000

-112° 41'

-112° 42'
348,000

-112° 43'

-112° 44'
345,000

-112° 45'

71.5 Mi

WATER
77.1 Mi

-112° 39'

351,000
-112° 40'

-112° 41'

348,000
-112° 42'

-112° 43'

345,000
-112° 44'

-112° 45'

2 Miles

10,000 Feet

2 Kilometers

8000

6000

1

4000

½

2000

0

¼

1,000 Meters 500

1000   0

TN
MN
GN

UTM Grid and 2004 Magnetic North
Declination at Center of Sheet
GN to TN 1.013° (18 mills)
TN to MN 12.873° (229 mills)

1983 North American Datum; UTM grid
zone 12
Generated by BigTopo7
(www.igage.com)
Map compiled from USGS Quads:
Robinson Canyon; AZ Grama Spring;
AZ

4,050,000
36° 35'

4,047,000

36° 34'

36° 33'

SECTION 13: 69.9–78.6 MILES

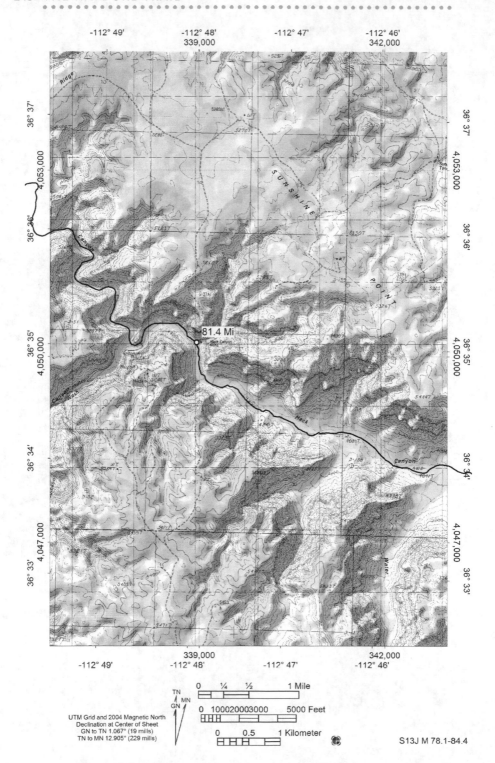

81.4 Mi

SECTION 13: 78.1–84.4 MILES

S13J M 78.1-84.4

UTM Grid and 2004 Magnetic North
Declination at Center of Sheet
GN to TN 1.067° (19 mils)
TN to MN 12.905° (229 mils)

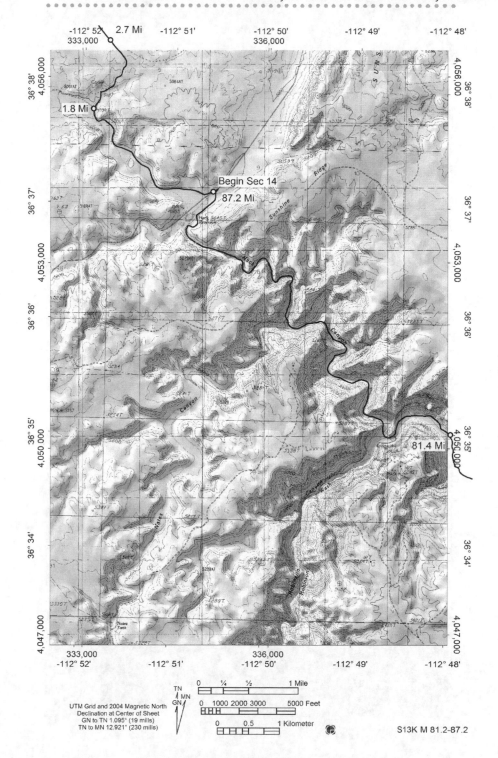

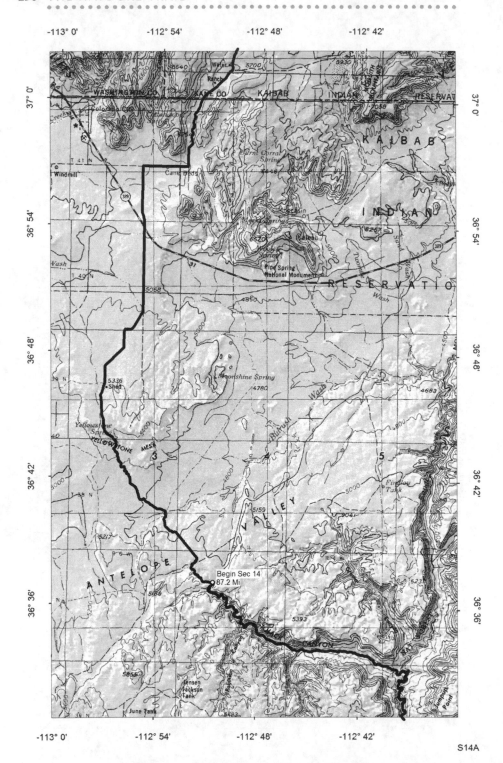

S14A

SECTION 14: OVERVIEW (continued on page 252)

Hack Canyon to the Weeping Wall, Zion National Park

• •

APPROXIMATE TIME: 9 days

DISTANCE: 69.9 miles

EXERTION: difficult

NAVIGATION: moderate to difficult

WATER: begins dry, ends moist

DESOLATION FACTOR: backcountry/out there

SPECIFIC HAZARDS: exposure, flash floods

PERMITS: Zion National Park requires permits for overnight backcountry use.

"What a wild pair of days. First, yesterday: we hiked a pack trail (complete with motorcycle tracks) through an amazing set of canyons, all in a wilderness study area. Red rock with domes, layers, stripes, and huge walls. Incredible! And that was just one of the formations. We wound up and down until we parted with all possibilities of motorized travel, where we descended into Squirrel Canyon, a cool, narrow place with crystal-clear water that we indulged ourselves with. Then it was into Short Creek, then Water Canyon, where we stopped for the night. These canyons were all so beautiful! We even saw cougar tracks that obviously showed pursuit of a deer, whose widely spaced tracks showed its efforts at fleeing. We never did find the outcome of that chase.

"Once again, we walked until dark, pushing our bodies to the brink. We ended up camping just outside the town of Hildale, a polygamist town, which we expected to be a strange little place. We weren't disappointed. We had to walk into town to go to the grocery store to get 2-liter bottles for water [these are still the strongest, most durable water containers that we know of]. This is what we found: occupied houses under perpetual construction (virtually all of them), silent children in nineteenth century garb, curious stares from unhappy eyes. We saw few adult men but

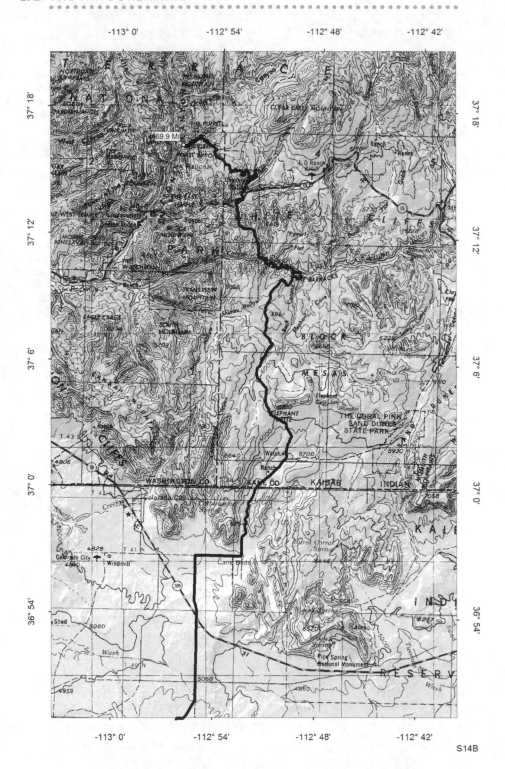

S14B

SECTION 14: OVERVIEW (continued from page 250)

many women in "Little House on the Prairie" dresses. We didn't see a single adolescent. Even the grocery store was like a time warp: nothing extravagant at all; we couldn't even get pop-tarts for treats! We purchased ten 2-liter bottles of soda and promptly poured them out in the parking lot and refilled them with water. By now we were feeling pretty weirded out by this place; we couldn't leave fast enough, it had such a strange vibe to it."

MARCH 6, 2000 [DAY 6 OF 101], UTAH/ARIZONA BORDER ON THE
ARIZONA STRIP

[Note: the trail does not go through Hildale. We were detoured there by the failure of some of our water containers.]

"Another cold, crispy night, this time surrounded on each end by extraordinary color. The sunset was the longest lasting, and one of the most colorful I have ever seen. It lasted at least two hours, until there was just a sliver of color on the horizon, in a sky otherwise dominated by the bright moon. The few clouds in the sky really did their part to add to the display. Every imaginable color was represented, even green. All this in such a vast panorama: the Strip, the Vermilion Cliffs, the Pine Valley Mountains, Mount Trumbull. It was a good thing that the show lasted as long as it did; it took that long to take it all in.

"A chorus of coyote calls, and a visit from some cows preceded the sunrise. Mitch spotted a band of antelope soon after, in the distance."

MARCH 19, 2000 [DAY 8 OF 101], ON THE ARIZONA STRIP

This section covers a large amount of vertical change, climbing up into the Vermilion Cliffs, then down into a river gorge, back up a few thousand feet, and finally descending to the bottom of Zion Canyon.

Leaving Hack Canyon, you will follow dirt roads all the way across the wide-open Arizona Strip. There is no consistent water source on the Strip, so plan accordingly. You may find evidence of earlier civilizations, fossils, and petrified wood out here; there are also quite a few critters running around. The big views out on the Strip may have a strange feel after traveling in the deep canyons of the Grand Canyon.

THE LONG ROAD ACROSS THE ARIZONA STRIP

GOING INTO THE VERMILION CLIFFS

You'll cross Arizona Highway 389 before continuing on BLM roads up into the Vermilion Cliffs and the area of the Block Mesas and Elephant Butte. Finally leaving the roads behind, a game trail along the shoulder of Rock Canyon leads down into the East Fork of the Virgin River, alternately known as Parunuweap Canyon and the Barracks. Water in the river could pose a difficulty, but only if there have been recent storms or snow melt. Plan on walking in the river bottom. An incredibly steep trail known as "Fat Man's Misery" will take you to the "top," scrambling through steep ravines and over repeated ridges and ledges. On our spring 2000 trek, we were hiking *up* the river but were shut down by too much water coming over a series of pour-offs. We had to find a way to climb out of the gorge early, finding a nearly impossible route to the top that we refer to now as "Mitch and Mike's Misery."

"FAT MAN'S MISERY" ROUTE GOES
UP THIS DRAINAGE

Once on top, you'll quickly enter the last park of the trail; originally established as Mukuntuweap National Monument in 1909, it was designated Zion National Park in 1929. You will work your way around Checkerboard Mesa and across Utah Highway 9 to a trail that skirts Clear Creek and brings you into Jolley Gulch and up by Cable Mountain. When we passed through here on our second trek, we were not too pleased to find a deeper than expected snowpack, with a nasty crust, up in these higher reaches of Zion National Park. We were finally forced to resort to making snowshoes from the limbs of a couple of unlucky juniper trees to negotiate the few miles of snowcovered terrain. This trail will bring you by Stave Spring and onto the Echo Canyon Trail, which leads down by Hidden Canyon to the Weeping

Wall in Zion Canyon and the end of both the section and the Hayduke Trail. Some people might be inclined, as we were on our first trek, to hike out to the entrance of the park. We don't recommend this, as there is no adequate walkway along the narrow road, which is essentially the only route out of the canyon.

Speaking from experience, no matter where you end your trek, if you've just hiked here from Arches National Park, you

HOMEMADE SNOWSHOES

will have an amazing sense of accomplishment, and a deep sense of satisfaction at experiencing travel through some of the most wild and beautiful lands anywhere. Congratulations!

■ **Resupply/Trailhead at Hack Canyon:** See previous description.

■ **Trailhead at Zion National Park:** The Echo Canyon Trail at the Weeping Wall in Zion Canyon, Zion National Park, Utah.

■ **Topos:** Robinson Canyon, AZ; Sunshine Ridge, AZ; Wild Band Pockets, AZ; Maroney Well, AZ; Colorado City, AZ; Moccasin, AZ; Elephant Butte, UT, AZ; The Barracks, UT; Springdale East, UT; Clear Creek Mountain, UT; Temple of Sinawava, UT.

ROUTE DESCRIPTION AND MILEAGE

If you aren't out to hike the entire Hayduke Trail, you may want to consider starting this section on the far (or north) side of the Arizona Strip. The Strip is a vast, brush-studded, sandy plain that extends from the Virgin Mountains on the west to the Kaibab Plateau on the east, and north from the Grand Canyon to the Vermilion Cliffs. Although the Arizona Strip is beautiful and interesting in its own way, and crossing it on foot is actually a really cool way to see what it has to offer, it may take you several days to do so, following dirt roads the entire way.

If you are through-hiking the Hayduke Trail, you will find that crossing the Strip by way of the "dirt road as existing trail" theory is by far the best way to go about it. If you have any doubt, just hike alongside the road for a while through the thorny brush, cow pies and blow sand with your freshly loaded pack on. You will soon be a believer, too.

It is dry out there on the Strip! Make sure you plan your water supply carefully. If you can't verify the flow of Yellowstone Spring before you head out, you better cache some water for yourself before you start.

1.8 ■ Head generally northwest up the #1014 road for 1.8 miles to a junction.

2.7 ■ Turn right at the junction and follow this dirt road generally northeast, then northwest, for 0.9 miles to another junction.

5.3 ■ Continue straight, or northwest, through the junction and follow the dirt road another 2.6 miles, generally north, to a second junction.

5.9 ■ Go right, or north, at this junction and go another 0.6 miles to the second junction in Bullrush Wash.

8.6 ■ Turn left onto this dirt road and follow it generally northwest for 2.7 miles, past some check dams (probably dry), until you are right beside Yellowstone Wash.

9.1 ■ Leave the road here and follow Yellowstone Wash generally north. In 0.5 miles you will come to a fork.

10.8 ■ Take the left fork and continue up the wash, generally north-northwest, for 1.7 miles to another fork.

11.1 ■ Go left again and follow this wash 0.3 miles generally north-west to a dirt road.

11.5 ■ Turn right onto the dirt road and follow it northeast, then north, for 0.4 miles to a junction just beyond a stock tank. *You should be able to find water at one of the many springs in this area, but be mindful that the land on either side of the road here is private property. Please respect the rights of landowners and don't linger or camp in this area.*

12.1 ■ **It could be a very long, hot 38 miles before you find water again in the East Fork of the Virgin River!** After you have taken as much water as you can carry, unless you have wisely cached water out there, continue going northwest up the road. In 0.6 miles you will come to a junction on top of this arm of Yellowstone Mesa.

13.0 ■ Go straight through this junction and follow the dirt road, first northwest, then north, for 0.9 miles to another junction beside a corral.

14.0 ■ Continue on this dirt road north-northwest, then north. After 1 mile you will reach another junction near a check dam.

15.1 ■ The road continues north, then north-northeast. Follow it another 1.1 miles to the junction at the Esplins Corral. *This is obviously private property. It's a really interesting-looking place, but only check it out from the road.*

16.1 ■ Follow the road north for 1 mile to a junction.

17.5 ■ Take the northeast road and follow it northeast for 1.4 miles to another junction.

18.5 ■ Go straight through the junction, then follow the dirt road north for 1 mile to the next junction.

18.8 ■ Turn right and follow this dirt road east for 0.3 miles to another junction.

20.0 ■ Take the left fork and follow the road north-northeast for 1.2 miles to the second junction.

24.6 ■ Now go north on this dirt road #239. You will pass Maroney Well and several road junctions, and in 4.6 miles you will intersect Highway 389.

28.0 ■ Cross the highway and continue north on road #239. After 3.4 miles you will come to the junction with road #237.

30.4 ■ Turn right onto road #237 and follow it east for 2.4 miles. Here the dirt road swings north. *The land on either side of the road is private property. Don't plan on camping anywhere between Highway 389 and the Utah border.*

34.5 ■ Follow the road north, then generally north-northeast, up Rosy Canyon. In 4.1 miles you will cross the Arizona/Utah border.

35.6 ■ The road is paved here. Follow it 1.1 miles northeast to a dirt road coming in from the north-northeast.

37.2 ■ Take this dirt road and follow it generally northeast, then north, for 1.6 miles to the junction at Pine Spring.

41.5 ■ Continue on the dirt road generally north-northeast, northwest, then north for 4.3 miles to the junction at Kane Spring.

42.7 ■ Go left at the junction and follow the dirt road northwest, then north. In 1.2 miles you will pass the unreliable Wyatt Spring.

45.2 ■ Continue on the dirt road generally north-northeast, then north-northwest, for 2.5 miles to a junction.

49.8 ▇ Take the right fork and follow this dirt road generally north, then northeast, for 4.6 miles.

50.4 ▇ The road that the most recent maps show has been closed off somewhere around here. Continue following the better road southwest, then west, to the edge of Rock Canyon and then around to the north. The road ends on the edge of the last drop to the East Fork of the Virgin River after 0.6 miles. If you have a high-clearance 4WD vehicle and are just looking for a killer 20-mile route through some of the best of the Zion backcountry, then this would be a great place to start.

50.5 ▇ Facing north from the end of the road, you will have Rock Canyon to your southeast and the river right below you to the north. There is a simple route, once you find it, down to the river in the draw to the northwest. *You definitely want to use this smaller draw; don't be tempted by the larger one to the west.* Find your way down the draw 0.1 miles to the bank of the river.

53.1 ▇ **The East Fork of the Virgin River is another one of those canyon waterways that can send down a ripping flash flood with no warning! Use extreme caution when traveling through this deep gorge and don't even think about camping down there!** Follow the river downstream, generally west-northwest. You will find yourself crossing the river repeatedly and eventually wading right down the middle of it. In 2.6 miles you will pass the mouth of Poverty Wash.

54.2 ▇ Continue generally west-northwest down the river. After another 1.1 miles you will come to a cataract in the canyon. The river here is blocked up by a rock fall and is funneled through a narrow opening. *It is usually too turbulent and deep to safely wade or swim through.* To your right, if you are facing downstream, is a giant boulder. Step up on top of it and you will see a large eddy on the far side of the boulder. This calmer water is a much safer place to wade or swim past the rock fall. If the water is low enough, you may actually find a way to keep your feet dry through here.

54.9 ▇ Keep following the East Fork of the Virgin generally west-northwest for 0.7 miles. You will come to a side canyon on the right that ends in a little waterfall.

55.6 ■ To the west is a crack in the canyon wall. Now scramble up through the crack to the top of the wall. *This route in and out of the river gorge is aptly known as "Fat Man's Misery."* Head north along the spine of the ridge separating the drainages to the east and west. In 0.7 miles from the river you will come to a knoll on the ridge.

56.3 ■ Here you will be crossing into Zion National Park. **Make sure you have your permit with you when you cross into the park!** Contour north, then north-northwest, past this knoll for 0.7 miles until you regain the ridge.

56.5 ■ Go north along this ridge another 0.2 miles.

56.9 ■ Leave the ridge here and go 0.4 miles, northwest across the wash below, then generally west across a small ridge to the bottom of the next wash.

57.4 ■ Continue another 0.5 miles, first west out of the wash to the southern end of Checkerboard Mesa, and then northwest along its base to the bottom of the draw that runs along its western side.

57.7 ■ Head for 0.3 miles up the draw to the saddle.

58.7 ■ At the saddle you should find a trail. This trail will probably have more cougar tracks than boot prints but is easy enough to follow. Take this trail 1 mile north down the bottom of the drainage to Utah Highway 9.

59.5 ■ Cross the highway and go down into the bottom of Clear Creek. Go up Clear Creek generally east-northeast. You will be roughly paralleling the highway, and in 0.8 miles you will come to the junction with Co-op Creek.

60.3 ■ Continue up Clear Creek another 0.8 miles, generally northwest, then north-northeast, until you can intersect a dirt road.

62.7 ■ The road turns to a pack trail as you continue generally northeast up Clear Creek, then north up Cave Canyon. Follow the trail as it contours back out of Cave Canyon and around into the bottom of Jolley Gulch. It is 2.4 miles to Jolley Gulch.

65.6 ▨ Stay on the trail and follow it 2.9 miles, first south out of Jolley Gulch and then generally northwest across the top of the plateau to Stave Spring.

66.1 ▨ Continue generally north-northwest, then northeast, for 0.5 miles to a trail junction.

67.6 ▨ Go left at this junction and follow the Echo Canyon Trail generally northwest for 1.5 miles down into the bottom of Echo Canyon.

68.4 ▨ Now follow the trail down Echo Canyon, generally southwest. In 0.8 miles you will intersect the East Rim Trail.

69.4 ▨ Go generally southwest along the trail for 1 mile down Echo Canyon, then down a series of switchbacks to the junction with the Hidden Canyon Trail.

69.9 ▨ Continue on the trail down the switchbacks another 0.5 miles to the parking area at the bottom of Zion Canyon. This is the end of this section and of the Hayduke Trail.

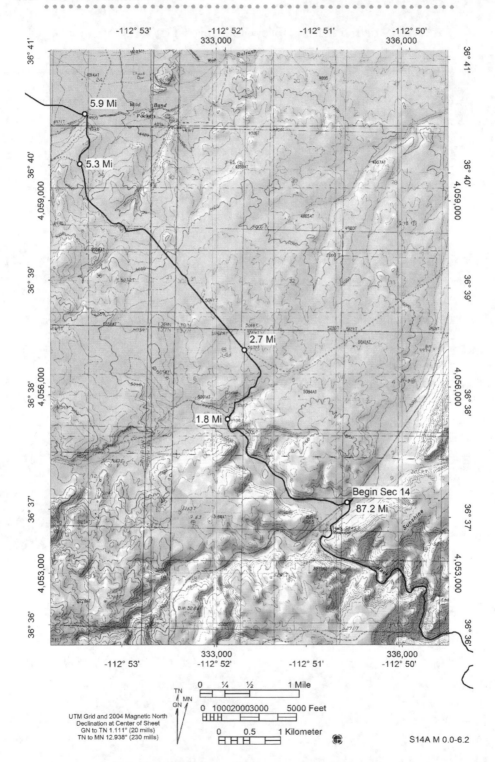

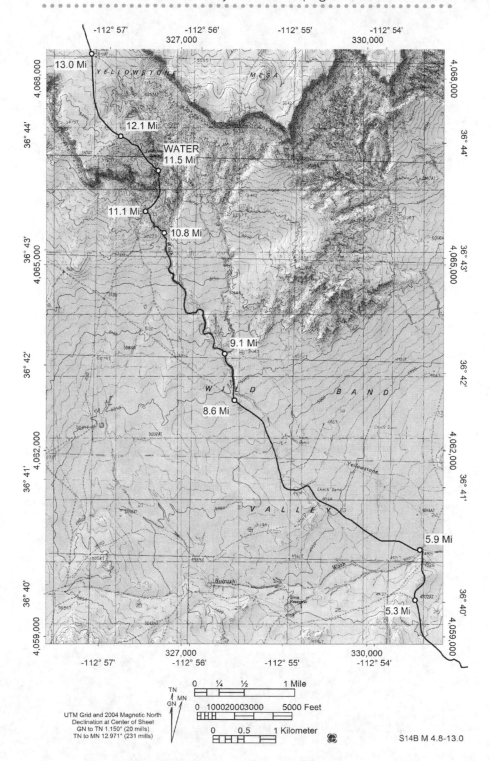

-112° 57'   -112° 56'   -112° 55'   -112° 54'
327,000   330,000

4,068,000

13.0 Mi

YELLOWSTONE   *MESA*

12.1 Mi

WATER
11.5 Mi

11.1 Mi

10.8 Mi

4,065,000

36° 44'
36° 43'
36° 42'
36° 41'
36° 40'

9.1 Mi

8.6 Mi

WILD   *BAND*

Yellowstone

Check Dams

5.9 Mi

Check Dams

VALLEY

Wash

Bulrush

5.3 Mi

4,062,000
4,059,000

327,000   330,000
-112° 57'   -112° 56'   -112° 55'   -112° 54'

0   ¼   ½   1 Mile

TN
MN
GN

UTM Grid and 2004 Magnetic North
Declination at Center of Sheet
GN to TN 1.150° (20 mills)
TN to MN 12.971° (231 mills)

0   1000 2000 3000   5000 Feet

0   0.5   1 Kilometer

S14B M 4.8-13.0

SECTION 14: 4.8–13.0 MILES

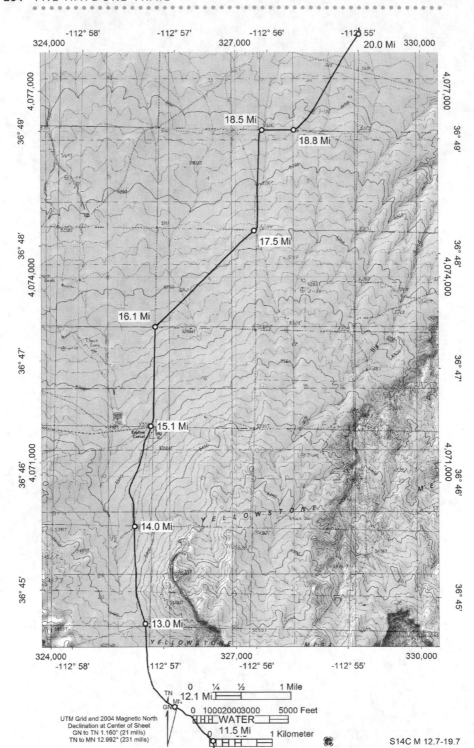

SECTION 14: 12.7–19.7 MILES

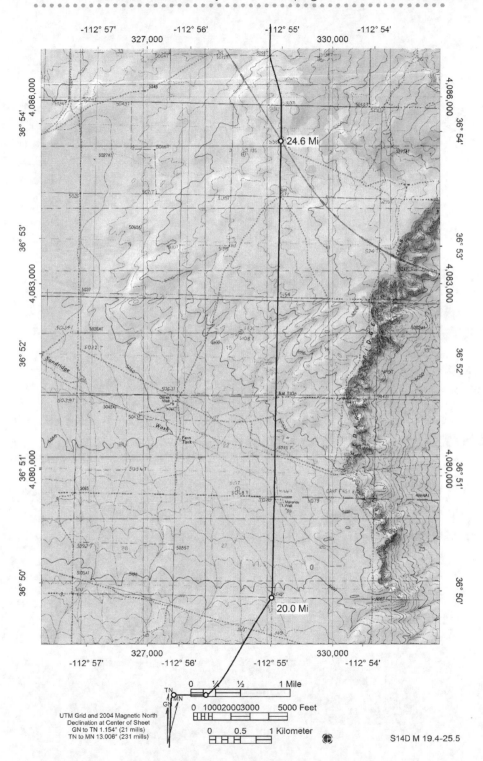

24.6 Mi

20.0 Mi

0   ½   ½   1 Mile

0   1000 2000 3000   5000 Feet

0   0.5   1 Kilometer

TN
GN
MN

UTM Grid and 2004 Magnetic North
Declaration at Center of Sheet
GN to TN 1.154° (21 mils)
TN to MN 13.006° (231 mils)

S14D M 19.4-25.5

SECTION 14: 19.4–25.5 MILES

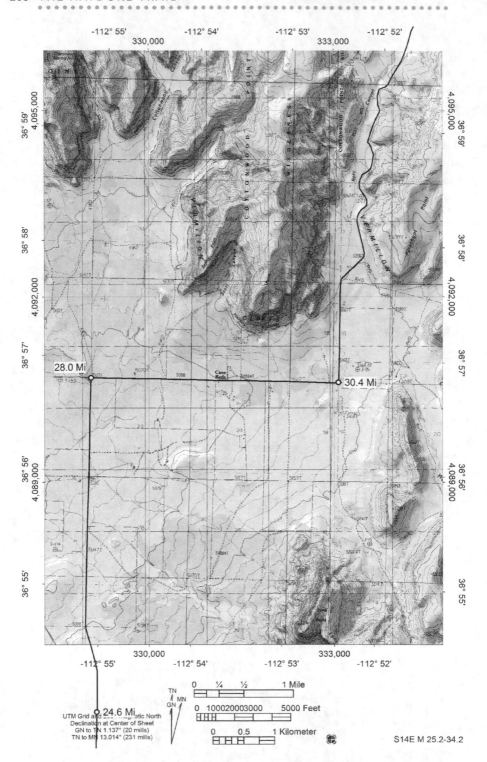

SECTION 14: 25.2–34.2 MILES

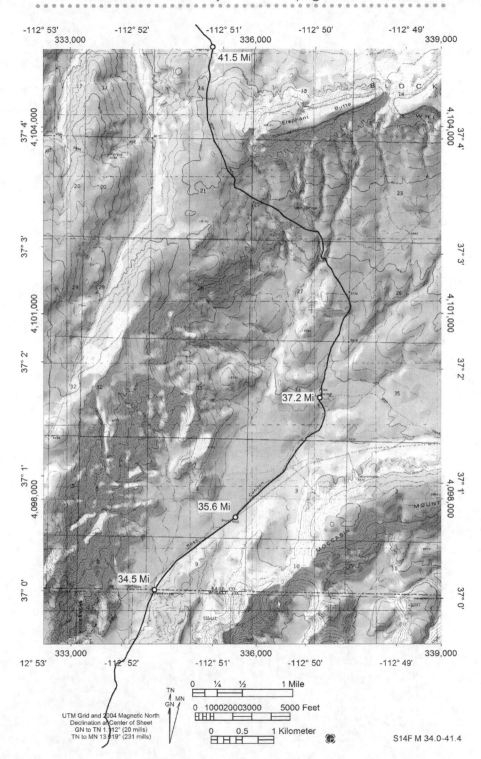

41.5 Mi

37.2 Mi

35.6 Mi

34.5 Mi

0   ¼   ½   1 Mile

0   1000 2000 3000   5000 Feet

0   0.5   1 Kilometer

UTM Grid and 2004 Magnetic North
Declination at Center of Sheet
GN to TN 1.112° (20 mills)
TN to MN 13.019° (231 mills)

TN
MN
GN

S14F M 34.0–41.4

SECTION 14: 34.0–41.4 MILES

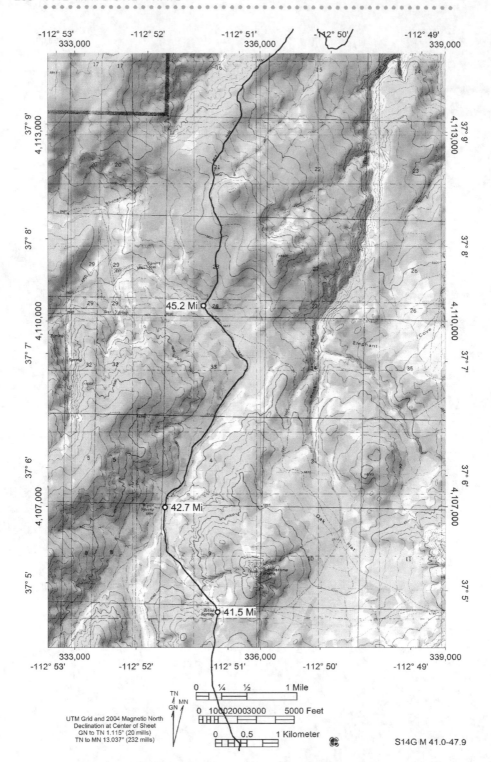

45.2 Mi

42.7 Mi

41.5 Mi

TN
MN
GN

UTM Grid and 2004 Magnetic North
Declination at Center of Sheet
GN to TN 1.115° (20 mills)
TN to MN 13.037° (232 mills)

0   ¼   ½   1 Mile

0   1000   2000   3000   5000 Feet

0   0.5   1 Kilometer

S14G M 41.0-47.9

SECTION 14: 41.0–47.9 MILES

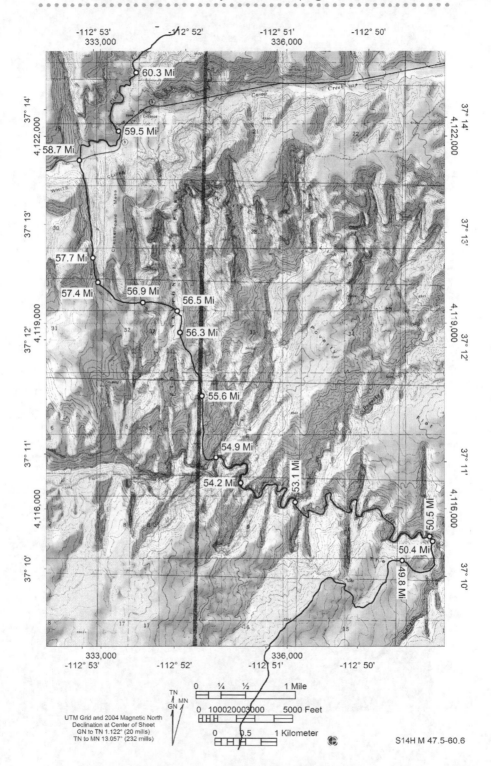

SECTION 14: 47.5–60.6 MILES

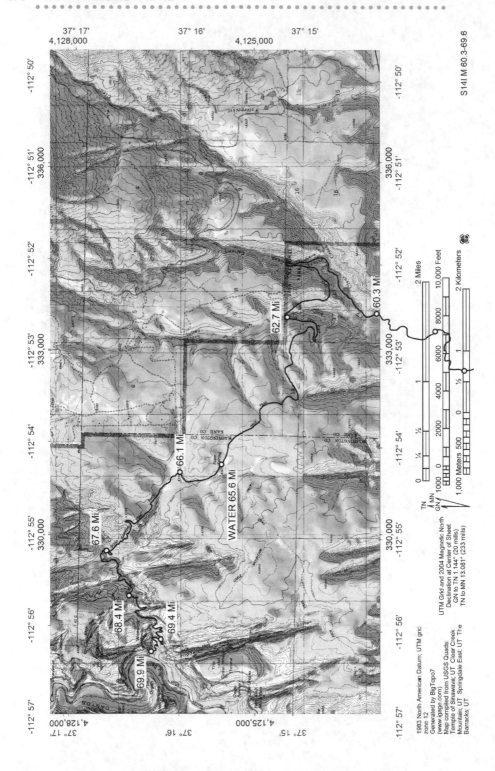

Acknowledgments

We would like to thank Glenn Pupura for his interchangeable Jeeps and for consistently finding us to deliver the fresh supplies that allowed our treks to continue; to Rachel Mitchell for all the goodies and support; to Brian Moody, Ross Hamilton, and Tom Wussow, who also met us out in the wilds with supplies; and to Mark Silver of iGage for his invaluable help with the maps for this guide.

We would also like to acknowledge the following businesses (in no particular order), whose help was instrumental in making this route a possibility: Boulder Mountain Lodge (Boulder, Utah), The Inn on the Creek (Midway, Utah), Slickrock Café (Moab, Utah), Adventure Medical Kits (and Dr. Eric Weiss), Osprey Backpacks, Cascade Designs, Powderwing Snowshoes, Thorlo Socks, Wyoming Wear, Kelty, Patagonia, The North Face, Red Ledge, Light As A Feather, Leki, Outdoor Research, Gator neoprene socks, iGage/All Topo Maps, Reliance Products, Gerber, Teva, Vasque, Princeton Tek, Grabber Bars, Clif Bars, Dermatone, Brunton, Cebe, Ursack. All photos were captured on Fuji film.

Suggested Reading

The following will give you some background information about the region and the skills necessary to enjoy and survive the Hayduke Trail. To get in touch with Mike and Mitch or to learn more about the Hayduke Trail visit www.deepdesert.com.

Abbey, Edward. *Desert Solitaire*. New York: Simon and Schuster, 1986.

———. *The Monkey Wrench Gang*. New York: Avon Books, 1975.

Allen, Steve. *Canyoneering 2*. Salt Lake City: University of Utah Press, 1995.

Barnes, F. A. and Michaelene Pendleton. *Canyon Country Prehistoric Indians*. Salt Lake City: Wasatch Publishers, 1979.

Brooks, Juanita. *Quicksand and Cactus*. Logan: Utah State University Press, 1992.

Butchart, Harvey. *Grand Canyon Treks*. Glendale, CA: La Siesta Press, 1970.

Calahan, James M. *Edward Abbey: A Life*. Tucson: University of Arizona Press, 2001.

Chronic, Halka. *Roadside Geology of Utah, Roadside Geology of Arizona*. Missoula, MT: Mountain Press Publishing, 1990.

Crampton, C. Gregory. *Standing Up Country*. Tucson: Rio Nuevo Publishers, 2000.

Cuch, Forrest, ed. *A History of Utah's American Indians*. Salt Lake City: Utah State Division of Indian Affairs, 2000.

Dellenbaugh, Frederick. *The Romance of the Colorado River*. New York: Time-Life Books, 1982.

Escalante, Silvestre Velez de. *The Dominguez-Escalante Journal*. Salt Lake City: University of Utah Press, 1995.

Fletcher, Colin. *The Complete Walker III*. New York: Knopf, 1984.

Lambrechtse, Rudi. *Hiking the Escalante*. Salt Lake City: The University of Utah Press, 1999.

Powell, John Wesley. *The Exploration of the Colorado River and Its Canyons*. New York: Penguin Books, 1987.

Steck, George. *Hiking Grand Canyon Loops*. Evergreen, CO: Chockstone Press, 1989.

Tawrell, Paul. *Camping and Wilderness Survival*. Missoula, MT: Falcon Press, 1996.

Van Cott, John. *Utah Place Names*. Salt Lake City: University of Utah Press, 1990.

Weiss, Dr. Eric A. *Wilderness 911*. Seattle: Mountaineers/Backpacker Magazine, 1988.

HOW TO VISIT AN ARCHAEOLOGICAL SITE

1. Stop, look, and think before entering a site. If a trail has been built across a site, stay on it. Remember that archaeological sites are part of our human heritage and also are places of spiritual importance to Native Americans.

2. Stay off the walls. The cumulative effect of people climbing, sitting, and leaning on ancient walls can destroy them in just a few years.

3. Leave artifacts such as potsherds and stone tools where they sit. Remember that every artifact tells an archaeological story, no matter how isolated and insignificant it seems.

4. Do not stack artifacts in little piles. It makes a nice photograph, but removing artifacts from their original context also removes valuable information on what activities occurred in which areas. It also can be an irresistible invitation for others to steal them.

5. Avoid walking on middens, the charcoal-stained soils usually located downslope from an alcove or cliff site. These are prehistoric trash heaps and contain valuable information on prehistoric activity, including treatment of the dead. Constant foot traffic erodes them and destroys information.

6. Do not reconstruct walls or other collapsed structures.

7. Never camp or light fires inside prehistoric ruins. Charcoal from your fire prevents radiocarbon dating of the site.

8. Keep your hands off the rock art. Chalking, rubbing, or tracing these ancient figures causes them to disintegrate. Creating modern "rock art" is punishable by law.

9. Check the site for trash and pack it out. Leave no trace of your own visit.

10. Report suspicious activities, evidence of vandalism, or exposed artifacts such as baskets and unbroken ceramics to the appropriate management agency. For example, the BLM Law Enforcement hotline is 1-800-722-3998.

Based on "How to visit an archaeological site without blowing out its walls," in "Documenting Destruction: Saving Utah's Disappearing Archaeology," by Jerry Spangler, Sports Guide, May 1994.